"Getting into the minds of some of our sport's brightest and best, Kelly has captured the attention to detail that is needed to succeed in the sport of dogs. Filled with passion, humor, and education, *Behind the Scenes of Best in Show* should be on the shelves of every sport-lover's library."

WILL ALEXANDER, HOST, THE DOG SHOW DRIVE, RETIRED PROFESSIONAL HANDLER

Compassionate Mind Collaborative
cmcollab.com

Copyright © Kelly Lyn Marquis, 2024
www.winall.us

All rights reserved. No part of this book may be reproduced in any form on by an electronic or mechanical means, including information storage and retrieval systems, without permission in writing from the publisher and author, except by a reviewer who may quote brief passages in a review.

This is a work of creative nonfiction.

Edited by Heather Doyle Fraser
Copyedited and Proofed by Hope Madden
Marketing by Jesse Sussman
Author Photos by Cynthia August *(cover)* and Debbie Wedderman *(About the Author)*
Cover and interior layout by Cindy Curtis

ISBN 979-8-9869419-7-4 (hardcover)
ISBN 979-8-9869419-3-6 (paperback)
ISBN 979-8-9869419-4-3 (ebook)

First Edition: April 2024

This paperback edition first published in 2024

Advance Praise

"The sport of showing dogs is a community built around the love of dogs, and it is unique in that ... pros and amateurs compete directly. The talents and skills of successful professional dog handlers have always been a driving force in establishing excellence in the care, conditioning, training, and presentation of top-winning dogs... Kelly Marquis has done a masterful job of compiling stories and insights from some of the most successful pros in the sport of dogs. She captures their voices as they share their insights and experiences ... an entertaining, informative, and inspiring book for dog lovers at all levels of involvement and experience."

DONALD STURZ, PRESIDENT, WESTMINSTER KENNEL CLUB

"Finally, a look backstage at the fascinating world of dog shows! This is a pure gem for the millions of folks who watch dog shows on TV or who are lucky enough to attend in person. Kelly's innate ability to explore the lives of key dog handlers—both past and present—exposes what really goes on behind the scenes of a Best in Show."

WAYNE FERGUSON, PRESIDENT, KENNEL CLUB OF PHILADELPHIA, AND PRESIDENT, MORRIS AND ESSEX KENNEL CLUB

"I have read a multitude of dog books, but never one so comprehensive, illuminating, and entertaining. *Behind the Scenes of Best in Show* digs to the very core of the sport. It features some of the stars of today, but also brings to life the architects and immortals of purebred dogs... and does it in such a humane and down-to-earth way as to be of interest and enlightening to the casual observer, professional handler, judge or the most accomplished breeder."

JOE PURKHISER, COL., USAF, RETIRED, AKC ALL-BREED JUDGE

"A must-read for everyone in the sport. The author's insights into the dedication of her fellow handlers make for a great read. I learned something new about each of them."

DOTTIE COLLIER, FOUNDER/VICE PRESIDENT, TAKE THE LEAD, MEMBER WESTMINSTER KENNEL CLUB, EXHIBITOR, BREEDER, AKC JUDGE

"I loved reading this book. The sections about Jane Forsyth and Mrs. Clark brought tears to my eyes as I remembered how wonderful they were and the influence they had on the sport. When I was establishing myself, these women were the people I wanted to impress with my dogs and my skills. I'm so pleased Kelly has put pen to paper to immortalize these dog show legends."

DAVID FITZPATRICK, PEKINGESE BREEDER, OWNER, HANDLER, TWO-TIME WESTMINSTER BEST IN SHOW WINNER, AKC BREEDER OF THE YEAR, DIR HANDLER OF THE YEAR, AMERICAN KENNEL CLUB BEST IN SHOW WINNER

"Kelly has expertly taken the reader into the lives and psyche of the great men and women in our sport. If they sound like world-class athletic coaches, it's because they are! When the masters of our conformation world share their stories, it is both educational and entertaining at the same time. A good read for all."

PATRICIA CRAIGE TROTTER, AKC ALL-BREED JUDGE, AUTHOR OF *BORN TO WIN, BREED TO SUCCEED*, BREEDER/OWNER-HANDLER

"In *Behind the Scenes of Best in Show*, Kelly Lyn Marquis brings many of our dog show stars within reach. Her interview subjects are masters of their craft, offering new and experienced exhibitors alike the benefit of wisdom in an easily accessible format."

LAURA REEVES, HOST, *PURE DOG TALK*

"Kelly Lyn Marquis is a conversationalist supreme! Her interviews with many of the top people in our sport are a must-read for every generation. Her style is warm, educational, and for those of us of an older ilk, filled with memories forgotten."

TOM BRADLEY, FOUNDER/VICE PRESIDENT, TAKE THE LEAD, MEMBER AND FORMER SHOW CHAIRMAN WESTMINSTER KENNEL CLUB, BREEDER, EXHIBITOR, AND RETIRED AKC JUDGE

"It is difficult for an author to write a book that has something for everyone, but Kelly Marquis has done it! *Behind the Scenes of Best in Show* is a how-to manual and dog show history book rolled into one interesting read. No matter your level of experience or interest in the sport of purebred dogs, you'll come away with a bit more knowledge and understanding of the sport after reading this book."

TOM GRABE, PUBLISHER, *THE CANINE CHRONICLE*

"*Behind the Scenes of Best in Show* is a remarkably authentic insight into the professional handlers who all have the same end goal but whose journeys towards that goal are so individual. The author does a deep dive into the thoughts, talents, and core values of the featured handlers. Whether you are a newcomer to the sport or already established, you will appreciate and be able to utilize the various takeaways the book offers. Kudos to Kelly for bringing this fascinating read to all of us."

PATRICIA PROCTOR, AKC JUDGE, FORMER AKC DIRECTOR OF FIELD STAFF, FORMER AKC FIELD REPRESENTATIVE, AND HANDLER

"Kelly Marquis's breakout release… takes readers on a journey with a dozen highly successful professional dog show handlers. This book is a unique and special gift that will help anyone in the sport achieve their goals."

AMY TOUROND, PUBLISHER AND EDITOR, *THE DOBERMAN NETWORK*

"Anyone who has ever been to a dog show can describe what they've seen: hurried handlers, imposing judges, cheering crowds, and ring after ring of seemingly perfect dogs. In *Behind the Scenes of Best in Show*, Kelly Lyn Marquis offers an uncommon glimpse at the unseen moments that take place before, during, and after every show. Each interview and every story reveals the kind of intimacy that not only encourages insecure dogs to become confident champions but also inspires talented handlers to dig deep and become even better versions of themselves."

DAN SAYERS, SHOWSIGHT

"Reading behind-the-scenes stories of these handlers is fascinating, and could only truly be told by someone who has walked this walk. It is so easy to think a handler's job is to run around the ring. To do a deep dive into all that is involved—the planning, passion, and persistence—is interesting, refreshing, and welcome."

BILL MCFADDEN, TWO-TIME WINNER OF WESTMINSTER BEST IN SHOW

"In *Behind the Scenes of Best In Show*, Kelly Lyn Marquis presents an unusual level of reflection and depth in a way never presented before … Here, we have the opportunity to explore the intricate and passionate world of dog shows, guided by someone who has lived and breathed this lifestyle. Kelly masterfully shares her own deep experience in dogs and weaves the stories of the "Masters" into a full open-curtain reveal of the joyful yet excruciating complexity and commitment required to succeed at the highest level.

This book is a must-read for anyone looking to understand the depth, dedication, and passion behind dog handlers' polished exteriors. It will become a centerpiece for Dog Show Mentor members, clearly revealing the relationships between breeders, professionals, and judges. It brings new meaning to the words 'commitment' and 'dedication,' previously not understood by the average exhibitor."

-LEE WHITTIER, FOUNDER, THE DOG SHOW MENTOR

"I was fascinated by this book. The author has selected a group of people whom I admire—many of whom are close friends. Insights into what makes a Best in Show winner and a Best in Show handler are always interesting, particularly when you have known these people as … exhibitors, know how they present their (dogs) and know how they respond to … [a judge's decision in the ring]. This book deals with people and should be a must-read for anyone in the dog world."

JAMES REYNOLDS, ALL-BREED JUDGE, CANADA

INTIMATE MOMENTS WITH THE MASTERS

Behind the Scenes of

BEST IN SHOW

HANDLERS AND THEIR SHOW DOGS

Kelly Lyn Marquis

Contents

FOREWORD BY DAVID FREI XI
INTRODUCTION: MEET THE MASTERS.......................... XIII

PART ONE: COMING TO THE SHOW

1. Janice Hayes: Curiosity and Observation 2
2. Frank Murphy: Ownership and Connection 12
3. Greg Strong: Commitment to Grooming, Dog Care, and Conditioning 35
4. Michael Scott: Strategy and Politics... 52

PART TWO: USING YOUR STRENGTHS TO YOUR ADVANTAGE

5. Michelle Scott: Innate Abilities and Managing Expectations.. 74
6. Katie Bernardin: Support Systems and Adaptability............... 88
7. Kaz Hosaka: Transformation 105
8. Andy Linton: Building Confidence and Establishing Trust ... 127
9. Taffe McFadden: A Spiritual Approach to Handling 142

PART THREE: ACHIEVING THE PINNACLE

10. Anne Rogers Clark and Kaz Hosaka: The Importance of Mentorship 158
11. Gwen DeMilta: A Force to Behold 185
12. Jane Forsyth: The Mother Who Inspired an Industry 209
13. Kelly Lyn Marquis: The Fuel That Feeds Champions 237

AFTERWORD: A COMMUNITY TO SUPPORT YOU..............261
ACKNOWLEDGMENTS.......................................264
ABOUT THE AUTHOR..270

This book is a token of my appreciation for everyone within the industry who either directly or indirectly helped shape my life and made me the woman I am today.

With heartfelt thanks,

Kelly

Foreword

BY DAVID FREI

Gather 'round, my friends—dog show fans, media, television viewers, show dog handlers, judges, breeders and owners, dog show professionals, dog show lovers, and dog lovers—you have a front-row seat for an unprecedented dog show ride. This book has never been written before.

Kelly Lyn Marquis, the author of *Behind the Scenes of Best In Show*, is your driver and tour guide. She is a longtime professional handler who has brought together many of our industry's top handlers in this book. To borrow a phrase, the people in Kelly's book are our "best and brightest." That's why she calls them "Masters." Talented and successful herself, she knows the questions to ask and the roads to take us down.

As we look at the dog show industry and the stories you are about to read, I would like to provide an enhanced and expanded introduction of the dog show players and the process originally put forth by Percy Roberts, a legendary dog show handler and judge from many years gone by.

- The standard (the written description of an ideal specimen of a breed) is the blueprint for how the dog should look and how it should perform.
- The breeders are the builders.
- The handler is the salesperson.
- The judge is the shopper whom the breeders, owners, and handlers want to turn into a buyer.

The handler has a key role in the competition—they need to prepare the dog, they need to present the finished product for the judging, and they need to make it look its best—somewhat like a real estate agent. The handler is the closer, the one who puts it all together in hopes of a happy ending for the breeders and the owners.

The judge (and the spectator, in person or watching on television) gets to see the dog in its two minutes in the ring. What they don't get to see is what leads up to that two minutes. It's a lot more than that time in the ring; it's pretty much a lifetime involvement and dedication that brings that finished product, and you will hear about that from the handlers featured in this book.

In *Behind the Scenes of Best in Show*, you will learn how handlers need to be equal parts psychologist (canine and human), athlete, parent, businessperson, artist, engineer, physical therapist, veterinarian, bellman, truck driver, and crate carrier. And more.

You are going to read about how each handler came to the industry (family background, accidental entrance, or right place-right time), who helped them along the way (mentors), and how they depend upon and have a role in their dog show community. You also are going to read about how they do what they do consistently, with different dogs, year after year.

Everyone asks us about the hit movie, "Best In Show" (released nearly twenty-five years ago)—"Is it really like that?" Those of us in our world laugh about the movie. We all join the joke when we say, "Yes, we know all of those people in our world." Most of us have probably had a "busy bee" episode of our own, and some of us even admit to being a little bit like each of the characters.

I always say—in only the most loving way—that we are indeed "a target-rich environment." The movie is a satire, of course, but still, we are flattered that such a talented group of movie actors and writers have targeted us.

But we are very serious. "When we go, we go hard," said one of the "Masters."

Through the years, there are some things that I have said often that seem to have gone unchallenged and unquestioned. Early in my own dog handling days, someone once told me that the best handlers are invisible, meaning that if they are doing their job well, you shouldn't even notice them. I probably say something like that on every telecast and in most interviews.

But the reality is that the masters use their knowledge, their hard work, and their "quiet hands" to get the job done. They are so good at this that you may not realize what they are doing until that beautiful finished product is standing there at the end of it all with a Best in Show title.

So, from here on, I'm going to have to put an asterisk next to "invisible," now that I have read the stories in this book, which have shown me how, as one of them said, "A great handler will draw you in." And besides, it's most certainly a good thing that these people you're about to read about are not invisible because you are going to learn a lot from them in this book and hopefully later in the show ring.

The talented handlers featured throughout *Behind the Scenes of Best in Show* bring magic to the dog show world every day. Well, it seems like magic, but behind what looks like magic is a strong work ethic, dedication, talent, heart, and certainly a "no fear" mentality. They believe in what they are doing, and they love and respect their dogs.

For these handlers, physically conditioning the dogs is a given. But they all constantly talk about conditioning their dogs mentally, as well. It's a recurring theme here, and you will read about it many times in this book: Great handlers connect with their dogs. Call it dog psychology, dog sense, being an animal communicator. In my therapy dog world, I say it all the time: we should worry more about what we learn from the dogs rather than what we teach them.

"Put your faith in yourself and your dogs" keeps repeating throughout Kelly's storytelling.

I am fascinated by the stories of the people featured in these pages. I am captivated by Kelly's weaving of her own experience and knowledge into her storytelling and her navigation through burnout with the help of her community.

The people you're about to hear from, through Kelly, are the best at what they do. Dedication, talent, and heart go into every moment they are grooming, conditioning, and training, as Kelly tells us and the "Masters" show us.

Along the way, she writes, this part of the dog show community can be combative, aggressive, hostile, and unreasonable. You will read how they are competitive, but they know that winning or losing does not define them. You will read how they are freely helping even their competitors and encouraging and training the next generation.

Kelly calls them a "motley group" toward the end of the book, but if you pay attention throughout, you know she says that lovingly and that she is happy to be a member of that motley group.

If you're a dog show handler at any point in that dog show life, or if you are a breeder/owner and a dog aficionado, I'm willing to bet that you won't be able to put this book down. I believe that you will have a lot of Post-its hanging out of these pages when you're done.

Keep it fun, the "Masters" all said. It's about the dogs, not the dog show.

DAVID FREI has been the co-host of NBC's National Dog Show Presented by Purina since its inception in 2002, where he is seen every Thanksgiving Day by more than 20 million viewers. It is the same role that he perfected in 27 years as the longtime (1990-2016) co-host of USA Network's Westminster Kennel Club Dog Show. He has been involved in the sport of dogs as a breeder/owner/handler and judge for nearly 50 years. He is the author of two award-winning books, *The Angel By My Side* and *Angel On A Leash*.

INTRODUCTION

Meet the Masters

Whenever I meet someone new and they discover that I am a professional dog handler, invariably the question most asked is, "Is the movie *Best in Show* an accurate reflection of what dog shows are really like?"

Usually, I laugh and admit, "Yup!"

Although the movie was designed as a spoof and a comedy, the truth is, much of what is brought to light does actually happen in the real world of dog shows… although to the people involved, it's no laughing matter. It is serious business.

While there are admittedly some funny tales to tell, this book has a different vision in mind. I aim to give you a rare, behind-the-scenes view into the hearts and minds of those who really do compete for Best in Show. In our world, Best in Show is not just a scene from a movie, it's real life.

To show you what it is like behind the scenes, I interviewed more than a dozen of the top professional dog handlers in the country. They volunteered their time in order to help me bring this book to life. My hope is that their stories will give you a feel for the immense dedication, talent, and heart required to become the best of the best. Even more importantly, I am excited to show you the deep connection, intimacy, and trust that is shared between handlers and dogs. At times throughout this book, you will notice the show dogs are masterful as well, teaching their handlers important lessons!

The Handlers Featured in the Book

As you'll learn from their stories over the course of this book, each handler has their own unique manner in how they handle, train, compete, conduct business, and interact with clients and peers. While much about them is different, they all embody a set of very special defining qualities that lead to mastery, such as passion, skill, talent, and work ethic. Those qualities, as well as their winning records and impressive stats, make them stand out in the vast sea of dog show handlers.

There is amazing work taking place at dog shows, and this book gives you a front-row seat. I share my perspective and the perspectives of others within my industry. You will see how each handler's life experiences shape the way they perceive and navigate the dog show world. Some handlers are born into the dog show culture and have great connections, some just get lucky and start with a great dog, some have the gift of gab, some thrive in competition and mental strategy, and most have a deep love and affinity for dogs.

HOW THE BOOK IS ORGANIZED

The book is divided into three sections, each containing several chapters. Each chapter features a specific professional handler. Although an entire book could be written on each handler, I chose to focus on several key aspects each handler embodies as a means to teach various handling techniques, dynamics, and strategies in an entertaining and provocative manner.

Part One: Coming to the Show focuses on how several different handlers got started in the industry and lays the groundwork for many of the foundational aspects required of a handler who is seriously committed to their job. It reveals where and how they dedicate their time and attention and shows the immense amount of work required, both inside and outside the show ring.

Here are the handlers we will meet in Part One:

- **Janice Hayes:** Curiosity and Observation
- **Frank Murphy:** Ownership and Connection
- **Greg Strong:** Commitment to Grooming, Dog Care, and Conditioning
- **Michael Scott:** Strategy and Politics

Part Two: Using Your Strengths to Your Advantage focuses on themes such as intuitive handling, managing internal and external expectations, the benefits of creating a healthy support system, working with a variety of different temperaments, handling alchemy, the vital role consistency plays in dog training, building confidence, and dog handling through a spiritual perspective.

Here are the handlers we will meet in Part Two:

- **Michelle Scott:** Innate Abilities and Managing Expectations
- **Katie Bernardin:** Support Systems and Adaptability
- **Kaz Hosaka:** Transformation
- **Andy Linton:** Building Confidence and Establishing Trust
- **Taffe McFadden:** A Spiritual Approach to Handling

Part Three: Achieving the Pinnacle focuses on a few people whose mere presence in a ring was, in my opinion, otherworldly: Anne Rogers Clark, Jane Forsyth, Kaz Hosaka, and Gwen DeMilta. Unfortunately, I did not have the opportunity to interview them (with the exception of Kaz) for this book, as they have all passed on. In an attempt to relay their significance, I interviewed several key people who knew them well and also drew upon my own personal experience with them and the way their legacy impacted me and the sport as a whole.

In Part Three, I also share my own story of navigating burnout within the industry–something that plagues many in the sport who make a career out of handling or spend a significant amount of time consumed in its intricacies. In addition to burnout, this final chapter looks at what fuels us as competitors and focuses on other potential areas of exploration as a professional within the industry.

My Hope for You

I hope you are entertained, enlightened, and intrigued by the material provided. To anyone new to showing dogs or looking to improve your skills both inside and outside the ring, I hope this book serves you and makes you a better handler. May you walk away with an open heart and an open mind, along with a whole new perspective on what it means to be a dog show handler on the path to mastery.

PART ONE

Coming to the Show

CHAPTER 1

Janice Hayes:
Curiosity and Observation

When I first met Janice Hayes, book writing was a new venture for me. We were from different parts of the country, and until I interviewed her, we had never had the opportunity to meet in or out of the show ring. When I approached Janice about featuring her in this book, I was excited about the material I wanted to present, but I had my doubts about how the dog show world might perceive my ability to write something noteworthy. Any apprehension I had just flew out the window when I connected with Janice. Her energy was so upbeat and supportive.

She quickly set me at ease, enthusiastically declaring, "I know you'll do a great job! I think everyone has a story."

This must be how it feels to be a dog in Janice's energy, I thought. Her enthusiasm, love, curiosity, and encouragement make you feel safe, loved, supported, believed in, and as though all amazing things are possible. When this is the place of BEING you come from, the

DOING is halfway handled. A place of safety for an animal leads to calm confidence and strength inside and outside the show ring. This is Janice in a nutshell. How did she get there, though?

Curiosity 101: Be a Resourceful Self-Starter and Embrace Your Thirst for Knowledge

Like many handlers, Janice fell onto her life path to dog handling rather serendipitously when her father found a Vizsla breeder who only had a show puppy. He wasn't interested in showing dogs, but he thought his young daughters might enjoy giving showmanship a try. Her dad purchased the puppy and then encouraged his girls to work with the puppy and train it to be a show dog. Janice did, in fact, give it a try, and in no time, it became a burning desire. By the age of nine, she was hooked.

She recalls that from the age of nine until seventeen or eighteen, each year, people would ask her what she wanted to be when she grew up. Each year, she would enthusiastically declare, "Same thing as last year, a professional dog handler!"

Janice adds, "My love of working with dogs was so intense, it may have bordered on being obsessive. My poor junior's dog–I just loved practicing with him."

When Janice refers to her junior's dog, she is referring to a dog she trained and showed in Junior Showmanship. This is a competition at AKC (American Kennel Club) conformation events for children aged nine and under eighteen.

Unlike other classes, in which a judge evaluates the conformation of a dog, its physical structure, and appearance, in this instance, the judge assesses a child's handling skills in comparison to other kids in their age group. This is a great way for kids to learn and improve their handling abilities. Many top professionals, myself included, competed in junior showmanship in their youth.

Janice says, "I trained my junior's dog every single day!"

Although her junior's dog didn't need to be trained every day, Janice loved doing it, and her beloved dog was a willing participant. She focused all her energy and enthusiasm on this one dog. At least we know he never suffered from neglect!

Unlike some families, who enjoy attending dog shows, Janice's family did not share her passion for showing dogs. Since her parents didn't enjoy attending dog shows and she was too young to drive, she had to be resourceful in terms of traveling to dog shows. She solicited people to give her rides, and in return, she would assist them in caring for, training, grooming, and showing their dogs. Determined to learn everything she could, Janice asked lots of questions, and worked for a variety of different breeders, owners, and handlers. She was curious, dedicated, and determined, doing her best to consume all the knowledge, practice, and skill she could in relation to showing dogs.

Janice's resourcefulness and experience working for a variety of different people provided another huge benefit.

"That's how I learned to perfect my craft," she explains. "I worked for different people. I didn't just show dogs in junior showmanship and then jump right into professional handling. I worked for multiple professional handlers over the years. I didn't go out on my own until I was twenty-five or twenty-six years old."

She discovered, "A lot of value can be gained by working for a multitude of different professional handlers." (See Chapter 10 on the importance of a mentor.)

This approach helped her to observe the business of dog handling as well as the nuances of the skill and strategy of showmanship. She soaked everything in, and while she was observing and adapting to the needs of different dogs and handlers, she learned what she did and didn't want to do when she began working independently.

Her enthusiasm for gaining a deeper understanding of how handlers work and what makes dogs tick appears boundless. She admits to being fascinated with learning from other handlers.

Janice declares, "I'm kind of like a creepy stalker!"

She says this offhandedly and with good humor, but in reality, it points to two very important skills that must be cultivated for dog handlers to be successful, not only with their dogs, but also with their businesses: curiosity and observation.

When Janice is around a handler who excites her with their talent, she watches everything they do. She asks questions and then applies what she's learned to her own dog handling and business.

"I will follow Taffe and Billy McFadden (more about them later) around. I love to watch Taffe show dogs. I learn something new from her all the time. Taffe has very quiet hands, and she is so in tune with her dogs. Taffe is talking with her dogs the whole time. Not with words. With her leash. With her confidence. With every movement that she makes. I find her fascinating."

Janice admires handlers that have "quiet hands." In this style of handling, the handler almost disappears, and all you see is the dog itself. Janice strives to achieve the same with her own dogs.

She explains, "Sometimes it's hard to look past their dogs and see what they are doing. I am so transfixed on their dog because the handler has put themselves purposefully behind the scenes."

Not only does she seek to learn all there is to know about training and showing dogs, but she also continually asks questions about the personal history of the judges to whom she will be exhibiting her dogs.

Knowing their background often helps Janice understand what the judges are looking for in the show ring. This can help her determine which dogs she feels will have the best chance of winning under that particular judge. Like all good handlers, Janice seeks to understand their preferences and accommodate those preferences when possible.

Helping Dogs Step into the Best Versions of Themselves: Motivation to Instill Greatness

Janice loves getting to know every aspect of a dog's personality–that's part of her strength as a handler. She tends to work with a lot of dogs that have "soft" temperaments.

By the term "soft," Janice is referring to a dog that is lacking in confidence or is timid, shy, withdrawn, or overly sensitive to various forms of sensory stimulation. Janice's excitement and enthusiasm are palpable as she describes the feeling of taking a dog that is soft and insecure, nurturing and building its confidence, and then witnessing this confidence explode in the show ring.

"There is nothing I like more than taking a dog that didn't have confidence in itself and making it into a rock star!"

How does Janice turn an insecure dog into a rock star? Part of her process lies in getting to know the personality traits of the dogs she is training. Her curiosity compels her to dig deeper than what you might see only on the outside with a dog. She wants to know what they enjoy most and what they don't like. When she is working with a dog, she fully tunes in.

Janice believes each dog is unique, and there is no one-size-fits-all formula that you can apply for training and handling. Instead, Janice observes her dogs and learns their tics and idiosyncrasies. This enables her to recognize when a method isn't working and then problem-solve creative solutions to get the result she wants. Each dog is different.

To this end, it is clear that Janice believes that all great handlers must have great dog sense, and I tend to agree with her.

She says, "You need to have enough dog sense that tells you when you are pushing for too much and need to pull back, or when a dog just needs an extra bit of encouragement or expectation that will propel them forward."

Also, how one trains is very important. When Janice trains her dogs, she plays with them, keeps the training fun, and lets them be dogs. It's clear that Janice trains using lots of encouragement, and her belief in her dogs' abilities shines.

She explains, "There is a brilliant moment that arises when everything I've been working towards comes together with a dog. When this happens, I make such a big deal out of him or her and what they just did. They feel so good about themselves. They just want to do it again and try even harder next time. That's what I love most."

When everything a handler has been building toward comes together in a dog, it's incredibly exhilarating. The handler knows it, the dog knows it, and as Janice says, "That moment is better than any Best in Show!"

For many of us handlers, it is why we do what we do!

As I listen to Janice talk about how she works with dogs, I can't help but think about how humans learn and achieve new skills and cultivate our strengths. Everyone learns differently, but what if we were allowed to embrace our humanity and our own idiosyncrasies in the ways we learn on the path to greatness?

Calling on Help and Discovering Innate Abilities

Although Janice is a masterful dog trainer, she too faces challenges with dogs–everyone who has been in this business for any length of time does. But here is another interesting quality among handlers: most of us are quite willful human beings. We don't give up easily. Janice is no exception. One challenge she faced really helped her grow as both a professional handler and as an individual. She explained this challenge with an English Springer Spaniel bitch named Liz.

She says, "Liz and I would kind of bump heads. I would show her on two different leashes depending on whether it was the breed or the group or what kind of mood she was in."

This developed into a guessing game for Janice, trying to decipher which leash Liz would offer the least resistance to. Frustrated, Janice turned to Taffe McFadden for help. Taffe advised her to contact a dog psychic named Jessica Montañez with the Holistic Being. Taffe explained that Jess was able to help her on many occasions when she ran into problems with dogs that she couldn't solve on her own.

Janice explained to Jess, "I don't know what to do. We are fighting over something we do every single weekend. I don't want to argue with Liz, but Liz can't constantly be deciding what leash she wants to be shown on."

After conducting an animal communication session with Liz, Jess reported back to Janice that Liz was fine with either leash. Janice just needed to pick one. Janice needed to make a decision and be emphatic about it.

Janice decided to give Jess's advice a try.

"I looked Liz right in the eye, and I said, 'This is the leash we are going to show on every single time.'"

She laughs, recalling Liz's expression, which seemed to indicate "whatever." But it worked, and Janice learned how important having a strong mindset can be when showing a dog.

The animal communicator pointed out another energetic dynamic that was causing Liz some confusion. What Jess identified in the session was that, when Janice went back to her set-up, feeling upset about losing in the ring, Liz thought it was her fault.

Janice felt terrible that Liz was blaming herself. Yes, Janice was frustrated, but not with Liz. When she lost with Liz, Janice felt extremely frustrated for several reasons.

She felt the judges were favoring males (also commonly referred to as simply dogs in show terms) and not giving Liz a fair chance because she was a bitch. She was also worried she didn't have enough political clout with the judges. Finally, she was concerned that she was holding back Liz's winning potential, thinking that maybe if Liz were with a more well-known handler, she would be winning more.

Jess also explained to Janice that Liz just felt she was not doing enough. Liz was trying to change things up.

When Janice received this message from the animal communicator, she thought, "Oh my God! I am not mad at her. It's not her fault the judges aren't pointing to her."

After that, Janice really changed her behavior. When she and Liz lost, Janice was mindful of her energy and what messages Liz might be receiving. From that moment forward, win or lose, Liz got to go back to the set-up and lay on the table and was told how pretty she was. That was what Liz lived for. She just wanted to be told how pretty she was. She knew how pretty she was, but she wanted to hear it.

Janice says, "When I really understood that Liz was feeling what I was feeling, it was a game changer. It made me more aware of what my actions and emotions were conveying to Liz. After that, it was a total team effort. We were no longer butting heads. It was, 'We are working together. This is what we are going to do, and we are going to stand out. We are going to make people see us.'

"Both Jess and Liz helped me figure out that, yes, we can take this to the next level. I can take Liz to the next level. I just needed to change a few of the things I was doing. Both Jess and Liz, they taught me a lot. I became a more confident handler."

Janice's experience with Liz and Jess was life changing. It changed how she shows dogs. And it didn't happen by accident. Janice was curious, and she sought out help and advice from someone she trusted. And then, after she received this advice, she acted on it. This is important when you are starting out and even later on in your career. No one has all the answers, but sometimes you can work together to find a solution.

Janice admits, "Jess gave me the understanding and confidence that I can communicate with dogs."

Although she sometimes doubted it, Janice always knew she had the ability to communicate with dogs on a very deep level.

She says, "I always felt I had a way better connection with dogs than I did with people. Dogs are just a more natural way for me. I was a very quiet kid. I wasn't confident in anything, and my dogs always gave me confidence.

"There was a period in time when I started doubting myself more, and Jess said to me, 'You are feeling what you are feeling because that is what the dogs are telling you. You aren't trusting what you are feeling. You are shutting yourself off from your abilities. You need to open yourself back up, listen, and trust.'"

Working with Jess forever changed Janice's belief in herself. Essentially, Jess gave to Janice what Janice gave to every dog she worked with. Janice discovered it wasn't just her imagination, she really was communicating with her dogs. They could hear her and vice versa. This validation helped Janice step up her game and believe in herself and her innate abilities.

With Liz, Janice discovered it was crucial to be aware of and manage her own emotional energy because her dog was picking up on it. Just as Janice observed others, she realized her dogs–particularly Liz–are also keen observers. Janice needed to take this into account and change her behavior in order for Liz to feel safe, comfortable, and confident. When Janice stepped into her conviction, Liz fell in line. When she doubted herself, Liz would fight her. Janice says that because of Liz, she learned how to brush things off and not get mired in self-doubt and blame. Working with Liz helped Janice learn to focus on what was within her control and let the rest fall away. Everything fell into place, and eventually, Janice and Liz went on to win the Sporting Group at Westminster in 2013. Due to the prestige of the Westminster Dog Show, considered the crown jewel among the dog show fancy, that moment in time was a precious achievement for Janice and Liz, a great outward result of a job well done.

Janice continued to grow in her confidence and handling abilities, and in 2023, earned the coveted distinction of winning Best in Show at Westminster Dog Club with a Petit Basset Griffon Vendeen (PBGV) named Buddy Holly. Holly was the first of his breed to win this distinction. The team will go down in history.

I love this story because I have come across countless examples of an owner or handler overcoming something personal for the benefit of their dog. Essentially, the dog was a catalyst in the owner-handler's personal growth. How beautiful.

CHAPTER 2

Frank Murphy:
Ownership and Connection

*"I have always been dog crazy, but I never
set out to do this for a living."*

—Frank Murphy

Frank Murphy did not intend to become a professional dog handler, and yet that is exactly what he became. Accidental entrance into dog handling is not an anomaly in the industry. Frank, like myself, had his sights set on higher education and the pursuit of a more traditional career. Yet passion, innate talent, and natural abilities opened a doorway to a less traditional career path.

After college, Frank worked as an electrician's apprentice for four years while attending night school to become a master electrician. Frank would indeed become a master … but not in electrical work.

While Frank was apprenticing and going to night school, he started exhibiting his own dogs on weekends. Showing dogs was fun for him, and it turned out he had a knack for it. Being the gregarious sort, he soon made friends in the dog show community. Before long, his friends were asking him to show their dogs.

"One day in 1991, I realized I was making more money by lunchtime at the dog show than I was taking home after a week's worth of work at my 'real' job, so I left," says Frank. "I decided to stop working as an electrician and dedicate my life to working with dogs."

As with many others in our industry, myself included, a favorite pastime morphed into a successful career.

People at dog shows gravitate toward Frank. He is passionate about this way of life and the people and dogs that give it meaning. His genuine nature puts people and dogs at ease. He is warm, open, and funny. He doesn't put on any false airs. He connects with highly educated people about global warming, the economy, politics, history, and literature just as easily as he connects with the guy who comes to dump the RVs at dog shows. With Frank, what you see is what you get.

He balances all these solid, dependable qualities with passion. Oh, and did I mention he is a redhead? Yes, he can be fiery, and that feisty spirit is part of his charm.

Fulfilling a Dog's Need for Human Connection

Dogs fulfill a variety of needs in people's lives. Like many in the industry, Frank is a big dog lover, but he views his connection to the dogs with which he works as deeper than that. He sees himself as fulfilling an important purpose in each dog's life while they are in his care; he feels honored to work with dogs. Frank believes dogs have a deep need for human connection and makes reference to the long history of the relationship between dog and man as proof. After all, dogs in prehistoric times followed people for days without eating and without the comforts of a home base just to be with them.

"I believe the thing dogs seek in life, more than food, fresh water, or warmth, is a relationship with a human being," says Frank.

If you think about it, that makes us as humans very similar to dogs. We have a biological need for attachment that can't be underestimated. It's key to our survival and our thriving in life, just like it is for dogs.

"The most rewarding part of a dog's life, for the majority of dogs, is the time they spend with their human."

Like most handlers, when Frank is hired to campaign dogs on a national level or to obtain championships, the dogs often live and travel with him, so he has seen and felt firsthand this connection.

Frank shares, "The most rewarding part of my job is being *that guy* with each dog. Maybe not all day, or even every day, but when I am alone with that dog, I know I am fulfilling that need for that dog. This may take place when I am giving the dog a bath, while showing in the ring, or while road-working him with the golf cart in the evening. I always try to be present with whichever dog I am working with during these times. I feel that whatever I give to a dog, I receive even more in return."

Not only does Frank enjoy the bond he shares with his dogs, he also enjoys the camaraderie he shares with other members of the dog show community. In a way, they are his pack! When not feeling gregarious, Frank escapes to his motorhome, which he describes as his man cave. A man cave inhabited by dogs.

He laughs, "I can't imagine too many jobs where I'd get paid to be with my own favorite dog most of the day and night!"

He also enjoys working in different places. It is great that Frank likes working in a variety of locations because there is a lot of traveling with dog show handling. Frank's workplace environment is always changing.

"I have been packing up the RV and leaving town every week for decades," said Frank. "I am not sure how crazy I would get staying in my hometown week after week. It still appeals to me to work in a different setting every week, in different conditions."

I, too, relate to Frank's appreciation for working in a variety of settings. Although sometimes traveling away from home can get old, showing dogs is never boring. The setting is constantly changing: the scenery, the weather, and the people.

In addition to living a nomadic life, the competitive aspect of the dog show world suits Frank's personality.

"We don't simply perform; it is our job to win. If you don't have a competitive streak in you, you will burn out," stressed Frank.

Moments that Transform a Career

During a career like Frank's, with so much success and so many top dogs, it's hard to pinpoint just one moment that defined or created a new path. As it turns out, when you strive to be "that guy" for all of your dogs, giving them the love, care, and connection for which they are searching, you will have several dogs play a key role in your career.

One day, while watching his Ridgebacks run in the backyard, Frank made a seemingly impulsive decision that would impact him in ways he could never have imagined. (Rhodesian Ridgebacks are the breed that got him into handling "by accident.")

"I remember watching two of my Ridgebacks running out in the yard. One dog I was watching was Corey, an eleventh-month-old, and the other was his dad, Pirate, who was two-and-a-half years old. I'll never forget that moment."

Frank had already entered Pirate in Best of Breed for the upcoming Florida circuit in January. As he watched the scene in his yard, though, his gut was screaming to take a different action.

Frank remembers, "Even now, I can picture Corey moving from point A to point B across my six-acre yard in Florida. I remember thinking, 'That's the dog I would put up.'

"I didn't care that he was still a puppy, and I loved Pirate, his dad. Pirate was a great producer and did some nice winning. However, watching Corey go across the yard that afternoon, I thought, 'That's the dog right there.' Right then, I called up the entry service and switched my entries. I withdrew Pirate's entries and entered Corey in his place."

Although this may sound like an impulsive decision, Frank was trusting his gut. When Frank made his first decision to enter Pirate, he was using his logic. Logically, it made sense to show Pirate because Pirate was a nice dog, structurally that is, and he was older and more mature physically. However, in that moment Frank took action on his gut instinct and it paid off in profound ways.

The Florida circuit is a big group of dog shows that starts off the New Year, and January 1 is when the stats for the nation's top dogs begin. These shows are important for anyone seeking national ranking because, in January, each dog campaigning on a national level starts with zero points. Every Best of Breed, Group Placement, and Best in Show award results in points accumulated for the total number of dogs defeated. Points are calculated January 1-December 31. Therefore, owners seeking national ranking for their dogs want to get off to a good start. High rankings are desirable for several reasons. Being the best is rewarding in and of itself. However, there is an added benefit.

Owners advertise their dogs online and in magazines. The magazines are targeted to dog owners, breeders, handlers, and judges. In fact, judges are given free copies as an incentive to owners to advertise to be seen by judges. Competitors want high rankings so they can advertise their rankings, essentially hoping to persuade judges and other dog show enthusiasts that their dog is the best. (Yes, it is a dog-eat-dog world.)

At eleven months of age, Corey won nine out of the first eleven breeds on the highly competitive circuit and even won the Hound Group once, in addition to several group placements. Corey soon became a bridge that brought a very important relationship into Frank's professional career and who would later bring in another important relationship that would have a tremendous impact on his personal life.

Not long after these wins, a man by the name of Sam Lawrence approached Frank and asked if he could own Corey. Sam Lawrence was a man of financial means who enjoyed discovering, owning, and financing dogs that had the potential to win big. A person such as Sam is referred to as a backer in the dog show world. Backers choose to own dogs, similar to how a person chooses to own a sports team… except unlike sports, backers don't make any money. Yes, that is shocking for most people to learn, but rarely is money awarded at dog shows, and if it is, it goes to the handler. People do NOT show dogs to earn financial awards. They show dogs for the sheer enjoyment of competing and owning a winner.

Backers often choose to take on ownership of a dog when the dog is older and has proven itself. Rarely do backers purchase a puppy. Often, the dog has an owner who has reared it from a puppy, yet that owner doesn't have the financial resources to campaign the dog, or perhaps doesn't want to spend the amount of money required to run an aggressive show campaign. National campaigns cost hundreds of thousands of dollars.

Backers often work with one or more professional dog handlers to show the dogs the backers own. At the time, Sam already owned many top dogs and worked with several different professional dog show handlers. Most highly successful professional handlers have one or more backers that they work with. However, relationships like this can be challenging to procure, especially if you are a handler who is unproven, meaning you've never campaigned a dog that achieved a number one nationally ranked status. Having a backer who is willing to put their money on you and the dog you are showing is a big deal. When that happens, a voice or feeling inside you might say, "This is my big break!"

"When Sam Lawrence asked me if he could own Corey, my Ridgeback, that became a life-changing moment. The decision to sign on a new owner-backer for a show dog can be very stressful. There can be the fear of losing control of the dog. If the dog is a female, it may require the previous owner to give up some or all breeding rights. Sometimes this is a sticking point because breeders that breed a high-caliber dog want to have the opportunity to continue breeding their line. Ownership changes are less complicated with males in terms of breeding rights because they are not limited to the number of puppies they can produce, like females. Aside from breeding rights, another matter that may need to be negotiated is which owner the dog is going to live with after it retires from showing. Aside from breeding and ownership concerns, there can be other stressors."

For instance, Frank was very hesitant about Sam backing Corey, but not for reasons you might think. Frank says, "I was reluctant to work with Sam, not because Sam wasn't a great owner, but because a person's dog is like their child. Corey was mine. What made me hesitate in working with Sam was that I had doubts in my mind. I questioned Corey's merits and my abilities. I questioned Corey, not because he wasn't a good dog, but because he was mine. Plus, I am not a good self-promoter. Corey was my dog, so it was personal."

Frank had no concerns about Sam. He knew Sam was a great owner and would offer both him and Corey a tremendous opportunity. He just didn't want to disappoint Sam.

They both got way more than what they bargained for.

After Sam took ownership, Corey went on to make breed history by breaking a Ridgeback record, winning twenty-eight Bests in Show. No Ridgeback had ever won more than nine.

"Corey tripled the record," Frank beams.

Corey finished the year with a ranking of Number Three Hound in the country.

"Corey and I had a very successful campaign. However, it wasn't a stellar year from Sam's perspective. Sam already owned dogs that won bigger," explained Frank.

But Frank and Sam's relationship didn't end when Corey retired from showing.

During the time Frank was showing Corey for Sam, John Wilcox, a highly accomplished dog handler, was showing a Pembroke Welsh Corgi in Washington State. John had already won a few Bests in Show on that Corgi, yet he wanted to retire from professional handling and make a career change. Someone offered the dog to Sam, and Sam asked Frank to handle him. But Frank surprised everyone by suggesting George Murray, another handler.

George is a professional handler from Ohio that Sam hired to show Kafka, Ch. Brunswig's Cryptonite, a famous top-winning Doberman. Frank immediately thought of George because he had a daughter in a wheelchair and a son with disabilities. Frank knew the additional income would be helpful to George and his family.

Frank could have immediately said yes to Sam, which would have resulted in more money in his pocket along with the benefit of another top-winning dog, but instead, he advocated for George, saying, "He could use a good dog. I'm sure George will find the Corgi easy to show, plus I think he can win with it."

But later that afternoon, Sam's then-wife Marion came to Frank, "Frank, what are you doing? You don't want to show dogs for Sam?"

"Of course, I want to show dogs for Sam," replied Frank.

She demanded, "Why did you tell Sam to send the dog to George Murray?"

Frank said, "Well, he doesn't have a dog right now."

Marion said, "That's bullshit. You tell Sam you want to show that Corgi!"

My guess is Marion didn't want Frank's altruistic nature to result in the dog being shown by another handler. She, too, wanted Frank to show the Corgi, so she stepped in and took over.

Frank says, "Marion must have gone back to Sam and told him I wanted to show the Corgi because the Corgi flew into the Orlando airport, and shortly after that, I started showing him."

The name of that dog was Forrest Gump. Like the character in the movie, he just "kept running" his way to more and more titles, racking them up like miles on an expedition. Frank, Sam, and Forrest Gump went on to win forty-six Bests in Show while earning the designation of number one Pembroke Corgi and number one herding dog.

Apparently, Marion's assertiveness paid off. All parties involved had the pleasure of achieving number one status, plus Frank and Sam's relationship deepened. Frank moved beyond showing his own dog for

Sam and stepped into a position where Sam sought out dogs to place into Frank's trustworthy hands.

A Passion and Talent for Finding and Cultivating Winners

When you look at Frank's show record, you begin to see unifying threads. One we've already touched upon is Frank's understanding of how we are connected to dogs and our pivotal role in their lives. Another is the ability and talent to find and cultivate winners.

"I think I am most proud of the fact that several times in my life, I have been given an opportunity to go out and find a dog of a specific breed, or of any breed, and get the dog on board and make a career for it."

Frank explains, "I have had number one dogs in their group, record breakers, national specialty winners, and of course, many, many Best in Show winners. Many factors go into this, not only the quality of the dog, but the dog's temperament, the owner's temperament, and the other dogs competing in that dog's breed and group at the time. Anyone can stand in the middle of the carpet at Westminster, hold the Best in Show ribbon, and say, 'This is the crowning jewel of my career.' The right dog, the right year, with the right panel of judges, can pull off a win.

"I've won some really nice Best in Shows. I've broken records with my dogs. I've won groups at Eukanuba and Westminster. But to me, the thing I'm most proud of is having the ability to see a green dog and be able to picture just how good the dog could be, given the right circumstances, then turning that dog into a winner or a record-breaker or a national specialty winner or recognized as a top dog in their group."

Not everyone is given that opportunity. For Frank, this opportunity arose over time as his relationship with Sam deepened.

Frank explains, "In the beginning, when I was showing dogs for Sam, he found the dogs. When we were finishing up Forrest Gump's show career, Sam's health was declining, and he began considering quitting dog showing. I called him one night and said, 'Hey Sam, I found the next great Corgi.'"

"Are you going to get him for that man in Miami?" asked Sam.

Earlier, another backer propositioned Frank. This other backer told Frank, "When you find the next great Corgi, I want to own it."

"Yes, I suppose I am," Frank said

Sam said, "What about if I owned him instead of that guy in Miami?"

Frank said, "Well, Sam, you always find your own dogs. This is one that I've found, and you haven't even seen him."

"Get the dog for me," Sam said.

As someone who has been in that position–in which an owner is willing to trust you and go all-in on you–it feels like a mixture of part excitement and part fear. It feels good to have someone who believes in you on your side, while at the same time you have the opportunity to pursue a goal with the dog of your choice. However, you must also face the fear of being wrong. What if this dog doesn't win? If things go wrong, it is on you!

According to Frank, this Corgi was the only dog that a professional handler showed for Sam that Sam didn't find himself. Their relationship shifted. Sam was now putting his faith in Frank and allowing Frank to take on a role he had never entrusted to any other handler. Was it the right decision?

"Sam wasn't a flowery speech kind of guy, so I put the dog in the truck at the end of the weekend," Frank remembers. "Probably the next weekend, I had all the dogs out in the x-pen when a big black Mercedes

(Sam's vehicle) drove slowly up to the x-pen. The window went down on the driver's door, and Sam said to me, 'Which one is it?'

"I pointed to the dog in the x-pen. All of a sudden, I am aware that there is Sam and here is this dog, but the dog doesn't look the way he could look. The dog was not entered in the dog show that day, so he wasn't bathed or appropriately groomed yet. Sam surprised me. I wasn't expecting him to show up at that moment."

I imagine Frank must have had a sick feeling in the pit of his stomach. Although he did nothing wrong, he must have wished he could have made a good first impression. I know I certainly would want the dog I had chosen to look its absolute best when the backer came to see it for the first time.

The window started going back up on the Mercedes, and Sam just said in a voice that was all business, "Time to put your money where your mouth is."

Frank laughs hard as he retells this story. "Oh my God, talk about pressure! When Sam found us dogs, not every dog he found worked out to where we kept it for a whole career. It was no sweat off my back because Sam was the one who was looking for the potential, and it was his name and his interest on the line. I got paid regardless.

"But now, I was the one under the pressure. I found this dog, and he was right, it was time to put my money where my mouth was. I thought, 'I'm not sure I'm ready for this kind of pressure!'"

FINDING A WINNER

Frank didn't choose this Corgi on a whim, though. He had been watching this dog win five-point majors from the bred-by-exhibitor class at specialties for a while.

Frank says, " I knew he was a good dog. I'll be honest. I did cheat. I went to Michael Sauve, who was an AKC rep in Florida and who was considered to be the Godfather of Pembroke Corgis. I said to Michael, 'Michael, I think I found the next great Corgi.'"

Michael said, "You did? Which one is it?"

"I think it's the dog that has been winning out of the bred-by-exhibitor dog class at specialties," Frank revealed.

Michael said, "I would give up my job at AKC for two years to special that dog."

So yes, Frank did see this dog and determined on his own that the dog would be a great Corgi someday, but he also used his resources—namely Michael—to verify his hunch. After that conversation with Michael, Frank recalls walking away, feeling like his instincts were spot on and a new relationship would be there for him if he chose to pursue it. That dog was named Kevin, Ch. Hummingbird's Keeping up Appearances.

Although he had potential, Kevin didn't come out like a house on fire. It took Frank time to find and cultivate that inner spark.

"Kevin didn't start out as a killer show dog," says Frank. "In fact, I remember one specific time in Orlando, Florida, at the beginning of Kevin's career. I was waiting to receive the blue ribbon for winning the group, and all that kept going through my head was, 'How in God's name am I going to drag this dog around the Best in Show ring?' Looking back on it now, it's hard to remember that feeling because he went to show his guts out for the next three years."

This is a testament to Frank's abilities. Not just anyone would have been able to figure out how to get Kevin to be a stand-up show dog, but Frank did. For many handlers, this is part of the fun, figuring out how to get into a dog's head and get it to perform.

CULTIVATING A WINNER WITH DOG PSYCHOLOGY

So how did Frank get Kevin to show like a rockstar?

Frank explains, "With Corgis, you can't set them up, you can't mold their ears forward, or scratch their tail up. They need to stand on the ground and do it themselves. The one thing I learned from Forrest Gump, house pets are not going to show their guts out. They might do it when they feel like doing it, but they are not going to do it 135 times per year, twice a day when they win the breed and three times a day when they win the group."

Frank decided to put Kevin in a kennel.

"He only came out to get a bath and to show. The highlight of Kevin's life was getting a bath or going in the ring and showing," Frank explains.

And Frank was always there, every single time, being Kevin's person, building their connection, being with Kevin in that moment. This connection was everything to Kevin, and it was something special for Frank too.

Kevin was a busy dog, so Frank also installed stall mats in the kennel to protect his feet from the constant running back and forth. He also had a coat that was difficult, so every single day the dog was shown, he got a bath.

"Every show dog knows when he's won," adds Frank. "I always wanted to win the last group of the day, so when I took him into Best in Show, he was still remembering his last win! On the other hand, if he won the first group of the day and sat around, waiting for Best in Show, I found by the time Best in Show came around, it was like starting from scratch. If he won the last group and then went right into Best in Show, he was still high from winning the group."

During Kevin's first year of showing, he was too young. His coat wasn't right. He wasn't mature. He still needed to fill out. One of Sam's friends got on Frank's case in front of Sam and said, "Yah know, Sam, you showed that dog too young."

Sam said, "No, I didn't."

They said, "Yes, you did. His coat wasn't right. He wasn't bodied up or mature enough. You showed him too early."

Sam said, "NO. I didn't, because I had fun!"

Frank realized Sam didn't want to take a year off, waiting for Kevin to mature, so to him, it was fine. By the time Kevin was through his second year of showing, he had thirty Bests in Show. Sometimes your intent isn't about showing a dog at the height of its physical maturity or breaking a bunch of records. For Sam, that first year showing Kevin wasn't about Kevin looking his absolute best or breaking a bunch of show records. For Sam, it was just plain fun having a dog out there on the show circuit with Frank.

Around the end of Kevin's second year of showing, Sam considered owning an Australian Shepherd as his next dog to back. If he procured the Aussie, he would have to agree to another handler showing the dog in another area of the country. Sam decided against backing the Aussie. His health was continuing to decline, and he was limited in his ability to travel. He felt there was no good reason for him to back a dog that he couldn't travel to watch compete.

Sam explained his thought process to Frank, "Frank, I don't want to just drop you and cut you off. Besides, if I own a dog, I want to be able to watch it show. You handle dogs in an area where I can drive to and participate in the dog show experience. Now, go show that Corgi!"

Then he abruptly insisted, "Just don't travel anywhere special for it."

Translation: we are not going to put a lot of time and money into a campaign because we don't expect Kevin to be a big winner, but we do want to keep him out showing with you because we enjoy working with you and participating in dog shows.)

That was it. Frank and Kevin were given another year with Sam. However, the implication was that they would be taking it easy.

Sometimes, though, life has a different plan.

The first two dog shows of that year were held in Deland, Florida, with entries of over 2000 dogs (a fairly large dog show). Kevin won both of them!

"By Monday morning after the conclusion of the show weekend, I knew I had the number one dog in the country, and I also knew that thing about not going anywhere special for the Corgi was out the window!" Frank enthuses.

Frank and Kevin went on to break the record for Pembroke Corgis. He won the group at Eukanuba and he won the group at Westminster. He won forty-four Bests in Show in one year. He was the number two herding dog at the time, and Dallas, a German Shepherd dog, was number one. With dog shows, you just never know where things will lead.

I always try to prepare newcomers to dog showing that in this industry, you can try to figure it out, but often, there is no rhyme or reason for why things happen the way they do. In this instance, if Sam hadn't been getting sicker, Kevin would never have had that third year because Sam would have taken on an Australian Shepherd, and Kevin wouldn't have achieved the success he accomplished in that final year. In fact, Kevin went on to break the record for the most Bests in Show won by a Pembroke Corgi, retiring with seventy-seven.

Learning from the Dogs

You learn different things from different dogs. One of the things Kevin taught Frank is that a long career doesn't have to be a drag on a dog.

"When Kevin won the group at the garden, that was his last show. He showed perfectly," says Frank. "But Sam kind of made me nervous about that as well because prior to Westminster in February, the last show Kevin had been in was when he won the group at Eukanuba in December. Sam kept saying, 'Don't you think you should show that dog once or twice?' He asked me this in January and then again in February, 'Are you sure?' he'd say."

This is a common misperception among owners. According to Frank, "Many owners often worry their great show dog will forget." He adds, "They don't! If any practice is necessary, it is often to settle the nerves of the owner, not the dog!"

I agree with Frank 100 percent! I've had this same conversation with many of my clients. Many owners are reluctant to trust the handler in this assessment, but it is true! Owners need to trust their handlers. No one understands the relationship between a dog and their handler better than the handler showing the dog. Trust that your handler intimately knows the dog they are showing and try not to second guess them.

"Sam asked me this so much, and each time, my response was the same: 'Sam, he'll be fine. He's a smart dog. He knows what he's doing. He'll be fine,'" Frank says. "But then I'm driving to Westminster and all of a sudden, my body breaks out in a sweat, and I start thinking, 'What if he forgot how to show? What if he's rusty, and he shows like crap, and I lose the breed?' My mind started reeling, and I thought, 'I need to put this out of my head.'"

As it turns out, the breed was a blur for Frank. In fact, he can't even recall it. My guess is that if Frank is anything like me, he was incredibly nervous. He was managing his emotions. He wanted to win. He wanted Kevin to show great and he wanted to make Sam happy. Being someone experienced with nerves, a handler learns to shut them down and focus on the task at hand. Nerves can feel very uncomfortable, especially prior to competition, but generally, for most handlers, once we get the dog in hand, get into the ring, and do our work, the nerves settle down and are channeled into getting the dog to put forth a stellar performance.

After the jitters wore off, the memory came back as well. Frank vividly remembers all of the details of what happened in the group.

"Jimmy Moses was in the ring with Dallas. All the top dogs were competing against one another. Lester Mapes was judging the group. He judged a lot the year before and gave all the top dogs at least two Group Ones each. He'd given Kevin and I two Group Ones as well. Nobody thought they had an advantage. All we knew was there were a lot of dogs in the group that Lester Mapes rewarded in the previous year, meaning everyone felt they had a good shot of winning, yet everyone knew their competition also had a good shot of winning!

"That night, Kevin showed perfect. He won the group. When we went into Best in Show, he was also perfect. Even though he showed hundreds of times throughout those three years, he still went out with a bang, showing his heart out. He wasn't bored. He didn't look old, lazy, tired, or disinterested. He looked perfect. The last year we showed him, we showed him 134 times and he won 134 breeds. Nobody beat him in the breed. That's my favorite stat in Kevin's career, in an entire year, he never lost the breed. He was undefeated in breed competition."

I loved hearing Kevin's story and even remember watching him show and competing against him during this time. Out of curiosity, I asked, "If Kevin had something to say to you, what would it be?"

Frank took a pause.

"In true Kevin form—always thinking of his person—Kevin's words to me would be, 'Didn't we have a great time?'"

UNDERSTANDING THE CORGI DYNAMIC AND WHAT IT REFLECTS IN US

Each breed and each dog has its own personality and temperament, just like humans. No two people are completely alike, but you can see some similarities among groups. Corgis are no different. They have a unique mentality, and once you begin to notice motivations and patterns, it becomes easier to understand them and how they will behave in certain situations. Frank, like many dog handlers, has made it his life's work to observe the dogs in his care and use the strengths of the breed and the individual dog's temperament to work to his advantage.

Frank explains, "Male Corgis are usually a little pissed off that they are so short. You have to use their mentality to your advantage. A dynamic I often found myself in with Kevin might go something like this: It's an outdoor show, it's hot, Kevin is feeling kind of ho-hum, or drained by the heat, whatever. If I sensed this in him, I'd scope out a ring that had some tough dogs, for instance, Akitas, standing around the outside of it. I'd walk Kevin toward the group of dogs, act like I accidentally wasn't paying attention, and I'd let his lead stray away from me. He would think I wasn't paying attention and would go glare at or lunge at an Akita. During my act of stupidity, Kevin would get all fired up because he had the opportunity to piss off a bunch of big dogs! And then I'd say, 'Hey Kevin, you shouldn't be doing that!' And then he'd go strutting over into the group ring and light it up, all full of himself. He loved having an opportunity to growl at an Akita. He'd strut around like a rooster. I understood his mentality, and I knew how to use it to my advantage."

I laugh as I listen to Frank telling this story of how he learned how to get this short-legged dog fired up and into his ego. As I imagine this scene in my mind (and I can totally see Frank pulling this off, by the way), I see a correlation between the two of them.

I say to Frank, "I find it interesting that you're working with a dog to help puff up his confidence while, at the same time, you're working on the same thing yourself. Sam had faith in you and trusted you to choose the next winner. You were hoping you would be able to deliver, and you sure did deliver–big time!"

Frank enthusiastically agrees.

"Yes! It felt good to do right by Sam. The experience with Kevin also gave me the confidence to land my next client. For the eight years that followed, I found all the dogs she owned. Kevin was the first dog that I found, acquired, and set in motion on a campaign.

"Two years after Sam retired, this woman came along and gave me the same options. We did Beagles, Pembrokes, Ridgebacks, and German Wirehaired Pointers. Having done it for Sam, who was more intimidating than anyone, gave me the confidence to be able to say, 'I can win with that one.' I'd have to credit Kevin with that, too. He changed how I saw myself in the dog show world."

Frank realizes what his life would have been like without those years of showing Sam's dogs. He would never have gotten the second client without having shown the dogs for Sam and winning the groups at Eukanuba and Westminster.

Enjoying the Journey and Its Surprising Paths

After Kevin's last show, Sam's health continued to decline. Eventually, he made the decision to no longer back dogs. Even after their professional relationship ended, though, Frank and Sam remained close. What many people don't know is that Frank lost his dad when he was only six years old. Sam had two daughters but didn't have a son. They each filled a hole in each other's lives. Sam lived about seven or eight years after he stopped showing dogs. Frank went and visited Sam often, even after their professional relationship ended.

"I don't know if you know this, but when Sam passed away, I was invited to the funeral. It was only for the family," says Frank.

Frank goes silent for several long minutes, recalling Sam's funeral. He gathers himself and his emotions together after having been surprised by the powerful impact of this memory with the family.

Frank surprises me when he further adds, "That's when I met my wife. I always say that even after Sam died, he was still doing things for me. As far as my career showing dogs is concerned, so much of what I have is because of Sam. The relationship that we had, and even meeting my wife and the clients I have now–all of it was because of Corey and Sam."

I choke back tears, hearing this heartfelt moment in Frank's life and feeling the impact of the synchronicities in his life and the connections he nurtured.

"It's funny, after all these years, I can still get stupid about all this," Frank says a bit bashfully. "That moment watching Corey in the yard was the beginning of something big. You never know. You make a decision that seems rather insignificant and then you find out twenty years later how that one decision helped open up roads you never could have imagined.

"Sometimes you let situations go by you, and you realize you missed out on the best part. The thing I am going to remember, and the thing that I'm conscious of now, is that these little moments are the ones to hold on to and remember. They are the ones that we often let slip by, but they are the best part of what you are going through. I am very grateful. I am very conscious of the fact that, being the dog lover that I am, this is the only job I could have where I actually get to be intimate with great dogs from all different breeds and from all different groups. I get to open up a door in this motorhome and get to be with whatever kind of dog I want to be with. For me to be here at this dog show, sitting in this parking lot, even though I lost today, is a gift." Frank laughs, "I am surrounded by dogs that I wouldn't otherwise be. It's a great thing!"

A BALANCED LIFE

Frank and Sam's business relationship developed into a very intimate personal relationship. My guess is that even though they became very close, they did their best not to let their personal feelings for one another affect their business decisions and vice versa. And their close working relationship developed into an even closer friendship after Frank stopped showing for Sam. It's important to remember that even though dog showing is fulfilling and exciting and can be all-consuming, you have to make space for other interests and relationships in your life.

"This dog show thing can really make you crazy!" laughs Frank. He adds, "It is really important to seek balance in your life and to have other interests outside of the dog world."

This mindset helps keep life in perspective. If you are not careful, dog showing can become all-consuming. Handlers work in a high-stress environment. Dog shows are extremely competitive, and any good handler is always out to win. That's their job. In addition, the job is very physically, mentally, and for some, emotionally demanding.

Frank says, "I feel very fortunate to have my wife. It's the first time in my life that I've ever been happily married. We've been married for seven years now. Recently, we had a couple of weeks off from showing. We went up toward Boon. We rented a cabin in the woods, and we went hiking in the woods for two days with our two house dogs. We enjoy riding our motorcycles up to the mountains whenever we have a day or two off. Taking time away from showing and enjoying some leisure time gives you more patience to handle all the demands you take on as a professional handler."

To me, Frank is an example of what it means to own your life and your vocation. That's what his life's work is for him. He also takes his cues from the many teachers he has had in his life–Sam, Corey, Kevin, and many others. Be in the moment. Use your strengths. Embrace your skills. Learn from your mistakes. Take the risks when you know you can and have the experience to back it up. Connect with the beings who mean something to you, and you will receive more back than you could ever have imagined.

CHAPTER 3

Greg Strong:
Commitment to Grooming, Dog Care, and Conditioning

When I think back to my first memory of Greg Strong, I am immediately catapulted into my teen years, a newbie in the dog show handling world. I was about fourteen years old, sitting outside a show ring next to my mom, watching Greg show a Terrier. He was tall, controlled, and quiet. His parents gave him a name that suits him well, he exemplifies both physical strength and strength of character. I remember noticing his big, strong hands and hearing his deep, calm voice. There wasn't anything showy about Greg—he was intent and disciplined. Many years later, I would compete against him and eventually stand as an equal to him in the Best in Show ring. And yet, up until the writing of this book, I had never developed a personal relationship with him.

The interview process for this book began at a cluster of dog shows in Syracuse, New York. I was nervous about reaching out to unfamiliar people in my industry and unsure of how I might construct the interviews. It was important to me that people felt safe and at ease with me when I reached out to them, asking them to be a part of my new endeavor. I saw Greg at that show and something about him intrigued me. My intuition was drawing me in, my brain busy trying to understand the reasons for this deep curiosity. Over the years, I had always perceived him as ethical, a quality I value. At the time, I saw a respectable businessman who might be able to guide me in structuring an interview process that would make the people I would interview feel safe.

I decided to do the unthinkable: ask a complete stranger for help. Had I lost my mind? As I stepped further into writing this book, I realized I needed to bring in the people who could help me create an accurate and broad picture of what it is like behind the scenes of the Best in Show world. Even though my mind yammered at me that I should be able to figure this out on my own, even though I was nervous, even though it wasn't my usual way of going about things, I finally just did it.

My dog show set-up, an area at dog shows where handlers and exhibitors keep and groom dogs, was close to Greg's set-up. I think I did a couple of drive-bys, meaning I walked by his set-up a couple of times, trying to get up the nerve to talk to him. I didn't want to be a bother. I didn't want to interrupt. Greg was always very busy and very intensely focused on whatever he was doing at that moment. Eventually, it became clear there would never be a good time since he never appeared to even pause, let alone have ten minutes to take a break. Finally, I got up the nerve and approached him. I simply asked, "Hey, Greg, I'm wondering if you would be willing to help me with a project I am working on."

At the time, Greg and his assistants were preparing an assembly of dogs that were lined up on a long row of grooming tables. He put down his stripping blade and gave me his full attention. I felt tender receptivity and kindness. It was unexpected from such a busy person.

I understood how his energy could calm timid, frightened, or worried animals. They would feel safe. That is certainly how I felt. I also felt that I was truly seen and that I mattered. Experiencing Greg's attentive energy gave me a whole new appreciation for how some dogs may experience their handler. It made me realize that this same attentiveness, this being valued, is a gift many talented handlers give to the dogs entrusted to our care. I felt an incredible resonance with Greg's energy. I could feel him, and yet I had a whole new experience of me, all at the same time.

Great handlers have the ability to offer both tenderness and strength. Although we have a wide range of emotions that we can draw from to hold space for our dogs, not everyone can tap into the full spectrum and do it at will. But Greg can and does.

When Greg commits himself to something, he goes all in. When he is not in the ring showing dogs, he attends to responsibilities that are many, varied, and daunting. He thrives in a fast-paced environment and is able to switch gears at a moment's notice.

In order to orchestrate all the demands of his life, Greg is very disciplined. In fact, in my view, he takes the requirements of a great handler to an extreme. Greg describes his work as a lifestyle, not a job. He admits his intense behavior can burn people out. However, for Greg, this lifestyle is a labor of love. And what he loves is dogs, competing, and making his clients happy.

Greg's story will give you a snapshot of an intense, highly-driven, successful handler. Since Greg always carries a large number of dogs, his days at dog shows are nonstop from sunup to sundown, and his weekly routines are just as hectic. Just reading about the details of his routines and schedule is exhausting, but giving a realistic picture of the day-in and day-out experience of a dog handler is necessary to accurately reflect the overwhelming demands some handlers manage throughout the course of their lives.

Although I too love the feeling of a hard day's work, I found myself feeling exhausted while I was talking with Greg. I kept thinking, "How does this guy keep this pace up? How does he find the energy?"

I found myself wanting to sidetrack him, or make a joke just so I could get him to ease up. I wondered what drove him to work so hard. I can be intense at times, but this man gives the word intense a whole new meaning.

As much as I wanted to change pace and get Greg to ease up, I just surrendered to it. This is a man who gets things done. I challenge anyone to try to keep up with him!

Several Irons in the Fire

Greg's daily allocation of time is most likely different from other professional handlers. Still, there are others like him, taking on more than the average bear! In addition to being a professional handler, he owns a very active boarding, grooming, and training facility, as well as several residential and commercial rental properties. He staffs his business and life accordingly, and relies on help to get things done. This doesn't save him from early mornings and late nights, though.

In fact, a typical day at the shows involves working from 6 a.m. to 10 p.m., taking only a dinner break. When he's not at the shows, he's up around 5 to 5:30 a.m. to exercise and ends the work day around 8 p.m. Rarely does he take a day off.

He explains, "We are consumed with the constant care of the dogs in our charge, twenty-four hours a day, seven days a week. There isn't much time for a personal life as most people know it. We have live animals to tend to and we can't just stop work because it's 6 p.m. Our responsibilities extend far before and after servicing our customers."

After working in the public's eye at dog shows and enduring long weekends of nonstop work, Greg returns home to his facility to attend to the grooming, conditioning, and training of his boarders.

Like many professional dog handlers, Greg wears many hats. He is a:

- Nutritionist: knowledgeable on the proper dietary needs of each dog, which can vary among individual dogs and breeds;
- Physical therapist: capable of overseeing the conditioning and maintenance of minor injuries;
- Psychologist: able to assess and provide the proper mental requirements for dogs (and owners!); and
- Veterinarian: capable of detecting, diagnosing, and treating many early-onset physical issues and even providing basic emergency care when necessary.

The job also requires a bit of athleticism to address the physical demands and endure the long hours. If all of that wasn't enough, Greg is also a successful businessperson with good people skills and the ability to manage and oversee bookkeeping and scheduling, employment details, and retirement planning. Being a Jack-of-all-trades is necessary to meet the complicated demands of professional dog handling and, in particular, the multibusiness lifestyle that Greg has created for himself.

Different Conditioning for Different Coats

Although he is a Jack-of-all-trades, Greg is also a specialist. Clients, owners, and peers seek Greg for his wide base of knowledge, ability, and commitment concerning one thing in particular. Greg is an expert on properly caring for, building, and maintaining a multitude of different types of dog coats (a "coat" refers to the hair that covers a dog's body).

As you will discover, caring for a show dog's coat can be extremely time-consuming. In my career, my specialty is showing Dobermans. Breeds like Dobermans are often referred to as wash-and-wear dogs. This is due to the fact that very little effort needs to go into maintaining a proper show coat. While talking with Greg, I was both in awe of his knowledge and commitment to coat care and maintenance and grateful that I didn't choose to specialize in a breed for which maintaining a coat is a huge undertaking. Many dog show enthusiasts believe that maintaining a proper coat is a labor of love, a work of art that relaxes them. I don't fall into that category, but have tremendous respect for handlers, like Greg, who do.

Greg began learning about proper coat care while showing his family's Lhasa Apsos and Afghan Hounds in both junior showmanship and regular conformation. Later, he apprenticed under top Terrier handlers. Through the years, he perfected his craft and is now highly skilled in caring for all different types of coats.

Different breeds require very different types of grooming. For instance, the grooming process for most Miniature Schnauzers is quite unique. Most are single-coated and the coat is stripped using a process called staging. In staging, the coat is pulled out in certain areas in a series of stages.

For instance, if a dog has a dip in its topline (a portion of their back located after their shoulders), the hard-coat, also referred to as guard hair, in that area needs to be pulled out first. This area is referred to as the circle. Two weeks later, the rest of the hard coat would be pulled off their body, along with a slight V up their neck. Two weeks later, the hard coat along the sides of the neck and down to the elbow would need to be pulled out. Lastly, all the undercoat, which consists of soft gray hairs, would be pulled out.

Once the staging process is completed and the new hair has grown to a showable length, there is about an eight-week window for exhibition in shows. After the eight-week time frame, the hair becomes too long, which is referred to as blown, and now must be stripped back out. The dog must once again go through the staging cycle before it is properly ready to enter competition. All of this is done to ensure the dog's coat and appearance reflect the ideal aspects of the breed (the standard).

This staging process must be used for the majority of dogs in this breed because they are single-coated, meaning they have only one layer of good guard hairs or hard coat, and all the rest is undercoat. They are not truly ring-ready until the staging process has been completed and all the hairs that have been stripped out have begun to grow back.

According to Greg, if a Miniature Schnauzer possesses a high ratio of hard coat versus undercoat (note this is highly unusual), the coat can be rolled. Rolling is another technique, a very tedious act that I'll explain later. It takes both a great coat and a highly skilled groomer to accomplish this technique with this breed. However, for most Miniature Schnauzers, their coat cannot be rolled and, therefore, must adhere to the staging process.

Terriers require a different coat care process. Most Terriers are hard-coated. One of two things needs to be done to a Terrier at any point in their life. One, strip their coat out completely. This means pulling all their hair out, completely down to the skin. Two, do what is called rolling their coat.

Unlike the stripping-staging process used on a Miniature Schnauzer, this rolling process enables the dog to look exactly the same for the next ten years or longer, as long as the groomer is committed to pulling about one-twelfth of their coat out every single week. This diligent process is necessary because the hair pulled out one week will grow long enough to pull out again in twelve weeks. This is the case with most Terrier breeds; however, there can be a slight-variations.

By the time the groomer gets to the twelfth week, the hair that was pulled out twelve weeks ago is now long enough to get pulled out again. This creates replacement layering that is a week apart. Every week, the longest hair is stripped off. This keeps the coat looking fresh and in a consistent showable length. These different lengths of hair create what is referred to as a carpet. This process makes a dog's jacket nice and thick, with varying lengths.

Again, in Terriers, the groomer must be committed to pulling one-twelfth of the coat every single week. If a week or two of grooming is skipped, the effects aren't seen immediately. However, in two months or three months, the effects will be visible. Either there will be no hair in places because too much hair was pulled out all in one shot, or all that hair that was stripped will be growing in at the same time, creating a big pack of hair. Consistent, diligent weekly grooming is a must. Without consistency, a poor outcome is guaranteed and highly apparent.

Certain supplements are instrumental in growing hair, and certain protocols help maintain healthy hair.

Also, different breeds have different types of coats. Welsh, Irish, and Airedale Terriers have coarse leg hair. It is hard and fragile, and there are special skills needed to grow and maintain a dog's leg hair. Greg compares leg hair texture in these breeds to uncooked spaghetti. Dry, raw spaghetti is not very pliable and breaks easily.

And dirt is hair's worst enemy. For instance, if a Welsh Terrier runs around in a dirt yard and comes in filthy, brushing the hair is the worst thing that can be done. This is because dirt in hair acts like sandpaper.

Just as sandpaper is effective in making wood or metal disappear, dirt has the same effect on hair. Dirt in the hair causes friction and makes hair break apart. This takes place when brushing a dry, dirty coat, or even if the dog is simply walking with dirt in its coat. It happens to long-coated breeds, such as Bearded Collies, as well. If they have a lot of dirt, dust, or other debris in their coat, even if it's not visible, those fine hairs with dirt on them brush up against each other like sandpaper and break.

The dogs in Greg's care are kept exceptionally clean. He says, "With the Terriers, we wash some dogs every single day: legs, face, and belly. We don't typically blow dry them. Instead, we towel dry them and put oil in their legs and face to soften hair, if necessary. Oil keeps hair soft and pliable, preventing breakage."

However, you must keep in mind that oil attracts dirt. For the majority of breeds, when using oil, you must also be committed to washing at least every couple of days.

With long-coated breeds, a lot of the same rules apply. With long coats, it is very important that several rules are adhered to in order to minimize coat breakage. Proper brushing and combing rules must be honored: Never brush a dry coat. Never comb a wet coat. Using a comb on long, wet hair creates too much drag, either pulling hair out or breaking it. Using a brush on a dry coat acts like sandpaper, damaging hair.

Most long-coated breeds in Greg's facility are bathed every other day or at least twice per week. He says, "We bathe dogs before they get matted, because anytime you get a mat, some hair will be lost. If a dog gets a mat in its coat, we don't simply pick it apart. We put the whole dog in the tub and wash, condition, and blow dry the coat."

A specific brushing technique must be followed while drying a long-coated breed in order to maintain healthy hair. Greg explains the need for this process.

"Visualize a dryer freely blowing hair. It flaps the hair like a flag in the wind. Similar to a flag in the wind, eventually, the ends of the hair get tattered. With hair, this happens more quickly because hair is much more sensitive than fabric. If the coat is not dried properly, the ends of the hair get snapped off."

He also explains the brushing process.

"We begin by brushing in the same direction the hair is being blown. Next, brush about halfway through the length of the coat and then roll the brush off and let the blow dryer help pull the hair out of the brush. Gently work through to the end of the hair. Do NOT rip through the entire length of the hair in one fell swoop; this damages hair. This is particularly important if the hairs get a little rain, water, or saliva on them, because then they collect dust or dander and those ends stick together. If the hair was placed under a microscope, you would see all those ends would be stuck together. Brushing right through those ends severely damages the hair."

At dog shows, Greg and his staff carry spray bottles containing water and conditioner, with anti-static sometimes added to the mixture. The spray bottles are used to wet dogs' coats before brushing. The staff continually works to minimize hair breakage and maximize hair quality and health. Greg's secret to hair growth is to grow hair faster than you break it. Therefore, precautions are always being taken to minimize hair breakage.

Many of their dogs are also washed at the shows, too. Sometimes, Greg's team washes the entire dog. Minimally, at least a third to a half of the dog—meaning one-third to half way up a dog's body—is washed, conditioned, and blown dry at the show.

With long-coated breeds, Greg uses a brushing technique. He rolls his wrist one way as he starts to brush. As he gets halfway through the hair, he rolls his wrist in the opposite direction to lift off of the hair. This technique avoids ripping out the coat. He lets the brush do the work.

He says, "Most people don't even know how to use a brush. For instance, they may be using a pin brush with sixty or more pins, but only utilize a few rows of the pins to move through the hair. You need to work the brush flat to the skin. The pins in the brush are designed to act like little fingers. When there is pressure on the pins, they push together. The pressure on the rubber that the pins are seeded in makes the pins spread back out again, helping break mats apart. You have to let the brush do the work, softly and gently, as you are moving through the coat."

Keeping the coat extremely clean and applying the proper brushing technique is highly emphasized for the dogs in Greg's care.

A GOOD COAT BEGINS AT THE SKIN LEVEL

Greg uses a lot of human products on his dogs because dog product manufacturers sometimes charge up to four times the cost for equivalent products. In Greg's opinion, many of these dog products don't deliver enough noteworthy benefits to justify the higher cost. He believes that growing hair—whether for a short-coated breed such as a Doberman, a long-coated breed like a Bearded Collie or a Terrier—begins at skin level. He says, "You cannot grow good hair unless you have good skin."

He also supplements coconut oil as well as several other products in the diet. Back in the 1980s, Greg was struggling to get hair to grow on a couple of his show dogs, so he began researching B-Complex vitamins. B-Complex contains four vitamins that help grow nails and hair: Choline-Bitartrate, Biotin, Pantothenic Acid, and Inositol.

"Most women should use it. If they did, they would never need fake nails again," Greg insists. "I give those four vitamins in their concentrated form. I've been asked, 'Why don't you just give B-Complex?' The reason is, B-Complex might only give 50 mg of Inositol and I may want 300 mg. I want to give that particular vitamin in a concentrated form. They are water-soluble, so they are safe even in concentrated doses. What the body doesn't use is excreted in urine. In dogs, it helps improve the strength and growth of toenails, hair, and skin."

Another product Greg uses frequently is called Show Stopper. He uses it primarily for growing undercoats on dogs. However, he cautions when the product is no longer used, dogs immediately begin to blow their coat, which means their hair falls out.

Supplementation plays a huge part in growing and maintaining a coat. Greg advocates that hair be fed and nurtured from within. A poor diet or unhealthy skin doesn't grow hair. It is as simple as that. And a skinny dog doesn't grow hair.

Greg has a masterful mind, always seeking opportunities to overcome challenges. Because of this, some of his grooming techniques are unorthodox. Many years ago, a successful Alaskan Malamute breeder and handler gave Greg her Best in Show winning Malamute with the instructions, "Don't ever wash him or he will blow his coat."

Greg says, "I don't have a dog in my kennel that doesn't get washed at least once a week, if not every day. So, I thought, okay it does make sense that warm water, brushing, and blowing pulls hair out. However, what would happen if I apply my Terrier knowledge? If I stripped one twelfth of this dog's undercoat every single week, what would happen when Mother Nature says, 'Hey, drop all that hair,' and there is nothing really old to drop or shed because it is fresh hair, since one twelfth of the hair is continually pulled every week. I tried it. That dog had a beautiful coat all the time."

He never blew his coat while in Greg's care.

Greg also insists this technique is effective when you pull a jacket on an Irish Setter. If you rake out that dull undercoat sitting in that jacket, you change the ratio of desirable, healthy, shiny coat versus undercoat.

According to Greg, this can even be done with a short-coated Doberman or Boxer. If you don't change the proportion of good guard hairs versus undercoat, you often have a bit of a dull look. Make it thirty percent undercoat and seventy percent shiny guard hair, and now you have a very shiny coat. And if you can make that ratio stronger or better in the guard hair department, it gets even shinier. This can be accomplished by washing a dog in the tub and using a rubber brush, moving it back and forth against the grain, and taking out whatever undercoat wants to come out. This keeps the coat looking its absolute best all the time.

Regarding his Irish Setters, people often ask Greg what kind of shampoo he uses to get the jackets so shiny. He usually laughs because it has less to do with shampoo and more to do with nutrition and knowing how to muck out (take out) the undercoat. The truth is, washing dogs in Dawn dishwashing liquid delivers better results than just about any shampoo because it strips dirt, grease, and product buildup from the hair.

As you can see, every dog's coat is different. In order to create and maintain show-worthy coats, Greg's team uses many different grooming techniques, proper nutrition, environmental controls (keeping coats clean), and changes the ratio of undercoat to guard hairs or hard coat.

Again, Greg encourages, "Don't be afraid to take out hair that wants to come out, such as in double-coated breeds like Border Collies and

Alaskan Malamutes. Mother Nature is only going to get rid of what needs to go, not fresh coat. Fresh hair is not dead… Mother Nature won't blow that."

Now take everything I have told you about maintaining a proper coat and multiply that work by thirty-eight! Yes, at one point, Greg had a lineup of thirty-eight dogs in his care in need of being prepared, shown, and exercised all in one day, every day, throughout the course of one year! At the time, he had three assistants.

He explains, "If we collectively did not have a strong work ethic and determination to be the best, there would have been far too many dogs to take on. We worked like a highly caffeinated, well-oiled machine and got the job done and done well!"

Although these details might seem tedious and overwhelming, they demonstrate the depth of knowledge and skill that Greg possesses, as well as the immense amount of time and commitment necessary to create and maintain different coats for different breeds based on breed standards (ideals). While Greg's commitment is one of the innate qualities that serves him well in this industry, his depth of knowledge and experience didn't happen overnight. These qualities have been developed over time as Greg has stayed committed to his passion and purpose as a dog handler.

I ask, "Is there ever a break, Greg?"

His response: "Mind over matter. And if you don't have a mind, it doesn't matter."

This is a big motto in Greg's life, and it plays out in a variety of ways. Although this motto helps him overcome seemingly insurmountable obstacles, it creates a few additional challenges as well.

He admits, "I've encountered major changes in my life because of how intense my lifestyle is. I am not laughing about it, because it is one of the downsides. Important people in my life have gotten frustrated, tired, and burned-out from my lifestyle."

Greg references two previous marriages. It's not just him, there are others in the sport that face this challenge as well. The travel schedule alone is often too much for couples to withstand, let alone all the other demands. Maintaining marriage and intimate relationships can be extremely challenging for professional handlers.

Being of Service to Clients and the Industry at Large

Even though maintaining relationships can be difficult, the sense of connection and appreciation Greg derives from putting in the effort is what often drives him to achieve more and more. This goes for both personal and professional relationships. For Greg, it's not about winning another ribbon; it's about taking care of the people in his life that matter to him, and that includes his clients.

"The enjoyment of working with the people I care most about, making those people happy, and helping fulfill their dream with their dogs is even more fantastic."

He adds, "That is what drives me. I want to serve my people and make them happy. I simply want to do the best I can do for them for as long as I can do it. That's what keeps me going.

"I'm very blessed to work with some of the greatest owners in our sport. They trust me, giving me their show quality house pet for up to three years in my care. Most every dog I show retires back to a bed or sofa from which they came to me. It is so comforting to know that the dogs I get so involved with and fall in love with retire back to a home I would want to live in myself."

Greg's compassion and concern for the well-being of others extends to spectators as well. He has a high level of sensitivity toward new people interested in our sport.

He says, "It is important to be kind and friendly because everyone that exhibits at dog shows started off new to the experience at some point."

Everyone who shows a dog was a beginner at one point. He is mindful of spectators, always listening and watching, considering how they might be experiencing the dog show, and seeking ways to make himself available to them. Often, exhibitors, whether they are owner-handlers or professional handlers, can become highly focused on their dog and winning, and as a result, act abruptly, harshly, or rudely to spectators.

Greg says, "I understand that competitiveness. I am competitive myself. I have found ways to curb that intensity around spectators because it is important to me that they have a good experience at the dog show."

He adds, "We are onstage."

And in his mind, being onstage comes with responsibility. Professional handlers are role models, and that holds true for many owner-handlers as well.

If he is outside the ring, waiting with a long-coated dog with its hair ready and looking perfect for the judge, and a spectator wants to pet the dog, Greg will say, "It's okay, you can pet the dog. I have a comb in my pocket."

He adds, "Obviously, you don't do that with a Standard Poodle. When I showed Bichons, I wouldn't let anyone touch them until I was done showing, and then I would invite spectators back to my set-up to touch them. I didn't want a child with a red lollipop in hand petting my Bichon. However, I do always try to find a way to keep the door open for spectators so they can have a pleasant experience."

A JOB WELL DONE

Greg's lifestyle, which he defines as a labor of love, has earned him the distinction of having won Best in Show on hundreds of dogs across all seven groups. He doesn't know how many Bests in Show he has won throughout his lifetime. That number doesn't matter to him. As much as he wants to win, when it's done, he moves on to the next challenge. He believes a win-loss column doesn't define you as a person or professional, that how you conduct your affairs is what truly matters.

He is a man of fortitude. His motto–mind over matter, and if you don't have a mind, it doesn't matter–gets him through life. He works harder than anyone I have ever met. He is a stand-up guy who takes great care of his dogs and the people in his life. His clients and dogs know that they can always count on him. He is not an attention seeker; he's the person that gets the job done well and done right. Feeling appreciated and fulfilling his clients' dreams motivates him to continually put in a hard day's work, each and every day, day after day. Greg is someone you can depend on.

CHAPTER 4

Michael Scott:
Strategy and Politics

I find it interesting to meet with someone who has experienced so much success within this industry and hear him say he "fell into it." Many of us try so hard to make something happen, yet Michael Scott says it "just happened." My interview with Michael left me feeling that maybe I had it all wrong. Maybe life need not be that difficult. Is it possible for success to happen without force?

According to Michael, he fell into dog handling because it was basically the family business. Ironic that someone who is sometimes viewed as arrogant by outsiders has such a simplistic explanation for how he came to be so successful in his career. Maybe it really was that simple.

When I spoke with Michael, I found his frankness surprisingly refreshing. Although his initiation into dog handling was effortless, don't mistake this simplicity for ease. Although the path was already laid out for him, Michael used all the resources available to him to attain his accomplishments.

Throughout his career, Michael has won Best in Show on a dog in every group. He won Best in Show at Quaker Oats. He has won multiple groups at Westminster. He has campaigned dogs to number one in five different groups. His success is not breed-specific; it spans many different breeds and groups. How did this happen?

Michael's parents started showing dogs in 1968. They were probably in one of the last waves of handlers licensed by the AKC, which stopped requiring professional handlers to be licensed in 1977. When they were kids, Michael and his brother competed in junior showmanship with Beagles. Michael's brother left dog handling to pursue a college degree. Michael also took time away but did not choose to pursue college. He admits he got into a bit of trouble during that time. After realizing his life was off track, he went back to work with his parents for a short time.

Soon after Michael came back into the fold, Ted Young, a close friend of Michael's parents, suggested that he take a job with Pat Craige, an Elkhound breeder/handler located in California (who years later went on to write *Born to Win, Breed to Succeed* by Patricia Craige Trotter and became an AKC licensed judge). When Michael left to work for her, he didn't know how long he would stay.

According to Michael, Pat was a breeder more than a handler, and she was intense. She was passionate about her breed and put a lot of time, care, and attention into how she conditioned and exercised her dogs. Biking dogs was an integral part of how she prepared her dogs' physical appearance and functionality.

"I learned so much about care and conditioning dogs from Pat in such a short period of time," says Michael.

Michael could have stayed out there working for Pat for years, but an unexpected opportunity presented itself. AKC offered Michael's dad, Ray, a job. And then, several of Ray's really good clients said that if Michael came back to the East Coast, they would like to hire him to handle their dogs.

"It was a great opportunity for me," says Michael. "I never really knew that I would be showing dogs for a living. It evolved that way."

Although Michael's story of how he got his start in showing dogs sounds fairly straightforward, it is important to note that he made key decisions at certain choice points. At each moment, he made the next best choice, and in time, one thing just "happened" to lead to another.

A Connection to Great People

According to Michael, he has been given the opportunity to work with some great dogs and great clients over the years. The people found him and the good dogs came to him.

He says, "I was fortunate to know the right people. My parents were well liked. I grew up in the sport at a great time."

Some of the people he refers to are Jane Forsyth, Ted Young, Anne Rogers Clark, and Mike (Michelle) Billings, to name a few. For those not involved in dog shows or those new to the sport, these were extremely influential people. They are considered icons in the sport.

The level of respect they garnered within the industry would be similar to the influence George Washington and Abraham Lincoln had on the United States of America. These dog show icons were very good friends with Michael's parents.

In later chapters, you will have the opportunity to read about some of these key figures. It will become clear that Michael's relationship with these people had a profound impact on him and how he conducts business.

"For me, one thing always led to another," admits Michael.

Again, although Micheal makes it sound simple, his ability to apply what he learned from them and implement their strategies is a huge part of his success. A great coach can tell a player how to play the game, but that doesn't necessarily mean that the player will have the ability to apply what's been taught.

Being a person who has spent a lifetime working hard to *make* things happen, hearing Michael's story and how his life and career seemed to be handed to him feels unfair. However, once you get to know Michael, it's hard to begrudge his success. Yes, he was given many opportunities that others would be envious of. Yet at the same time, he worked hard, fully utilizing his natural talent for fostering and nurturing relationships.

He is also obsessively passionate, dedicated, and disciplined in his work and with the people in his life. He values people, and the people in his life value him. In addition, once he finds the right dog, he drops into a new gear, and a whole other side of Michael takes over.

GREAT SHOW DOGS ARE BORN, NOT MADE

Michael says most of his great dogs didn't need a lot of training, they simply needed fine-tuning. He says, "I feel there was something certain about them, something special. They knew they were great."

Michael mentions Bebe, a Corgi, who was one of his first top-winning dogs.

"Bebe was a push-button dog. She was so in-tuned," he says. "Matisse (a Portuguese Water Dog that Michael handled, winning 238 Bests in Show as of February 2015 and ranked Number One Dog, All Breeds in 2014) was wonderful. You just rack him up. The dog had such an amazing aura. People couldn't walk by him without stopping to look or comment on his appearance. Even people who didn't know a thing about Portuguese Water Dogs were in awe. Those great dogs didn't need me. I could have turned them loose in the ring and they would have just gone out there and done their thing. They were so smart and self-assured."

There is no doubt in his mind when Michael says, "Great show dogs are born, not made."

He chooses these dogs because he can identify this aura and their winning nature. This is part of his strategy, and it allows him to focus his energy on doing what he does best... more on that later.

And yet, Michael's approach sounds too easy. I find myself resisting the simplicity of his business model. I've always viewed a big part of my job as my ability to find the greatness within a dog, and then I help to bring out this greatness. Many of the dogs I work with have issues, and it often takes a lot of work to find their confidence and help them express that in the ring. I have shown many dogs that are great structurally, but they don't carry themselves in a way that garners attention. One of the things I do as a handler is to help them become more confident and project their energy so the judge and spectators notice what a good specimen they are. It is very clear to me that, although Michael and I share commonalities as handlers, we experience our role as handler much differently.

From Michael's perspective, his dogs don't need him in order to be great show dogs. This leaves me wondering how this belief may energetically influence his dogs in the ring. Is he energetically influencing his dogs? And to what degree? When I am handling, I am constantly sensing and feeling what my dogs need and making adjustments based on the energy I receive from them. So, I'm very curious about how

Michael's energy impacts his dogs in the ring. Does his belief in the dogs he handles contribute to their confidence, as it might with humans? For instance, when you exude confidence in someone—as Michael is confident in his dogs—often that person steps up and becomes exactly what you believe them to be: successful.

I ask, "Do you have to change how you approach a dog, depending on the dog in front of you? Do you tailor your approach in any way to the dog, or do you always just show up the same way, as Michael?"

Michael looks confused by my question. He then says, "I think so."

Michelle Scott, his wife, who also handles dogs professionally (more on her in Chapter 5), jumps in and adds, "He commands something from his dogs and they come around."

I still find myself trying to figure Michael out. So, I explain, "If I have a dog that has too much energy or can't handle a correction, I respond differently to that dog. I adjust my energy in order to get the dog's energy to come into balance."

Michael immediately understands, laughs, and says, "Yah, I give those dogs to Michelle!"

In all seriousness, he then adds, "Maybe when I was younger, I worked with more of that… but Michelle is so much better at the neediness than I am."

He laughs, then adds, "With both the dogs and the clients!"

I love how Michael owns who he is. He is wise enough not to waste his energy in areas that aren't his strengths or don't appeal to him. Again, I find myself shaking my head, thinking, this seems too easy. Why couldn't I have had this conversation with Michael back in my twenties? My life would have been so different!

According to Michael, his top dogs didn't need someone to make them into great show dogs. What they needed was someone who was willing to work hard to campaign them, and this is another of Michael's fortes.

FINDING THE NEXT GREAT ONE: SPEARHEADING A CAMPAIGN

When I ask, "What do you love most about showing dogs?" He says, "I love being with Michelle, my wife!"

He laughs, and so does Michelle. He then gets more serious and says, "I love being able to work with the dogs. I love being able to find that next great one. I think I really get involved and excited when I feel like I have that next great one. When I find it, I get obsessed. If you give me a project, I will get totally involved in it. Once I have that, it's all I think about 24/7."

Hearing this outpouring, I sense a perfectionist nature in Michael. After stating that to him, he admits, "Yeah, I'm a little neurotic that way. Everything needs to be in its place. It needs to be the way I want it."

Not all handlers enjoy the demands of running a top campaign, but Michael does. In fact, he lives for it. He's a master strategist who loves the mental aspect of orchestrating a national campaign. He admits it can make him crazy at times, sitting in a rental car after going Best in Show and trying to make the decision, should I stay here with this panel of judges, or are my odds better traveling to a different show, under different judges at a different location? Strategizing and making crucial decisions like this is what really gets Michael fired up.

This is a key job requirement all highly successful handlers must commit to if they choose to take their handling to another level and run a national campaign. They constantly need to determine which show among many being held across the country offers the best odds of their dog winning. Often, this can be quite a gamble because there are so many moving parts to consider. It is similar to a game of chess, only you are playing against multiple opponents.

Factors that require consideration for a successful strategic campaign might include (but are not limited to) the following:

- Who is the local favorite in each area?
- How strongly do I believe this judge will like my dog?
- Who will be my competition at each show?
- Will this judge's decision be swayed by other judges on the judging panel?
- Will the judges be influenced by one of my competitors or do I have an edge with that judge over my competition?
- Out of the judges I am considering exhibiting to, who are their friends?
- What judges are highly influenceable and by whom?
- Who are the judges friends with on Facebook and other social media?

A good handler knows the answers to these questions, and if they don't, they ask someone until they find the answers. This is all part of the game of dog shows!

Not only does the handler have to determine the likeliest place they can win, but they also need to take travel time into account. Smaller dogs have an advantage in that they have more travel options since they are allowed to fly in the cabin with their handler. Handlers of larger dogs have the extra concern of having to expose their dog to flying in cargo unless their owner flies them on a private jet (which sometimes happens). Most handlers decide to fly a dog cargo at some point, but it's not a choice any handler makes lightly.

Michael describes some of the pressure he faced while campaigning Matisse. He recalls sitting in a rental car in his driveway or at a show, trying to decide whether he should stay or go. At times, he would have a crew of people waiting for his decision. In several instances, he rented a car and then turned it back in because he changed his mind.

He says, "Other days, I was at a certain show and realized I was at the wrong show and I needed to be somewhere else."

Making decisions like this can be extremely stressful, yet Michael enjoys it. He admits it is demanding on so many levels.

He says, "There is the mental scrutiny and the physical exhaustion that can come, not just from all that needs to be decided, but also the physical demands of driving from show to show. It is constant. The driving requirements that are incurred pursuing a campaign for number one dog are exhausting. Just getting from place to place can be very draining and demanding on the handler."

Plus, Michael adds, "A good handler needs to provide the dog with great care and conditioning."

This, too, is something Michael is well known and respected for, providing high-quality personal care and attention to his dogs–again, part of his strategic mindset. The dog you are campaigning is your biggest and best asset. It needs to be at its best at all times and in all ways possible, which means the handler needs to provide exquisite care and attention.

I say to Michael, "It's clear you enjoy planning and strategizing the best shows for each dog you campaign, but what are you thinking about when you are with your dog in the ring or outside the ring? Do you plan everything out before you go into the ring?"

"Oh yeah," says Michael. "I'm a thinker. I know everyone who is in the ring with me. I know the players and who I need to beat that the judge might like. I do all my homework. When I was campaigning for number one working dog, I could tell you who was judging the Working Group at every show in the country any day of the week. I would think it all through constantly. It was painful driving with me! I was obsessed with figuring out where I needed to be and who I needed to beat."

When Michael campaigns a dog, his mind is spinning like that 24/7. His dogs probably sense this and know, "Michael has got this!"

I believe some dogs are born to win, to entertain, to light it up. I believe some of these dogs love being with someone like Michael, who understands them and helps them shine their light to their fullest potential.

He explains, "For instance, Michelle might look at the Canine Chronicle and say, 'oh, Kelly won Best in Show on her Dobe.'"

He will then ask himself, "Did that judge put up that handler because it was the local favorite? Can I beat that dog in their area under a certain judge?"

All these factors come into play–once again, strategy at work. He says, "You need to mentally store all that information. You have to remember it weeks and months in advance."

I ask, "Do you remember all this, or do you write it down?"

Michael says, "I remember it! Sometimes I forget what it was, or occasionally I'll say, 'I missed that.' But overall, I know everything that is going on at every dog show around the country whenever I campaign a dog. I want to know everything!"

He says, "When I was campaigning Matise, I knew the judges coming up all across the country as far out in advance as you can find out."

Michelle adds, "The funny thing is, he doesn't have a good memory in terms of remembering names!"

We all laughed at that, but really, this points to how seriously Michael takes his job as a handler. He is hyper-focused when it comes to the competition and the win. If it isn't about the competition, it's not nearly as important.

"When we go, we go hard," says Michael. "But we still have a good time."

When he says this, he is referring to his owners and his wife, Michelle. Michael and Michelle travel together as much as possible, which can be challenging because they each have clients of their own.

"Yes, campaigning a dog hard is exhausting, but we enjoy it," says Michael.

He starts getting all fired up again and says, "Milan, Matise's owner, wanted to play hard. Milan was always watching what I was doing with Holly (a top-winning Pointer Michael showed in 2008). When he got Matise, he knew he wanted to play hard, so he called me. He loved my competitiveness."

Michael also believes it is important to have a good working relationship with the handlers you are competing against. In fact, often handlers team up to take out a common opponent. Michael is a master at this.

They each benefit by working together. He gives credit to Jimmy Moses, a highly accomplished handler most widely known for all the winning he did with German Shepherds. In the 1990s, Jimmy handled Mystique, winning 275 Bests in Show, which designated them as one of the top winning teams of all time.

Michael says, "I learned so much from Jimmy. I remember when I showed Bebe, the Corgi. Jimmy would call me to ask me where I was going to show."

He didn't want to compete against Michael's dog, so he would find out where Michael was going so he didn't have to compete against him. That way, they both could win.

"He was showing his dog, and he would want to know where I was going so he could win. We would talk about it. He would tell me, 'Don't go show to that judge, let me go there, you can hit them at this other show and go Best in Show there.' I learned so much from Jimmy about campaigning dogs because I always had the Corgi in the Herding Group, and he had the Shepherd. We would talk all the time. I was younger than him. I give a lot of credit to Jimmy for having taught me a lot about the intricacies of how to campaign a dog. He was a master strategist."

Once again, it is clear how Michael's motto, "It's all about who you know," shows up again and again in his career. Michael is very strategic in putting himself in line with the right people to help him get the job done.

Three Essential Ingredients for Success

Michael says he always remembers the words uttered to him by Annie Rogers Clark, an icon in the sport (see Chapter 10 for more on her role, particularly as a mentor).

"You've got to start with a great dog. You need a good handler. The dog needs to be owned well. These are the three ingredients necessary in a successful campaign."

Michael took these words of wisdom to heart. He believes if he is going to take the next great dog to the top, he needs to assemble these three key ingredients.

Michael says, "That's how it is with me. It has got to be all or nothing. I'm always looking for the next great one. I like finding the dog. Once I do that, I find the right owner with enough money to make it happen."

A majority of what I write about in this book describes the attributes of great handlers. I suppose a whole book could also be written on what it means to be a great owner. To be a great owner, one must have money, a lot of money. Campaigning dogs at the national level is extremely expensive. A good owner must have financial resources, and it is extremely helpful if they are well liked and respected within the sport. In this sport, as in much of life, people are more willing to do for people they like and trust. It's human nature.

Over the years in this sport, I have repeatedly heard judges say, "If all things are equal between two dogs, then my deciding factor will be to put up the handler, dog, owner that I know and like."

Many judges work hard to separate their feelings for their friends who show dogs to them. It is their intention always to put up the best dog, but sometimes you have two or more dogs who are equally great or of equal quality. Most judges admit, under those circumstances, they will award their friends' dogs. So here, in addition to having a lot of extra money to spend showing dogs, it is equally important that owners be well liked and respected within the sport.

GREAT OWNERS

Michael only works for owners that honor and respect his abilities as a handler. Not surprisingly, he describes his "great owners" as good business people.

During the interview, he asks me, "You know how some clients want to get involved and help you pick judges?"

I nod my head, acknowledging how frustrated I felt working for clients who "need" to be part of the decision-making process. Michael explains, "My clients let me do my job."

My whole body feels a big sigh of relief when Michael says this. What resonates is how good it feels to work with clients who trust my ability to make good decisions, who don't second guess my decisions and don't feel the need to control things.

Michael says, "I make the decisions about which judges to show to. That's my job. Yes, I talk about it with my clients, I value their input, but they let me make the final decision."

Michael also explains that he rarely makes the decision to fly dogs he is campaigning. He drives everywhere. He says, "My clients give me the ability to do what I want to do. They let me do what I feel I need to do. We talk about the details of the campaign."

Michael isn't told what decisions he needs to make, but he is open to hearing suggestions when he is unclear or undecided. He is given the freedom to do his job in the manner he feels is best.

According to Michael, clients should allow the handlers to make the decisions. Michael emphasizes that a client hires a handler to engage in professional service, and part of a professional handler's service is the ability to properly select the best show circumstances for the client's dog.

Sometimes a handler needs to make a decision, and it is hard for them to explain their reasons. There may be unseen factors that need to be taken into account. Michael elaborates, "Handlers have gut feelings and we need to be able to follow them."

He shares a conversation he had with a fellow professional handler. At the time, this handler told Michael he was considering retiring from handling dogs professionally and offering himself up as a campaign manager to help people determine where they needed to show their specials. This handler was pretty excited about the idea, but Michael wasn't convinced.

Michael went on to explain that no one except the handler "knows each handler's personal relationship with various judges. For instance, if they showed to a judge and walked out with an attitude and offended the judge. Then maybe they can't go back to that judge for a while. Maybe it's a judge they've always been a good sport with and have a great relationship with. Someone else can't possibly know all those intricacies and see the whole picture."

During this discussion with Michael, I recall a series of events during the national campaign I ran with a Doberman named Raisin (Ch. Blue Chip Purple Reign, also commonly referred to as Reign) when I went with my gut instinct, and it paid off. But first, I am going to tell you about a time I allowed myself to be persuaded by a dog's breeder to make a decision that went against my best judgment.

The breeder begged me to show Raisin in her local state of Pennsylvania because those were "her favorite shows" and because the shows in Pennsylvania were much larger in numbers and more prestigious than the shows where I wanted to exhibit in Maine. I was against showing in Pennsylvania because one of the judges on the panel in Pennsylvania was a Doberman breeder who was very influential. He was a very knowledgeable dog person, well respected, and extremely persuasive. When he was on a judging panel, you could see the influence he had on the choices other judges made in the selection of dogs they chose to recognize and reward.

I knew he was not an advocate of Raisin's. Even though I generally fared well whenever I exhibited dogs to the actual breed judge, I didn't think my good-standing relationship with her would translate into a breed win for Raisin in Pennsylvania under those circumstances. Therefore, I told the dog's breeder that I felt we would lose the breed in Pennsylvania, and I wanted to show her in Maine instead. In Maine, we had a great lineup of judges who would likely lead to Raisin winning at least a couple of Bests in Show.

My concern in this case—my gut instinct (and logical intelligence)—was valid, and I didn't listen to it. I went against my own informed discernment and acquiesced to the breeder. Not only did we lose the breed that day, we weren't even in contention for the win. We were completely dismissed from competition, which is the ultimate insult for a top dog.

Two months later, I found myself in an interesting position. I was showing in Ohio. The same judge that dismissed Raisin in Pennsylvania was scheduled to judge the breed in Dobermans the next day in Ohio. My original plan was to leave Ohio and drive to another show immediately following Best in Show judging. My motorhome was packed up and running. However, something unexpected happened.

As I was walking Raisin back to the motorhome, holding the Best in Show ribbon we had just won, I turned around and saw a group of judges standing around excitedly talking. It "felt" like they were all talking about Raisin and how much they loved her. How do I know that? I didn't know it for a fact, it was a gut feeling. They were all smiling and looking in my direction. And among that group, excitedly smiling herself, was the breed judge that I had been avoiding.

I said to my mom and the breeder, "We are not leaving, we are staying."

They both looked at me in shock. They both knew Raisin had recently lost under that breed judge. However, something about the look on my face made them not challenge me.

Out of curiosity, my mom asked, "Why?"

My answer was, "I can't really explain it, I just know that we need to stay."

There was something about the smile on the judge's face and her body language that made me feel she would award us the breed. The next day, we won the breed easily and went on to win another Best in Show.

A great handler needs to strategize AND follow their gut. Even a "thinker" like Michael listens to his instincts and the wisdom that goes beyond mental logic. Because Michael recognizes his own strengths in this, he doesn't allow his clients to interfere with his decision-making process.

An Industry Built Around Dogs and Relationships

I've been in this business in one form or another my whole life. One thing that fascinates me is how differently people perceive the purpose of a dog show and how its mission should be executed. Many exhibitors are quick to cry wolf when their dog doesn't win. Often these exhibitors believe they were taken advantage of because a judge picked a dog based on political reasons. Extremists like this commonly say, "Who will win has nothing to do with the dog."

Do politics play a role in dog shows? Yes, absolutely. However, I would like to think it is not as often as the extremists would have us believe.

Politics are everywhere. They are a part of life. So yes, they are a part of dog shows. If you are an exhibitor, junior handler, owner-handler, or professional handler, you are going to need to learn to accept this on some level. You can fight it, hate it, rage against it, but in the end, you will need to somehow come to terms with it. It is up to you as to how you will respond to it.

I certainly had to. Politicking wasn't my thing, especially when I was younger. I felt very uncomfortable talking with strangers. I felt uncomfortable in new situations, and I wasn't a good self-promoter. (Frank Murphy admits this as well in Chapter 2.) I was aloof, serious, and guarded (not qualities that set people at ease). Yes, I embodied several Doberman characteristics!

What did work in my favor was that I didn't allow my struggles to paralyze me. Instead, I focused on always presenting my dogs to the absolute best of my abilities. I felt like the underdog (which was modeled to me by my mentor, Gwen DeMilta–more on her in Chapter 11) and was always highly motivated when an obstacle was put in my path. My determination took me a long way and even helped me overcome a severe handicap: my lack of people skills.

One of the many things I appreciate about Michael is that he doesn't beat himself up over what he isn't. He knows who he is, he knows his strengths, and he knows how to utilize them to his advantage. Michael shows beautiful dogs and applies his knowledge and knack for building relationships with judges to give his dogs an edge in competition. Much of what Michael values in this business is people and relationships.

He adds, "A huge part of your job as a handler is your relationship with the judges. The judges have to want to point to you and your dog."

As we have already explored, when it gets down to a judge deciding who will win Best in Show, Michael believes in the three key ingredients: a great dog on the end of the lead; a respected owner; and a respected, well-like handler.

"The whole team has got to be something they want to reward. As I got older, I especially realized the importance of this."

There is a whole lot more to showing dogs than the dogs themselves. Besides the dogs, there are owners, judges, handlers, sponsors, breeders, kennel club officials, AKC reps, and many other players. There is undeniably a very large people component to showing dogs. And this people-driven industry, much like other industries, favors those who are good at building mutually beneficial relationships. Call it politics. Call it relationship building. Whatever you call it, Michael is very good at it.

After interviewing Michael, I appreciate how naturally he allowed his innate strengths and people skills to serve him in his profession. He doesn't get caught up in what dog is right and what dog is wrong. That is the judge's decision to make. He lets the judges do their jobs. It isn't his job to preserve the breed standard. My guess is that Michael believes that is the responsibility of a good breeder. From Michael's perspective, it is his responsibility to condition and take care of his clients' dogs well, to present them well, and to show them to the proper judges. That is his job. He is clear about what he expects of himself, what he expects from his clients, and what his clients can expect of him.

One of the many things I have learned in writing this book is that all great handlers are passionate about their work. However, as individuals, they feel passionate about different things. What lights one handler up may bore or frustrate another. Michael loves finding the next great dog, orchestrating a campaign, and building the relationships he needs to accomplish those two goals. Whereas Michael's wife, Michelle, enjoys nurturing and fostering confidence in her dogs. That's what lights her up. That's how she feels fulfilled in her work.

Michael and Michelle are like the sun and the moon. Equally great handlers, but they bring different strengths to the table and are fulfilled in different ways by their job.

"It's Just a Game!"

Michael also holds the unique view that dog showing is a form of entertainment. It's a sport. It's a game we play. In a sense, his clients hire him to entertain themselves. After all, people watch dog shows for entertainment.

My guess is that some serious dog show exhibitors are cringing at this. That's okay. I get it. I used to take this all very seriously as well. From my perspective, I think it is part of my responsibility and the judge's responsibility to have a thorough understanding of the Doberman standard and to judge accordingly in order to protect the integrity of the Doberman breed. Gwen DeMilta, one of my mentors, who you will learn about in Chapter 11, modeled this way of thinking. She was very serious about everything. However, Michael makes a valid argument. Dog showing is a sport that dog show enthusiasts participate in for entertainment. Perhaps this is how Michael keeps his role as a dog show handler in perspective.

For Michael, things just fell into place, and one thing led to another. Some of it has to do with luck, and some of the simplicity Michael speaks of in his career trajectory is because he knows who he is and who he isn't. He knows what matters to him. This keeps things simple for him. This helps him strategize and strategize well.

I really appreciate Michael's clear-cut approach. When he is not campaigning a dog he is passionate about, his perfectionistic drive eases up and he returns to idle, conserving his energy until the next great dog comes along. He knows that his passion is strategizing a national campaign, and that is where he puts all of his energy. His energy isn't wasted. It is focused on what matters to him.

As he states, he had the good fortune of being surrounded by several key people. When you read about Jane Forsyth (Chapter 12) and Anne Rogers Clark (Chapter 10) and how they conducted themselves and business matters, it becomes clear that Michael modeled himself after these great women. He was a quick study, applied all he learned from his past mentors, and made a name for himself, serving his clients and his dogs well.

Although success did happen for Michael, he also happened to life. Michael had the wisdom to wait for life to happen, and then he made his own destiny. He recognized when opportunities presented themselves, always took the next best step, and utilized his talents and resources to get the most within his power out of the circumstances. That's not just good logic but also hard work and wisdom at play.

PART TWO

Using Your Strengths to Your Advantage

CHAPTER 5

Michelle Scott:
Innate Abilities and Managing Expectations

"Great handlers really know how to connect with their dogs. It's not easy to explain this. For me, it's just instinctive."

—Michelle Scott

Michelle and I both grew up on the East Coast, mostly showing dogs in the New England area, and we crossed paths often. She is a couple of years younger than me and mainly showed working dogs in her younger years. Although never close friends, we watched each other grow up in the sport. I am very familiar with Michelle, how she handles and cares for her dogs, how she interacts with her peers, and how she conducts herself as a fellow professional. To work with Michelle is truly an honor.

When she is working with her clients and their dogs, she is quiet, kind, sincere, warm-hearted, compassionate, and comforting.

Michelle's true joy begins in the training phase with her dogs. She likes to start with a clean slate. Like an artist with a piece of clay, Michelle sees the beauty within the animal.

She says, "I love creating from scratch. I like to condition a dog mentally and physically. It is very rewarding to me. I am very much about the underdog. Getting a new dog and making it into something special is one of the most satisfying things about my job."

When describing the attributes of a great handler, Michelle says, "I think there is a natural talent that just happens. Having compassion, truly loving the dogs, and having a strong connection with them is huge. It's innate for me. Great handlers really know how to connect with their dogs. It's not easy to explain this. For me, it's just instinctive."

Michelle's innate talent led to several outstanding achievements in her career, which include winning Best in Show at the highly prestigious Westminster Kennel Club, not just once, but twice.

Michelle states, "I have been incredibly blessed. I think it was fate. Success found me."

Michelle's first Best in Show win at Westminster was with a Newfoundland named Josh.

"Josh was such an exceptional dog," says Michelle.

In fact, Michelle believes she is the lucky one when it comes to Josh. As she reflects on her experience with Josh, she describes him as an old soul and a true gentleman. Michelle humbly remembers, "I just felt so honored to be his dance partner. We carried each other. We worked together."

Although Michelle says it must have been fate, the road to winning Best in Show at Westminster was not easy. Fate or not, there were many challenges along the way. For instance, while showing in the Working Group at Westminster in 2003, during the individual exam, Josh pulled away from the judge and broke out of his stack, practically lying down on the carpet.

Stop for a moment and picture this. Josh is a big dog! For those of you unfamiliar with Newfoundlands, males generally weigh up to 150 pounds, sometimes more. When he resisted the exam, he was too large for Michelle to hold him up and keep him steady.

When he pulled away, Michelle did her best to reassure him and get him back on track. In addition, Josh was startled and unnerved by all the spotlights. Most dogs never encounter spotlights while in the show ring, but Westminster is different.

Despite the mishap, they went on to win the Working Group.

This wasn't their final foray at Westminster. Michelle and Josh planned to compete again for Best in Show the following year. She realized that if they had a second chance at this, she would be going back into an environment that caused unease in her dog. Just like humans, dogs remember stressful situations, particularly those that take place in a new environment. When they reenter that same environment, fear naturally arises within their bodies and brains, putting them on high alert because they are anticipating a similar negative experience. This natural response would help them detect danger out in the wild.

Michelle needed to come up with a plan to address Josh's fear and unease. She says, "We wanted to be sure that if we were lucky enough to be in the same situation again with the spotlights, that Josh would feel more comfortable."

And since they had no access to a big arena with spotlights, there would be no way to train or prepare for this in a tangible way. What's more, as we've established, a Newfoundland is a very large and powerful dog. If he were spooked or he suddenly attempted to escape the ring, there would not be much Michelle could do to hide or redirect his behavior. Because of his size, Michelle would be at his mercy. She would be reentering the lion's den, so to speak, and she would be doing so with little to no preparation as the world witnessed. Talk about pressure!

Taking all these concerns into account, Michelle decided to consult with Jess Montañez, the same animal communicator who worked with Janice Hayes (Chapter 1). Jess worked with Josh intuitively to prepare him for what would be taking place at Westminster the next year. Jess also identified the cause of another issue Josh was having.

He was resisting judges opening his mouth for the physical exam. This deviation in behavior seemed to come out of the blue. According to Michelle, "This was highly unusual for him."

By connecting with his energy, Jess identified that while running in the yard with another dog, Josh accidentally bumped into a tree and needed a chiropractic adjustment to his jaw. Luckily, this issue of pulling away from the judge during the physical exam could be overcome with practice, training, and healthcare.

"That was not something we would have been able to figure out for ourselves because it was so unusual," explains Michelle. "Jess helped us figure this out, helped get him healthy by suggesting a chiropractor adjust his jaw, and then we were able to get through the physical exam more smoothly."

Now that that issue was resolved, there still remained the concern of the spotlights. How could Michelle prepare to show Josh under those conditions without any tangible way to practice? Other than seeking Jess's expertise to counsel Josh energetically, there didn't seem to be anything that Michelle could really do, but presence goes a long way with a dog.

"I don't think it was anything specific that I did," says Michelle. "It was more a matter of us both anticipating what to expect and giving Josh the reassurance that I was there with him. That was enough to make the difference.

"I also knew to talk to him a bit more out loud and say, 'Hey, here we go. The lights are going to come on.' Maybe that was for my own security and comfort, but I do believe dogs understand things. Whatever it was, all things came together beautifully, and he had an incredible performance."

This is also a testament to Michelle's fortitude. Truly great handlers are like athletes. When they step into the ring, they have the ability to tune out the world, manage their emotions, manage the reactivity of their dog, and maintain a clear, strong focus throughout their entire performance. It requires a tremendous degree of mental and emotional control.

Michelle has the capacity to appear soft and sweet on the outside while being a pillar of unwavering strength for her dogs. Spectators can't see the inner dynamics at play. A good handler, like a great poker player, doesn't show their hand. The fans in the stands and the viewers at home simply saw a handler smiling affectionately at her dog with all the love in the world, not knowing the level of strength and faith that Michelle channeled to deliver that unforgettable performance.

Cherishing Moments that Define Us

There are moments that stand out and are forever cherished by handlers. It's no surprise that one of Michelle's most cherished memories occurred with Josh at Westminster.

Many handlers, spectators, and judges remember watching Westminster Best in Show 2004. Burton Yamada was the judge. He stood in the center of the ring. The lights were dimmed down low, almost dark, and there was a hush in the stadium. Seven handlers and their dogs awaited their turn to enter the Best in Show ring as reporters with cameras and video cameras huddled together to capture the culmination of this annual event. Suspense and excitement were in the air. Who would be the winner?

Each handler had their own routine to prepare themselves and their dogs, both mentally and physically, while all eyes watched each individual performance. This moment for each handler is like a sacred event. Like the Triple Crown of Thoroughbred Racing, the opportunity to win Best in Show at Westminster only comes once a year.

As Michelle begins to describe the night Josh won Best in Show at Westminster, she gets choked up. Although many years have passed since that memorable evening, her emotions bubble to the surface as if she is reliving the experience again.

Michelle and Josh entered the ring, and as the spotlights centered on the pair, the vision seen by the world was a big, black, sweet dog floating around the ring as his handler smiled at him. It appeared they were both relaxed without a care in the world. As Michelle and Josh arrived at the center of the ring, Josh nailed his free bait. Then to Michelle's surprise, Josh let out a huge, exuberant bark.

At that moment, Michelle could have reacted in a variety of ways. Should she calm him down and not risk him escalating into uncontrollable barking? Michelle read her dog's energy perfectly. She captured a spontaneous moment brilliantly and rode the wave. She smiled, stepped back, and allowed Josh to take center stage. The crowd erupted with applause.

"So many people thought that I told him to do that. I didn't. That was all Josh. I was so proud of him. All I could say to him was, 'It's all you. This is your moment, buddy… just go for it!'"

At that moment, he stood there as proud as could be and let that bellow go. Michelle stood tall, smiling at him, and kept repeating, "It's all you, buddy!"

Michelle's success at Westminster didn't end with Josh, though. In fact, the following year, she went on to win Best in Show again with a different dog. This dog was a German Shorthaired Pointer named Carlee.

Michelle describes Carlee's performance as the stack heard around the world. She says, "That bitch would typically go into the middle of the ring, yawn, and then step up into her four-square. She had been shown for so many years that she knew the routine by heart and seemed bored with it all, but this was just her temperament. On that night, though, we went out onto the Garden floor, she hit her free stack as usual, and just stayed there, and the crowd went nuts! Then the judge, Linnette Saltzman, started walking around her. I swear, Carlee's whole body puffed out, and she cocked her head, and I just said to her inside my mind, 'You got this, girl!' And she just ate it up.

"You know, it's just so amazing when you are out there on the Garden floor; there is so much electricity and energy. In both situations, with both Josh and Carlee, I completely stepped back and said, 'This is for you.' I will never forget those two moments."

What both of these moments have in common is the connection and communication Michelle felt with her dogs–and it isn't just with Josh and Carlee. This is part of Michelle's instinctive nature that she just can't describe. What she does have words for, though, is the feeling she has with her dogs.

Michelle describes her connection, "Somehow when I'm showing dogs, they set something off in me, and then I feed off of them."

She admits that for her, it is mostly intuitive and innate. She can't remember when she first felt it. Michelle says that she's not sure what it is, but she does know that when her dogs feel comfortable enough and good enough with whatever energy, love, confidence, or encouragement she's giving them, they take these feelings in, gain confidence, and you can see it in how they perform in the ring.

Michelle Describes Her Greatest Achievement, and It's Not What You Might Think!

For Michelle, who thrives on the connection and the energy she exchanges with her dogs and their owners, success all comes down to the basics. Michelle says the level of competition isn't the driving force for her—local, regional, national, or international—it's the relationship and connection that is built on the way to competition.

"For me, the basic stuff satisfies me the most, even at the local dog show level. For example, I had three young dogs, one a Bernese Mountain Dog and two Portuguese Water Dogs. My job was to get them trained and socialized for their first debut in the ring. I worked really hard with these dogs. They won… but it wasn't so much about the win as it was about the fact that it was my job to socialize, train, and prepare them for the ring. I did that, and it resulted in them all performing remarkably well. Those are my proudest moments and achievements.

"Another example is a new special that I've had. It's taken me months to roadwork, condition, and train him and now he looks incredible. The owners are thrilled. The owners can see the difference. That is one of my greatest achievements."

Michelle also revels in working with the shy dog that can't get into the ring, and building trust to help that dog move past the fear and resistance. These are the things that feel good down to the core of Michelle's being.

She explains, "The ribbons are always great and, of course, the statistics. But for my temperament, it's always about helping the underdog and working with the ones that need the extra help. That's what gives me the greatest satisfaction. Michael (Michelle's husband and the professional handler we met in Chapter 4) and I are very different. He likes to find beautiful dogs that he can run all the way with, and he does great things with them. For me, I'm happy with the shy dog or the new dog, the one that needs the extra effort and more connection. I help them through the resistance and get them where they need to be. That's my happy place."

HANDLING DOGS AND LIFE WITH EASE, GRACE, AND BALANCE

While Michelle is completely devoted to her work and loves what she does, she also recognizes that there is more to life than dog shows and the industry. She admits that completely separating herself from the dog show world is difficult because you have to be committed, and it's non-stop work almost all the time. However, Michelle truly does strive to strike a balance.

She explains, "At the end of the day, I enjoy having that glass of wine and just hanging out with Michael. I reflect a lot on what's happened, and I do a lot of planning for the future."

As someone with a helpful nature who tries to please those around her—dogs and owners alike—sometimes things can get out of balance, but knowing when to say when is important. Michelle reflects that she does try to make everything "perfect," even though this ideal will always be out of reach.

"I guess that's who I am. I just don't turn off very often. That being said, I would also say I am not so single-minded about things that I can't stop and switch gears. It's important that when you come home, you do other activities outside of dogs."

For Michelle, maintaining balance in her life is very important, and one of the ways she maintains this is by not having her sole focus be on dog shows and ribbons.

"We work hard and play hard. Our vacations are about experiencing the world, and new places, amazing food, and culture. So, that is how we balance it, and that is what makes me who I am."

Michelle also tells me it's important to be a good winner and a good loser. Even though she strives for that perfection, she is realistic and pragmatic when it comes to walking into the ring with her dog. She's mindful that you can't win every time. It's a big priority for her to always be a professional.

She says, "I know I can't win all the time. Knowing when it's time to just walk away is important."

That work and life balance she craves is also something her husband believes in, and this makes life and work easier for both of them. Michelle feels grateful to have a partner who is in the same business so they can help each other and talk things through. It helps her keep things in perspective. Michelle is strong in her convictions about how to keep this professionalism alive in her work every day.

"I always walk away saying, 'I can only do my dog.' My job is giving the best performance, the best condition, the best of the dogs. I am not in the ring, pointing the finger. At the end of the day, it is simply my job to do the best I can with everything within my control. That's all I can do."

Although Michelle doesn't take credit for this, as an experienced handler myself, it is clear to me that Michelle's dogs are well aware of her perspective. They know she just wants them to do the best they can. Whatever happens in terms of wins or losses is almost irrelevant. I believe this is one of the reasons Michelle has so much success with emotionally sensitive dogs. She doesn't put any additional pressure on them to perform, and this philosophy and her presence give them a sense of comfort and trust in her.

Michelle says, "I never want my dog to sense that it was their fault or that they did something wrong if we don't win. I just want my dog to leave the ring feeling positive about him or herself. For their benefit, I want them to feel good about themselves at all times."

INNER PRESSURE TURNS TO PRESENCE

Many outsiders aren't aware of all the pressure and emotions that go into showing dogs. Michelle explains, "I recently had an experience with an owner. I was showing a dog that had a few months where it wasn't doing well in terms of wins. It's really tough making those calls to the client. It's great when you are winning and everyone is happy, but when all of a sudden, you are not winning and you are not doing so great… Well, that's not an easy call to make.

"Not being able to make people happy is hard for me. When I can't meet their expectations, I get really frustrated. It helps when the owner's response is encouraging or sympathetic to the emotions that you are feeling. For example, I recall telling one client, 'I know that you are at home and you are frustrated with what is going on, but just be aware that I am the one here in the moment. I am the one living it and it is incredibly hard and frustrating and emotional for me as well.' Sometimes, the owners aren't aware of this emotional toll that we as handlers experience. We're not just going through the motions of showing dogs. There is a lot of inner pressure we put on ourselves. There is so much that we are putting out there, trying to do the best that we can. We are committed to our jobs and want our dogs to do really well."

In an industry where winning is always the ultimate goal, it's easy to become hooked by the competitive mindset and forget about creating a balanced life amidst the chaos. Michelle is well aware of these pitfalls and even falls into them herself at times. Few people would ever witness this side of Michelle because she is a true professional. No matter what she's feeling on the inside, Michelle walks, talks, and embodies the qualities of a professional, ensuring her clients and dogs know they are valued.

It takes a lot of discipline to be able to conduct yourself at the caliber Michelle demands. This discipline, as well as her honesty when it comes to communication with her clients, is a true reflection of her character and the integrity she brings to the sport of showing purebred dogs. Her authenticity allows her to be vulnerable with her clients while still maintaining professionalism.

Michelle reflects on how the dog show industry has opened her eyes to her own needs and ways of being.

"Dog shows have taught me that I am more sensitive than I realized, and I really appreciate when a client says, 'Thank you so much for all your hard work. I appreciate all you do. We'll get 'em tomorrow.' As handlers, those times when a client encourages you, especially when it's not the news they wanted to hear, really goes a long way."

Michelle adds, "We have one client that we've worked with long-term, campaigning their dog, which is highly competitive and stressful. And right in the exact moment, without even realizing it, this client sends a text that says, 'You guys are the best. I appreciate all you do.' It's super motivating ... it's just HUGE! So many of us really do want to make our clients and the dogs happy. That's what we love doing, and hearing, 'I believe in you!' works every time!"

This understanding of what makes a difference for Michelle–knowing that her clients believe in her and trust her with their dogs–translates in how Michelle interacts with the dogs and builds connection with them as well. Michelle is a selfless handler. While there are many handlers who may be tempted to step onto the carpet at Westminster and make it about them, Michelle naturally and truly fades into the background to let her dogs shine. Michelle makes it about them.

I believe they sense that from her. I also believe her dogs shine for her because they sense that she is someone who doesn't feel comfortable in the limelight herself. Michelle's belief in her dogs is so strong and unwavering that it helps them step out there under all that pressure and say, "I got this!"

They deliver in the ring just as much for Michelle as for themselves. The dogs Michelle works with step up really big so she can fade into the background, where she is most comfortable. When I share that insight with Michelle, she says, "I think you may be right."

Not only does Michelle verbally speak to her dogs, but her whole body speaks volumes as well. She admits to being aware of the fact that she has talked to her dogs her whole life. It's only recently, though, that she realized there are other ways she's been communicating with them as well.

She said, "A few weeks ago, someone said to me, 'Do you realize that every time you walk into a ring, you smile at the dogs?' He said, 'You are always smiling at them.'"

Before he pointed that out, Michelle never realized that about herself.

She added, "That's true. I realized, even when I am not verbally communicating with them, I am communicating with them. Now I'm self-conscious of how much I smile at my dogs! He was right, I do it all the time!"

Have you ever noticed how you feel when someone genuinely smiles at you? It feels good. Michelle's gentle way of smiling at her dog has a very powerful effect on how they perform in the show ring. It says, "You are free to relax, you are safe with me." Or, "Let's have fun, I believe in you."

There is so much going on behind that gentle smile of hers. Michelle's presence takes the lead, and the dogs feel as if they are in a safe haven, even in the spotlight and pressure of the ring.

There is a big give-and-take between Michelle and her animals. You can see how much she gives them and how much they give back to her. She isn't interested in the limelight. For her, it's more about creating the best experience for her dogs and clients. Like a caring mother, Michelle patiently and intuitively holds space and faith for a dog, gently encouraging them to become their best.

CHAPTER 6

Katie Bernardin:
Support Systems and Adaptability

Wallflower personalities don't really cut it in the dog show world. It's a competitive environment that culls the timid. They don't rise to the top. The majority of handlers showing dogs are strong, self-assured, and carry a certain power. They command respect. Yet that's not Katie, at least at first glance. Even from observing Katie from afar before I had conversations with her, I could see a tender softness inside that made me want to get to know her better. Her soft blond hair and big brown eyes draw you in, as well as her sweet, kind energy that makes you just want to hug her.

When I first started dabbling in writing, Katie was the first dog show person to approach me and say, "I read your article, and I loved what you wrote. I needed to hear that."

When I think of Katie, I have visions of a mother goose with her goslings. Picture Momma Goose with fuzzy little goslings waddling behind her. Doesn't that just warm your heart? What you don't see in Mother Goose is that under that sweet exterior is a hardy creature that can withstand changing climates. She can fly great distances, she can float gracefully along the water, and walk along the shore. She's adaptable. Oh, and by the way, if you threaten what is near and dear to her, she'll expand into her full wing capacity and challenge you! Do not misinterpret her reserved nature.

This is Katie, a woman who is kind, warm, and loving while also being resilient, capable, and fierce. She's a mix of quiet strength AND vulnerability.

This quiet strength teamed up with a big black alpha male of a Giant Schnauzer named Ty. Together, they were the Alpha and Omega. For those who don't know Giant Schnauzers, they are deeply loyal, bold, valiant, alert, watchful, courageous, and devoted. Their black beards and deep-set eyes shrouded by long, black eyebrows give them an intimidating, fierce look. They don't back down. And that's what this team did, they didn't back down. In fact, they rose all the way to the pinnacle of success, Number One Dog All Breeds—an incredible distinction for any dog and handler.

Before we jump ahead to the grand finale of Katie and Ty's remarkable accomplishments, let's go back in time to how Katie came to be a dog handler. Katie's parents weren't into dogs, but her grandma was. Grandma, her dad's mother, was big into obedience when Katie was growing up. She co-bred Miniature Schnauzers with another breeder by the name of Carol Goremaker, who lived in Nebraska.

Both Katie's parents had full-time jobs, so Grandma played a huge part in raising Katie. As a baby, Katie traveled around dog shows in a carrier on her grandma's back. There is a photograph of Katie at four years of age in a sit-and-stay with a lineup of dogs. She remembers grooming stuffed animals on tables and walking them on leashes.

Later pictures show Katie on a step stool, drying the Miniature Schnauzers' beards, putting chalk in the dogs' coats, with big amounts of chalk ending up on her as well!

Katie fondly recalls, "Whatever I was allowed to do, I did it!"

By the age of seven, Katie received her first opportunity to go into the ring and show a dog. Carol Goremaker entered one of her dogs in the show as a filler. A filler refers to a dog that is entered for the purpose of creating more points for another dog to win. Carol informed Katie that if she wanted to show the filler dog, she would be responsible for grooming the dog and preparing him for the show ring as well.

Katie and her filler trotted into the ring and won Winners Dog for the major. (A win is termed a major when three to five championship points are awarded by defeating a larger number of dogs. To obtain an AKC championship, a dog must win a total of fifteen points, with a minimum of two majors.) At that moment, Katie was hooked!

Although Katie appears to navigate dog shows with confidence and self-assuredness, she tells me she actually is quite reserved. She cherishes her alone time, when she can slip away into a book, disconnect from the world, and recharge her batteries. She admits, "With dogs, I don't have to put on a façade. Dogs allow me to be me. I don't have to do my hair and make-up. They love me regardless."

Although she enjoys being able to relax with her dogs, she also enjoys the feeling of control she experiences while showing dogs. Control is a necessary part of a handler's job because each dog has a variety of mental and physical needs that must be met in order for them to perform at their best. One of the reasons Katie needs to disconnect from the world is because she puts so much into her dogs. She takes her job seriously and strives to present each dog to the best of her ability. She and her husband, Adam, work as a team, showing a variety of different breeds from several different groups.

She says, "Adam and I show anything from Brussels Griffons to Irish Setters to Bearded Collies to Airedales to Giant Schnauzers."

Katie adapts her handling style to each breed. She explains, "At Westminster one year, I was held up in Giant Schnauzers, and I needed to get to my Labrador. With Giants, you have to be fierce, strong, and stern. If you don't, they will take advantage of you, and the other working dog handlers in the ring will try to dominate you. After showing the Giant Schnauzer, I had to immediately jump out of that ring and run to the Labrador ring. Before I took the Labrador in, I had to take a deep breath and be calm. One must be calm with a Labrador and talk sweetly. Sometimes, I sing to my dogs to get them to wag their tails. It was such a huge switch to go from fierce, fierce, fierce, push, push, push to sweet, good boy, you are such a good boy!"

But that's how Katie's days go, moving from dog to dog, breed to breed, different personality to different personality, being intentional and grounded in her inner wisdom. She needs to constantly change her energy depending on the breed and personality of the dog she is showing.

She adds, "With Brussels Griffons, you have to be gentle, and you have to build them up. They can act like big dogs, but you can't be too hard on them because they will melt. Bearded Collies require you to be their security blanket. I need to say to my Beardies, 'It's okay, I've got you. Nothing bad is going to happen to you. We can do this together.'"

Katie communicates this way, utilizing more than just words. She communicates this nonverbally as well by shifting her energy, posturing her body a specific way, and changing the tone of her voice.

Then she's off to Golden Retrievers, where she needs to be a cheerleader. Goldens need a happy yet controlled vibe. Pointers require the handler to be firm yet soft. You have to make them think they are confident enough to run out on the end of the leash and be beautiful. They are supposed to project the appearance of nobility.

With Irish Setters, you need to accept you will never win a battle. You need to make it seem like what you want them to do is their idea and tell them how beautiful they are.

Springer Spaniels are different, you can manipulate them and be more commanding because they can be crazy and require a firm hand to control and settle their energy. As you can see, some of these "truths" about different breeds seem contradictory, but therein lies the mastery.

"It is a lot of balancing, and juggling, and bringing yourself up and down," adds Katie. "You are exhausted at the end of the day. You have gone through so many emotions and so many highs and lows. You need to feel the energy of each dog, go with it, and know how to control it so that you can control them."

It takes a lot of talent to move in and out of different personalities at will, yet that is what great handlers do, and they make it look easy. A master handler such as Katie is constantly adapting to meet the needs of her dogs and her environment, whether spectators realize it or not. It is a subtle yet difficult skill.

Katie loves the challenge of navigating the personal needs of each dog she handles, and she does it with ease and grace. One of her greatest joys and an area where she likes to exert her abilities is in taking a shy dog or a dog that isn't confident and growing together with that dog.

"When I have a puppy that I have been training, and it walks around the ring flawlessly for the first time–that's what I love! I have always loved taking puppies and growing them up. Yes, it can be frustrating at times, but I just love to watch them grow mentally and physically. Whenever they grow, it feels like I grow too."

She adds, "I have always said that about Ty. I found so much of myself in that dog. He helped me grow as a human being and as a handler."

Prior to showing Ty, the most success Katie experienced was being ranked Number 2 Sporting Dog. Although a nice distinction for someone her age, her husband Adam had achieved more at a younger age. In his mid-twenties, Adam showed an Irish Setter named Emily that he piloted to Number One Sporting Dog, Number Three All Breeds. In fact, the original plan was for Adam to show Ty.

Adam showed Ty to his championship and also won his first group. However, at a show in Canfield, Ohio, before Ty began to be shown intensely as a special, Adam showed Ty in the breed on an extremely hot day. It was clear Ty didn't want to show, his attitude was indifferent and lackluster.

Adam asked Katie to show Ty because Ty was shutting down on him and not feeling as receptive. The next day, Adam went to the ring to watch Katie show Ty. Adam knew Ty would show well enough for him. But when he saw Ty with Katie, he could see the dog would do whatever Katie asked of him, so he said to Katie, "The dog is yours."

Katie says, "Adam had a lot of success when he was young. He was always used to being the star, the one that won. So for him to give me the lead was a huge moment for both of us in terms of trust. It helped both of us grow as individuals and as a couple."

Adam was an experienced handler with a proven track record, and he knew how physically and mentally demanding a national campaign can be on a dog. If Ty was going to be campaigned hard, he was going to need to have a strong emotional bond with his handler. My guess is that Adam saw that Ty had a strong connection with Katie and sensed that, once their emotional bond for each other was deepened, the team would be formidable.

Despite initial hesitation, Katie found her courage and showed Ty, and the twosome went on to win the National under respected judge Doug Holloway.

Katie says, "All I remember is watching Adam pace back and forth outside the ring. At one point, Maddie, our assistant, grabbed him and told him he needed to sit down. She could see he was making me and everyone around him a nervous wreck."

Although Katie and Ty won the Giant Schnauzer National, there was still much for this twosome to overcome and accomplish. The following December, Katie showed Ty in Orlando and lost every breed. However, Katie grew a lot as a handler during Ty's campaign, thanks to the help of several key people along the way. One such person was Carissa Shimpeno, or Rissa, a personal friend of mine who is well known for her success in Dobermans.

Carissa had shown Ty a couple of times when Katie or Ty had a conflict, well before he became famous. With her extensive experience in working dogs, Rissa had some advice for Katie to help minimize Ty's unfavorable habit of sidewinding. (Sidewinding is when a dog runs at a slight angle instead of a straight line.)

Katie found Carissa's advice helpful. "I came from sporting dogs, where my focus was on having them run fast and look pretty. Carissa taught me how to get him to move correctly, in a straight line. She taught me to slow him down, make him look at me, and make him go at the correct speed. She also helped immensely with how strong I needed to be mentally with Ty."

Not only did Carissa help in this way early on, but she continued to help Katie throughout Ty's campaign, even though she had a top

Doberman bitch special of her own competing against Ty in the Working Group.

Katie says, "Carissa always took the time to help me. Whenever I had a question, she was there to help. She was instrumental in teaching me how to become a working dog handler. She helped me develop the strong, fierce demeanor that I needed to be an equal force with a working dog such as Ty."

Katie says Angela Lloyd, a multibreed handler whose predominant success is with Hounds, was also a big help.

"Angie has been around and worked for a lot of different handlers before going out on her own as a handler. She is able to see many different sides to challenges handlers must face. She enjoys helping others and always demands the best out of herself."

Katie says both women helped mold her into the handler she is today, and she looks up to them.

Her husband also continued to be her main support and guide. As they began planning for the new show calendar year, they knew they would be edging for a top position. At this point, Adam realized that Katie needed some space and breathing room to figure out how to best work with Ty if they were going to take it to the next level. Katie needed to find answers to some of the following questions: What did Ty need from her? How hard could she push him? What was the best way to present him?

In order to accomplish this, Adam suggested that Katie fly out to the West Coast for three weeks of dog shows. He believed this would help Katie tune out everyone else and figure out what worked for her and Ty.

Katie got to Portland, and when she arrived at the show, she felt like a small fish in a big ocean. It was a huge show with the top winning handlers. At first, she felt young, inexperienced, insignificant, and lacking in political connection and savvy. She felt she was in over her head.

Initially, she was awarded a couple of group placements but not first place. She called Adam, feeling frustrated and disappointed. Adam counseled her, reassuring her that she was doing fine.

He then asked her, "Are you figuring out what you need to do with Ty? Are you figuring out your timing in the ring with him? Are you learning how hard you can push him? Are you learning what he needs from you? Those are the questions you need to keep asking yourself. That is why you are out there, to help you and Ty sort those things out on your own."

With Adam's words echoing in her head, Katie persevered through her frustration. And she learned something interesting.

"I was watching *The Walking Dead* in my hotel room, and I remember at one point suddenly realizing it was super important that I find ways to help Ty completely shut down. He was always on guard. He was my protector. If we went for a walk, he was on guard. If I had the lights on in the hotel room, he was always staring at the door. Any movement outside the door, and he was on his toes."

With that insight, Kate developed a routine at dog shows to help Ty relax his guard and decompress.

Kate said, "I would close the blinds, shut off the lights, and get Panda Express! We also had our Netflix and chill days because I believe that is what he needed. And I needed to chill as well! I needed to shut down and turn off too."

By the last leg of that trip out west, Katie and Ty found their rhythm.

Katie says, "Every time I got self-conscious or doubted myself, Ty showed up for me strong in the ring. We got stronger and stronger as time went on. I knew how to keep Ty happy, and that dog knew how to help me be strong. That was the most important part of that trip."

Katie adds, "I remember flying back from Arizona, feeling overwhelmed with the heart of that dog. I remember thinking, 'Wow, he is doing this for me. He's underneath the plane (in the cargo area), and I'm up here.'"

Katie spent much of the flight writing out her feelings because there were so many emotions coursing through her that she needed to express. She says, "It was really overwhelming to know he tried so hard for me. He taught me, and we learned together."

When she returned home, Adam saw the two of them show and said, "Wow! You learned what you needed to learn!"

Adam knew he made the right call showing his faith in his wife and her dog by setting them free to find their way in each other. Katie had a great support system, with two males who were very protective of her and just wanted her to believe in herself, fulfill her potential, and accomplish her goals.

The Best and the Worst of Times

In 2017, Katie and Ty earned the distinction of Number One Dog All Breeds All Systems. This was the pinnacle of success. Despite this, though, they lost the breed at the last show of the year in Orlando. It was a tough way to end the year, being number one yet getting defeated in the breed at the very last show. But that is dog shows. There are always disappointments, and for Katie, that was a tough pill to swallow.

Katie says, "Losing the last breed of the year when Ty was Number One Dog crushed me."

Typically, dogs retire when they are Number One All Breeds All Systems, as it is the highest possible ranking. It is the very height of achievement. In this case, though, Katie, Adam, and the owners had another goal in mind, which was to win 100 Bests in Show.

The following year, while pursuing their goal of 100 Bests in Show, tragedy struck.

They were in Canfield, Ohio, in August of 2018 when Katie made the decision to leave the circuit early and return home. The shows were outdoors, the weather was super hot, and it was affecting Ty. At home, the following Monday morning, Ty was happily running around in a paddock, playing with an English Setter bitch. Adam walked to the paddock and opened the gate, like he had so many times before, while Katie stood at the kennel door waiting for the dogs to run back to her. Often, the dogs would take a lap around the front yard before running to Katie. Every day, they did this, probably at least two hundred times without incident. Yet this particular time, both dogs darted behind two parked cars, and all Katie remembered hearing was the sound of Ty suddenly shrieking in pain.

"It still haunts me," said Katie. "All I heard was Ty screaming. Adam ran to him, picked him up, and carried him into the house."

They examined Ty, guessing he hurt his shoulder because he couldn't put any weight on his foot, yet his foot didn't appear injured in any way. It was possible he hyperextended his shoulder or maybe pulled or strained a muscle. Once they could see he was calm, they gave him some Medicam for pain and inflammation and put him in his crate to keep him quiet and give him time to rest. Later that night, they hoped to see improvement, yet Ty still wouldn't put any weight on his shoulder or his leg.

The next morning, Adam took Ty to their good friend Debbie Torraca at Wizard of Pawz in Colchester, Connecticut, a company that specializes in canine physical rehabilitation. During the exam,

Debbie was able to determine that Ty suffered an injury to his pastern (the area on a dog's leg before the foot, the equivalent of a human wrist).

Debbie detected a lot of swelling and advised, "You need to take him to the Veterinary Orthopedic & Sports Medicine Center (VOSM) in Annapolis, Maryland. You must see Dr. Sherman Canapp."

The earliest appointment available for Ty was two weeks away. In the meantime, Ty was kept in a splint to prevent further injury. When the time came, Adam drove Ty down from Connecticut to Annapolis. An ultrasound was performed on Ty, and he was diagnosed with a grade three sprain. He popped two of his side tendons behind his pastern and partially sprained the tendon that goes up the front of his leg. Ty's injury was probably the most severe case the center had ever seen.

The clinicians were surprised that Ty's injury occurred simply by playing in the yard. The only other time they saw an injury in that area of that magnitude was when a police dog named Porter jumped off the roof of a three-story building. Adam was instructed to follow the same protocol set forth for Porter. Ty's leg was shaved so bone marrow could be extracted and inserted into his pastern. Regenerative medicine was utilized in which Ty received stem cell therapy with platelet rich plasma (PRP) injections. Ty was given only a fifty-fifty chance of being able to walk normally again.

Part of his treatment also included sessions with Debbie. At Wizard of Paws, he received water treatment, laser therapy, and stretching techniques. Even if Ty's tendons did heal properly, there was still a concern about how much flection he would have, which would affect his movement in the long term. Katie and Adam were doing everything they could, but they still feared Ty might never be able to function the same way again.

Katie says, "All I kept thinking was, I am a reader, and this book, this chapter, can't end this way."

After a month and a half of hyper-vigilant care and rehab, Katie drove Ty back down to Maryland to receive his prognosis. The doctor walked Ty to the exam room while Ty's owner, Carol, and Katie anxiously paced the waiting room. Doctor Canapp returned with Ty and said, "I don't know how to tell you this… but it worked! Everything healed the way we were hoping it would. The tendons reattached themselves!"

HOLDING HOPE FOR A HAPPY ENDING

Katie needed to make a decision. Should they enter Ty in the Eukanuba dog show in Orlando, Florida, in December? This would be the same show where Katie and Ty, at the completion of a stellar year, lost in breed competition the prior year.

Would Ty be sound while moving? Would Ty's hair grow back on his leg enough to be ready for competition? Would he be able to gait well and without a limp? Katie describes being on the phone with her best friend Kelly (whom she relied on for support throughout her campaign with Ty) while in the car with Adam. They were all part of the decision-making process. They questioned the odds of whether or not Ty could show and win at Eukanuba. They were unsure. It was Adam who said, "Enter him."

It was decided that Ty would be entered in the show, but if he didn't look the part in time for the show, he would not be shown.

Although there were four days of competitive events prior to Eukaneuba, they didn't enter Ty in any of the earlier days. For Ty to show his best, Katie knew she needed to stay focused and remain calm for herself and for Ty. At that point, not even knowing if Ty would be shown, she was full of nerves.

Adam said at the time, "If we get Ty out of the crate Sunday morning and he's lame, you are not showing him. If he is off in any way or not looking his best, you are not walking in the ring with him."

Katie wholeheartedly agreed with Adam.

Sunday morning rolled around. Adam informed Katie that she and Ty could just relax and stay in bed. He would handle the details. He was going to the show and would send someone back over to get Ty. Ty wouldn't be showing until 2:00 p.m. Adam said, "I want you guys to sleep, relax, and take your time."

One of their assistants came over around 10 o'clock to bring Ty to Adam so Adam could trim him and get him settled in. Although Katie was doing her best to remain calm, centered, and focused, she had a conflict. Bearded Collies were being judged at the same time as Giant Schnauzers. While she showed her Bearded Collie, her assistants ran back and forth, keeping her updated. When it was almost time for Ty to enter the ring, Adam then came to show the Bearded Collie so Katie could show Ty.

Jen, one of Katie's assistants, had Ty ringside. There was a massive crowd around him. Katie recalls, "There were so many people."

The crowd was excessively large. It was after 2:00 p.m. on Sunday afternoon, and the only other breed being judged was Bearded Collies, so there were lots of spectators gathered to watch.

After taking in the crowd, Katie looked at Adam and said, "All I want is for people to see Ty and how incredibly strong he is—what he came back from. Many people thought he would never come back from his injury. Even the vet didn't think he would come back."

Katie adds now, "I had dreamed about being able to walk into the ring with Ty one more time."

This was Katie's chance to make that dream come true. She says, "As soon as I walked Ty into our place in the line-up, he stepped into his stance strong and perfect."

So far, so good. Ty felt confident, but would he be able to gait like his old self? Katie hoped so. The first moment of truth arrived. The judge asked the dogs to gait individually around the ring.

Katie explains, "Ty and I took our first steps in the ring together, and the place erupted with applause!"

Katie remembers hearing the crowd roar, and she felt so supported.

"After I gaited Ty around the ring to the end of the line, my team was there, waiting for me, watching intently."

Ty felt great moving, but Kate was worried and hoped he looked his best. She asked, "Was he lame?"

They collectively agreed, "No, Kate, he was beautiful."

She began crying. She was having a hard time controlling her emotions. She was so happy, so grateful to be back in the ring with Ty. She wanted this moment with him so much.

Next, Ty needed to complete his individual examination. Katie proudly says, "During his individual examination, he gaited back to the judge and nailed his free stack."

Every step was perfect! He went on to win the breed.

Katie says, "It was the biggest high I have ever felt. I came out of the ring crying."

People swooped in to congratulate Katie on her win and Ty's performance. Jen, being an attentive assistant, focused on getting Ty back to the set-up so he could relax and rest his leg. The team wanted Ty to be at his best for the Working Group competition that would be held later in the evening.

It was such an emotional high for Katie. She feared never having the opportunity to show Ty again. Walking in the ring with Ty again was a dream come true. And winning the Working Group later that night was icing on the cake!

Pam Burns, who judged the Working Group, allowed the handlers and dogs to showcase themselves. She asked each contender to perform a free bait. Ty's free bait was awesome.

Katie says, "I had the cheesiest smile on my face when he nailed it. It was perfect. He was perfect."

She says, "I will never forget that moment in time. I kept crying. Being about to tie a pretty little bow on it, put it on the shelf, and feel completed. It was what I needed. I felt so incomplete for the past year. I needed to feel that the final chapter was done. And it was."

Time to Be

Katie was completely at peace with where her journey ended with Ty, just thirteen wins shy of the 100 mark.

"I did something few people have been able to do. I was surrounded by so many great people. Maybe if I hadn't been surrounded by so many amazing people, the result would have been different."

Either way, she no longer feels the need to prove herself. She used to worry that she would never be successful or never be able to win everything she wanted to win. It felt so far out of reach.

She says, "That is what Ty taught me. He taught me to believe in myself and know that I am good enough."

Katie believes that her time with Ty helped her grow in many ways. She feels more comfortable in her own skin now and even more comfortable in her relationships. She feels stronger and able to stand up for what she believes in and what she wants.

She says, "Before, I would hide. When Adam and I first got married, I bottled everything up–until I couldn't handle it anymore."

Now, if something is on her mind, she speaks her truth. She credits not only her campaign with Ty for helping her with that, but also the support of other handlers like Carissa Shimpeno and Angie Lloyd, who encouraged her to speak up for herself and to say what was on her mind. She found her strength and courage and learned to believe in herself.

Because of all of Katie's experiences, she believes in passing on the support and encouragement that she received. She tells the young girls who work for her, "Work hard, do your job the best you can do, and you will have your day in the spotlight."

She enjoys encouraging the girls to believe in themselves. She is also able to relax and enjoy the simple things that bring her pleasure, such as nurturing and training puppies or fine-tuning a special by getting into their head and figuring out what makes them tick.

All of this work of being a great handler requires tremendous patience. You must have patience with the animals and with clients. Patience with yourself, your partner, your help. And yes, even with judges. Lots of patience is required.

Katie says, "Some people want to react and yell and scream and hit things when they don't get the result they want. That gets you nowhere. You need to control it. We are not just responsible for twenty-something dogs, we are also responsible for the kids that work for us. We are responsible for dogs, in which most people think of their dogs as if they are their kids. We are responsible for each other. We are also responsible for a truck and a trailer and keeping it safe, clean, well maintained, at the perfect temperature. There is a lot we are responsible for."

CHAPTER 7

Kaz Hosaka:
Transformation

Kaz stands about five feet, eight inches tall with alert brown eyes, thick, well-groomed dark hair, and a body of balanced athletic proportions. His temperament at a dog show is a highly focused, well-contained explosion of energy. Born and raised in Japan, his culture comes through in both his appearance and his demeanor. At shows, his dress is impeccable, and so are the Poodles in his husbandry.

When Kaz commands the lead of a Poodle in the Best of Breed ring, he is practically unbeatable. His precision is unparalleled. If a handler wants to win a breed in Poodles and Kaz is at the show, they know Kaz and his dog are the biggest obstacle standing between them and the ribbon they desire. When it comes to Poodle handlers, Kaz is the king who stands at the top of the mountain.

Although he stands at the top of the mountain now, Kaz faced tremendous opposition along the way and had to do a lot of climbing to stake his claim. The way in which he conquered this mountain had a lot to do with the qualities that are important to him: honor, respect, deliberate and focused action, and fortitude.

Before interviewing Kaz, I didn't know him personally, but I could see those qualities at work in everything he did. Based on my observation of him, I expected Kaz to be a bit dry humored, for how could someone who appears to take life so seriously have a sense of humor? I was shocked to discover that there is so much more going on beneath the surface of this man! I felt an immediate kinship with Kaz when we spoke, and he both surprised and delighted me at every turn.

Transforming a Poodle Special Is Like Tending a Japanese Bonsai Tree

What truly fulfills Kaz is the transformation process of bringing a dog to its highest potential. He is often amused by the reactions of other people when they first see a new dog he is considering campaigning as a special.

He says, "People will ask me, 'Is that your new special?' And then they laugh and look at me in disbelief. It is funny how often people don't believe me!"

A year later, when they see him and that same dog, they look somewhat shocked, "Is that the same dog?"

Kaz laughs and admits he truly enjoys discovering a diamond in the rough and transforming it.

He sees the underlying potential. He finds this process of seeing potential and then participating in the transformation deeply fulfilling, and it's what keeps him engaged and passionate about his work day after day, year after year.

He evaluates his abilities as a handler on how his special looks and performs the first day it walks into a show ring versus how it looks and performs on the last day it shows. In his mind, a visible transformation must take place in order for Kaz to be satisfied.

He says, "The last day I present my dog as a special dog, it must look ten times better than when it started. That's my goal every time."

That is how Kaz rates himself: his ability to transform a dog, both mentally and physically, so that at the end of the dog's career, a dramatic transformation is evident.

Kaz says, "You cannot make a great show dog overnight. It takes a long time to achieve excellence."

He explains his philosophy in terms of a Japanese bonsai tree. He says, "In order to be perfect, a Japanese bonsai tree is touched every day. My Poodle special is special. I want it to be perfect. Therefore, like a Japanese Bonsai tree, I touch my special every day."

The way he tends to his Poodle special is special indeed. Although he doesn't trim his special every day, he touches it. He brushes the coat and changes the top knot. He gives his time and attention thoroughly and methodically.

Kaz is constantly thinking about what needs to be done mentally and physically in order to prepare his special for an upcoming event. While he brushes his special, he mentally envisions being the best.

He says, "I am always thinking about the dream."

In his mind's eye, Kaz knows which judge is judging the breed at Westminster and who is judging the group and Best in Show. He thinks about the judges he will be showing to, how he wants his dog to look and perform, and what he needs to do in order to properly prepare them.

In 2008, Kaz won the Toy Group at Westminster with a Toy Poodle named Walker. The prior year, Walker refused to go next to any table that had the Westminster logo. At Westminster, tables are decorated with purple curtains with the kennel club logo of a Pointer, pointing. The following year, Kaz placed a Pointer logo in the grooming room of his kennel so the dog was exposed to this disconcerting stimulus every day. Eventually, Walker got used to it.

In a careful, well-thought-out manner, Kaz desensitized Walker. After listening to Kaz talk about his Poodles, it became apparent to me that desensitization is a common part of his training practice. With Walker, it was the Westminster logo. With other dogs, Kaz focuses on other things like flower arrangements (more about that and his dog Spice in Chapter 10). His Poodles get acclimated to seeing the Westminster logo and flower arrangements long before they show at Westminster.

There are many things that could impact a dog's ability to show when the pressure is on. Many years ago, Kaz identified that when Poodles see silver tape on the mats at dog shows, they jump over the tape. Therefore, Kaz places silver tape in the runs at his kennel to help his Poodles get used to seeing the silver tape and walking on it. Kaz anticipates and plans for potential challenges and makes adjustments along the way. He prepares his dogs by controlling the variables that he can control.

He laughs, "Show Poodles, especially Toys, can sometimes be dumb, so you need to do these things and plan and prepare in this way to make them perfect!"

Kaz's patience is apparent in all he does. He takes whatever time is necessary to get something right. In fact, he gets his special generally a year in advance to begin preparing them for entry into the specials ring. According to Kaz, it takes a long time to get them right. Kaz starts looking for his next special when he begins campaigning a new special.

Kaz says, "It takes time to find the next best dog to campaign."

Most of the dogs Kaz finds are in Japan, and he brings them back to the United States, or he breeds his own Miniature Poodles. Once he starts a new dog, he is looking for the next dog. While he is campaigning a dog, he is often simultaneously grooming and training his next one as well, acclimating the dog to all the circumstances that will be required of them as a show dog.

As I listen to Kaz explain to me all the time he takes to expose his Poodles to different circumstances, I interpret this to mean that Poodles don't like surprises!

Kaz says, "A Poodle special needs time to adjust to traveling as well. In Japan, there may be one or two dog shows here and there and there is not much traveling. But here in the US, we have 150 shows, and sometimes ten hours of driving. It's a lot of shows and a lot of driving. Show dogs need to learn to eat on the road as well as at home."

For some breeds, if a dog doesn't like eating (yes, that happens quite often!), handlers will do what is referred to as stuffing or force-feeding. In this case, a handler will form food into a torpedo shape, place it in the back of the dog's mouth, and then ease it down into the back of the throat. The dog then swallows, and the food travels the rest of the way down. Many dogs are surprised by this at first. Most simply come to accept it. Some even seem to enjoy all the extra attention of being held and petted as they are given their food by hand.

A dog may need to be force-fed for several reasons. Males often stop eating when a bitch is in season. Young males can just plain be disinterested in food. They may eat small amounts here and there, but they don't have much interest in food and, therefore, aren't eating enough calories to maintain proper show weight. Other times, a dog may get nervous when it is away from home and will lose its appetite for a period of time until it adjusts to its new environment. Knowing a dog's eating habits is very important, and good handlers have lots of experience in getting dogs to eat and maintain proper show weight in order to look their best.

Kaz explains, "Toy Poodles are not good eaters. They need to adjust to traveling in the truck, eating on the road, and staying overnight away from home. There are lots of things they need to learn before they begin showing. Mentally, there is a lot to overcome."

Even for owners seeking a championship on their Poodle, Kaz requests six months to prepare the dog for competition.

Usually, Kaz retires his specials at the Garden, then starts showing a new special in March. He believes it takes six months to get things figured out with a new dog. By the end of the year, his new dog begins showing well and hopefully has started winning more consistently. The following year is when Kaz puts his sights on being ready to start campaigning and winning. Sometimes, he'll show for a third year. In general, he will campaign the same dog for roughly two and a half years, which translates into most specials being with Kaz for three and a half years, since it often takes a year to prepare the dog in the first place.

As I observe how Kaz pursues his dreams, I see how much he achieves through planning, patience, and perseverance. Perseverance requires persistence, an ability to endure challenges and remain steadfast to get through to the other side. It is clear when I listen to Kaz's story that Poodles are full of challenges!

Kaz balances his steadfast nature with the softness of patience, allowing his dogs adequate time to adjust. Something about Kaz's steadfast, patient nature and also the level of patience I witnessed in Andy Linton's approach to training made me want to look up the meaning of the word patience. I was surprised by what I discovered in Webster's Dictionary.

According to Webster's Dictionary, "Patience means the quality or habit of being patient." Patient is defined as, "Enduring affliction or pain without anger or complaint." I found this definition shocking yet perfect! What Kaz overcomes with his Poodles, some would consider a painful process! Yet Kaz always perseveres through the pain and the struggle because it is a value for him, it is in his nature, and he wants what is on the other side of the challenge.

I see an inherent understanding and acceptance in Kaz that there are always obstacles to overcome, and he allows himself the necessary time to overcome and reach the peak of each mountain in his path. This man is an expert in Poodles for a very good reason. Few will attain his level of mastery because so few have the discipline it takes to persevere at this level. In fact, most don't even try. Kaz is practically uncontested in the Poodle ring because most don't have the talent, skill, dedication, and desire to do what needs to be done at the level of mastery Kaz has attained.

POODLE KNOW-HOW: HOW TO TRAIN THEIR BRAINS

According to Kaz, you can't introduce anything new to a Poodle and expect them to handle it with ease and grace!

Kaz says, "Most show Poodles don't have a brain! They need everything to remain the same."

That puts the responsibility on the handler to control the variables that you can control and keep your routine the same in every way, every day.

Kaz has an EXACT routine he goes through with each dog. He places the dog on the table the same way each time. He places the dog on the mat the same way every time. He does not place them on the floor, he places them on the mat. He lets them shake. Then he fixes the ears, then fixes the leash, then says, "Look at me. Lets' go."

That is Kaz's routine with each Poodle. He insists, "I can't change it. It has to be the same every single time."

I asked Kaz to compare how much of his time is dedicated to preparing a Poodle mentally and how much of his time is dedicated to preparing them physically and grooming them. According to Kaz, catering to a Poodle's temperament is the most important aspect of his job. Catering to their temperament is essential because often, they are not good show dogs to begin with. Most of them have been raised to be pets and serve no other function than to be their owner's companion.

Kaz says, "Show Poodles, not properly raised and socialized, can be very spooky. You can groom a Poodle perfectly, but more important is teaching and training their brain to be show dogs. Yes, grooming is important. You need patience to groom a Poodle properly, and one should never be lazy about it."

His routine is the same with his class dogs. He dislikes using oil and dematting dogs. Instead, he brushes his dogs out every single day. All his dogs. At times, he had thirty to forty Poodles in show coats. All thirty to forty Poodles would be brushed every single day. His approach reminds me of Greg (see Chapter 3) and the endless hours spent on doing things right. Neither one of these men got to where they are in their careers by cutting corners. They are perfectionistic in nature.

Kaz is extremely efficient in his grooming and states, "If a dog is not matted, it doesn't take much time to maintain their coat on a daily basis. It takes roughly ten minutes for a Toy Poodle or Miniature Poodle and up to thirty minutes for a Standard Poodle."

While it takes roughly ten to thirty minutes to simply brush a Miniature or Toy Poodle, washing and drying require more time–usually forty minutes (Toy Poodles) to an hour (Miniature Poodles). Washing and drying a Standard Poodle usually requires between two to four hours. The time involved in performing these tasks is also dependent on how one grooms and dries.

THE PERFECT SHOW TRIM

There are a hundred different ways to trim a pet Poodle. Everyone has a different way of trimming a Poodle.

Kaz says, "When trimming a pet, the goal is even scissoring and a clean cut. Show trimming is different. There is only one perfect trimming fit for each show dog. Every dog is different. Each dog's show trim is very unique. The groomer must assess a dog's qualities in order to determine the correct trim and then cater the trim to each dog."

Some of the questions Kaz may be assessing when he is determining how to trim a show dog include: Does this dog move close behind? Does this dog have a low tail set? Does it move wide in front?

Kaz says, "In Poodles, there are a lot of ways a groomer can fix the appearance of their structure. Not 100 percent. We can create an illusion. We can't actually fix things, but we can create an outward appearance that enhances certain qualities and makes faults less obvious or noticeable."

When Kaz first gets a Poodle, how he trims it will change over time. For instance, a year later, that dog may be moving differently, the carriage is different, and the trim work needs to reflect and honor these changes.

Even the dog's attitude can affect how a dog needs to be trimmed. If a dog's attitude improves and it carries itself more confidently, the trimming will need to be adjusted. Similarly, if a dog isn't reaching as much in the front, or is moving close behind, or carrying its head in a particular way, the trimming will need to be adjusted.

Kaz says, "A Poodle handler needs to understand its dog's strengths and weaknesses in order to determine the proper trim. You can't just look at a dog and say, 'Here is my special. She is perfect.' No. No dog is perfect. I've never seen a perfect dog. Most dogs have two or three or four faults. They are still really good specials, but there are always areas that could be improved.

"With all Poodles, you have to know what you have and you need to know your dog's faults so you know how to hide them with your trimming. You need to be able to create an illusion of ideal structure. Yes, even an ignorant judge can see bad feet, but an ignorant judge cannot see correct shoulder blades, or proper front-end assembly."

Certain things one cannot miss. For instance, a Poodle should be sound coming and going, and Poodles are supposed to be a square breed. They can't be long.

Kaz says, "Even a bad judge can see a bad head or flat feet. If you have a special, you need to have at least a decent head and decent feet… you can't hide those things. The rest you can fake, mostly!"

For Dobermans, you can't do much with grooming, but with Poodles, you can.

Kaz says, "You want a Poodle's tail carriage to point to two o'clock."

He admits there were times when he had a Poodle that carried its tail at one o'clock and it took him a long time trimming to create the appearance of a tail carried at two o'clock. It takes a lot of patience to create an illusion such as that.

Kaz says, "I can look at a Poodle and I know which handler is showing that dog based on how it is trimmed."

Truth be told, Kaz says, breeding for show Poodles often becomes focused on what is pretty and eye-catching, and often, temperament is not the first priority when determining breeding stock.

Additionally, the way they are raised and cared for has a significant impact on a Poodle's temperament. That is why Kaz must develop a very strong relationship in which his dog trusts him. Trust develops over time and with consistency. Kaz and Andy Linton both believe that building consistency and structure into a dog's day-to-day living environment creates a feeling of safety within the dog, resulting in a bond in which the dog knows it can trust the handler.

Kaz does not allow anyone else to touch his Poodle special (except to hold it ringside). One reason is that it's important to Kaz that his Poodle special spends time with him. Every day, Kaz maintains his special's overall well-being by feeding, grooming, washing, and trimming. He does this both at home and while at the dog show. After the show, he washes the top knot himself. He doesn't allow anyone else to perform that task. Nobody else ever grooms his special. He laughs, saying that after Best in Show, when the majority of handlers and owners and spectators have vacated the building, he is still there washing the top knot and drying the coat.

Another reason Kaz performs all these tasks himself is because a lot of money is being spent on his Poodle special's campaign, and he feels it is too much responsibility to put on an assistant. His Poodle special is a top dog. He needs to be the one responsible for all of that dog's needs.

Not only does Kaz physically touch his dogs every day, but he is also highly attentive to what they need mentally and how to accommodate their unique dispositions. After having trained with Anne Rogers Clark and watching her show her own dogs, Kaz does not make excuses when something goes wrong. (More on that story in Chapter 10.) A handler must be responsible and take ownership of everything within their power. You have to do the best you can do under the circumstances.

"This is what makes a great handler," says Kaz. And that is what he expects of himself every time he interacts with one of his dogs while in a show ring.

PRESENTATION MATTERS

Poodles are described as being very "Poodly" or being "Poodly in appearance." Whether it is a Standard, Miniature, or Toy Poodle, a Poodle stands proudly as a true aristocrat. All Poodles must carry themselves, according to the standard, with an air of distinction and dignity. As a Poodle handler, it is Kaz's job to ensure his Poodles always look "Poodly." There are a number of ways Kaz creates this Poodly appearance.

Since many show Poodles aren't necessarily smart and obedient and often don't have a long attention span, Kaz trains them in a very specific manner. His goal is to show powerful movement for three to five seconds. In my mind, Kaz is trying to create a snapshot or a series of snapshots versus a whole reel of film.

I get excited when I hear Kaz talk about presenting a dog this way. I know that with my Dobermans, I have a similar intention… to create a perfect picture… and maintain it for as long as the judge is looking. A handler can do this with a Doberman because a Doberman's temperament is ideally very stable, disciplined, and focused. The Doberman standard describes a Doberman as being eager to please. Similar to a Poodle, Dobermans are described as poised and dignified. With my Doberman special, I aim to create a reel of film. However, this reel of film often begins with the creation of a series of snapshots like the ones Kaz creates with his Poodles.

In fact, this series of snapshots is how I approach training puppies as well. I ask for three to five seconds of perfection, and each time they make progress, I tell them they are amazing. Dobermans were bred to be obedient and, as I said, eager to please, so doing what their owner or trainer requests is part of their genetic makeup. Working as a team with their owner or handler is part of what makes a Doberman feel good about themselves and actively builds their confidence.

As Kaz described his training process, I continually discovered correlations to mine. Perhaps his beginning years as a Doberman handler and trainer influenced how he trains his Poodles.

He says, "When gaiting a Poodle, all I need is three to five seconds of perfect movement. I never long-walk my Poodles. They may trot okay while long-walking, but that is not the type of gait I am trying to create in the ring."

I begin envisioning a Poodle trotting freely, and compare that to how I see Poodles gait with Kaz. Yes, there is a big distinction. With Kaz, Poodles have a lot of energy and purpose as they move. They appear upbeat and happy.

I can see and understand how Kaz creates this purposeful gait with his show dogs. The AKC standard describes the ideal Poodle gait as, "A straightforward trot with light, springy action and strong hindquarters drive. Head and tail carried up. Sound, effortless movement is essential."

Kaz uses play to create energy and excitement. He says, "I throw a toy so they can run and grab the toy and bring it back."

But utilizing play, showing and training are fun events his dogs look forward to. You can see their enthusiasm in everything they do.

Kaz is always talking to his dogs. He'll say, "Let's go!"

That phrase is backed with energetic enthusiasm, such as an eager look in his eyes and an energetic body posture that portrays forward movement. Another energetic strategy Kaz institutes is that he never brings his dog ringside himself.

He explains, "I groom them perfectly, get everything perfect, but I don't bring them ringside. My assistant does. I do that on purpose."

His assistant takes his special ringside and holds the dog. Kaz shows up at the last minute. While with the assistant, his dog is often looking for Kaz to appear, and when he does, his dog suddenly becomes excited. When Kaz and his dog enter the ring together, his dog is vibrant and excited because Kaz is there once again.

I often do this with dogs, as well. Unless a dog needs to be with me to settle, I don't like to hold dogs ringside. I want my dogs to have the mindset that when they are with me, they are always working. And working is fun! When I am working with my dogs, I work them intensely, and each time they get something right, I tell them how wonderful they are. Often, someone else—an assistant, or even an owner—will be holding their dog, and the dog's energy builds up watching me train other dogs. They become excited and eager, anticipating their time with me and their turn in the show ring. Obviously, this isn't the approach I use on hyper dogs. My goal is to help them release energy productively, not create more energy in a system that is already bursting at full capacity.

Although Kaz and I have similar training techniques, he has several additional challenges that I have no experience with. For instance, you can't just hand a Poodle to a bystander. Their coat must be properly handled. In addition, they need to feel mentally safe with the person that is holding them. Plus, you must be very mindful of how a Toy Poodle is placed down on the floor or outside.

Kaz only allows his dogs to be held by trusted assistants. He teaches them to be very careful. With other breeds, such as very large dogs, you do not need to worry as much about a baby carriage, or a spectator backing into or stepping on a dog. With a Poodle, especially a Toy, you have to worry about everything that can go wrong and be very careful.

Kaz says, "I don't want anything dangerous going on around my dog when my assistant takes the dog ringside. That is very important."

In addition, his assistant is trained to be hypervigilant about what is going on around his dog. For instance, the assistant needs to ensure there is not too much wind blowing on his dog, or that the dog is not overheating in the direct sun, or standing on a hot surface. You must also be very careful about Toy Poodles jumping. If they jump, for instance, off a table, they can easily break their leg.

Kaz believes that the first goal with a Poodle is always to get them to focus on you. Kaz says, "If a Poodle is focused on you, they are less likely to get distracted by something else."

Kaz trains his assistants to look for possible problems outside the ring that may potentially distract, unsettle, or even spook his dog. His assistants are required to handle outside ring distractions whenever possible. For instance, if someone is standing ringside and Kaz's Poodle notices that person and becomes startled, Kaz's assistant will ask the person to move because they are distracting his dog. His dog may notice someone wearing a certain color, a raincoat, or a hat, and his Toy doesn't like it or becomes transfixed by it. In cases like these, Kaz's assistant will often ask the individual to move to another space.

Kaz and his assistants are always vigilant about potential problems, visuals, or noises that may alarm or distract his dog. That is why his Poodles must always look at him, all the time in the ring. This is one of the reasons why you never see Kaz talking to other handlers while he is in the ring. He needs to keep his Poodles really focused.

Although I have never handled a Poodle, I have handled lots and lots of dogs that are easily distracted, unsteady, or spooky over the years. I approach my Dobermans, Boxers, Great Danes, and several others in much the same way. I keep their focus on me.

Unlike Kaz (because he has a coat to work around), I am also able to attend to insecure mentalities in a dog by reassuring them with my hands. I hold them firmly and assuredly while running long strokes down their body, gently brushing my hand along their eyes and muzzle, placing my finger in their ear and massaging it, and rubbing the underside of a dog's tail to relax them. Everything in my body and being is communicating to them that they are safe and that they can relax.

Kaz tends to his Toy Poodles' spooky disposition in a variety of ways. Because he spends time grooming his dogs every day, they have lots of exposure to one another, and deep trust is built.

He says, "Every day we groom, brush and change out a dog's top knot. Every day we wash the legs, we dry them, we brush them, and trim them. Day after day."

Kaz's dogs receive a tremendous amount of care, and this care translates to safety, consistency, and trust.

Creating the Moment

Kaz says, "For me, a great handler is fun to watch. A great handler has timing."

One of the things he appreciates with handlers he admires is that there is a moment just before they move their dog in which they share a quiet moment with that dog. To me, this means collecting and gathering that dog's focus and uniting with that dog so the handler and dog are working in unison. Kaz says, "If a handler can make that moment, they are a good handler."

Kaz explains, "One attribute of a great handler is timing. When it is their time, they control the moment, they own the show for five or ten seconds and make it theirs. When a great handler is showing, you watch them. You may not know why, but you do."

Kaz describes this in a way that makes me visualize a moment in time being captured, owned, and controlled by a handler. There is a certain presence to what he describes and an ability to create that moment. He says, "Some handlers may go through similar motions, yet you don't notice them… they don't draw you in. A great handler will always draw you in."

Kaz continues, "The judges notice it too. The judge may find themselves thinking, 'I have to watch this dog, because I have to watch this handler. There is something special about them.'"

Kaz says, "Kelly, you are the same way. The way you move that dobie, the first step, the second step. Dog's legs, your legs, … there is unison and symmetry in how a talented handler comes into perfect symmetry with their dog."

I love Kaz's description of movement. I do often find it amazing to see photos of myself moving with a dog (and it's not just me; I see it with many others). I can't see myself in the ring, yet when I see photos, my leg is always reaching with their leg. Even a bad-moving dog, I will find a way to bring us into rhythm. I point this out in this way because I don't consciously seek to match my legs with theirs, but as I seek to find rhythm with them, this is the natural result. Some handlers have a gait that never changes and the dog must conform to the handler, but handlers that are gifted in moving their dogs are adaptable. They will naturally shorten or lengthen their stride to come into alignment with the dog. Just as Kaz's trimming makes constant adjustments to the uniqueness of a dog, so does a great handler's gait. Even if a dog has an undesirable, short, choppy gait, a great handler will find harmony and bring themselves and their dog into a rhythm that looks pleasing to the eye.

When handlers pause and bring themselves into symmetry with their dogs, the connection is felt and is powerful. When dogs work with me, they know we will not do anything until I have their full attention… Perhaps I just hate to be ignored! If their attention is distracted or on something else, I will wait until they focus back on me. They don't control the show, I do.

There are times that I see their attention is elsewhere and I know I can make that work, so I fall into rhythm with them. When a dog is not looking at me, I may sense that, although they are looking at something else, they are aware of me as well. I can see a stillness in their body as if they are waiting for me to come into sync with them, and so I join them rather than expecting them to join me.

I have heard many handlers describe great handling as being a dance. This is true, for at times, I can feel a certain confidence in a dog I am showing, and I don't try to control it. I allow them to lead, and I follow. (Michelle Scott did this with Josh, the Newfoundland that won Best in Show at Westminster in 2004.)

A handler that is too controlling can shut down the magic. Handlers, like the majority described in this book, know how to dance, adjust, and adapt, and this leaves them open to capture a moment and own it. There is wisdom in knowing when to control and when to surrender. Knowing when to lead and when to follow. Witnessing a moment in which a handler releases control and surrenders is truly magical!

Kaz says, "You witness a story when you watch a great handler capture a moment."

FOCUS ON BEING THE BEST YOU CAN BE, NOT WINNING

Kaz says, "A lot of young handlers don't know how to capture the moment. They all look the same to me. When I am handling, I am not in the ring to talk with other people. In the ring, my dog has all my focus. Times have changed."

Kaz describes the good old days as he recalls them. While at dog shows, handlers would be combing through the AKC Gazette (a magazine that lists dog shows being held across the country and the judges that will be judging them) in search of upcoming judging panels. They would eagerly look to see what highly respected judge would be coming up that they would have the honor of showing to. (This will become very apparent in Andy Linton's Chapter 8, when he describes in detail how he dedicated six months to preparing to show Sera to Anne Rogers Clark.)

Kaz feels much of this reverence has been lost, and most of the great judges are no longer with us. He sees a lot of upcoming young handlers more focused on talking to judges than on doing the fundamentals such as conditioning, care, and grooming. Breeders, owners, and handlers used to hang around the show talking about breeding, grooming, and handling.

Kaz explains, "Dog shows used to be busy after Best in Show. Now all that is left is Poodle handlers washing top knots. Everybody else goes home. People are not learning from one another anymore."

Kaz says others that have been in the industry for a long time feel the same way. They believe twenty years ago, things were better. People wanted to learn. There were excellent handlers with great dogs that were fun to watch.

If adolescents involved in junior showmanship want to learn from past generations, patience and planning are repeated themes embodied by both Kaz and his mentor, Anne Rogers Clark. Mrs. Clark was an avid writer, and people often requested interviews with her, hoping to tap into her deep knowledge and wisdom. She was quite vocal as a judge about her frustration with exhibitors who were not properly prepared. She called attention to the fact that, as a judge, it frustrated her to witness immaculately groomed puppies being shown to her that were not lead-broken. She was bothered when she saw an exceptional dog that was not in the right hands.

Kaz warns against the desire for immediate success. Instead of focusing on winning and getting ahead, focus on getting everything right.

He says, "Mrs. Clark would always ask, 'Did you do a perfect job? If not, go back and work harder and get everything right. That's why you didn't win. If you did a perfect job, then you can think about the other things that didn't work out, but always you must ask yourself, did I do everything perfectly? If you made a mistake, stop right there. That's what you focus on.'"

That is what Kaz grew up with. In fact, he gets upset if he wins Best in Show and his dog shows terribly. Doing a terrible job handling and winning is more upsetting to him than losing and getting everything perfect. Kaz's focus is always on getting everything right.

Kaz says, "There are roughly 150 plus shows per year. You and your dog may hit everything perfectly four or five times in a year if you are lucky. Mistakes are always made. I shouldn't have lagged behind the dog. I moved too fast. I didn't hit the turn right. I always think about it, what mistakes I made and where I can improve."

One of the things that has led to so much success for Kaz is his intense focus on each present moment. Each time he walks into a ring, his mind is focused on creating the moment and doing everything within his power perfectly. Kaz says, "That's the first focus... not winning, but getting everything under your power right."

Advice to New Handlers in the Industry

It's important to spend time every day with your dog, especially Poodles.

Kaz says, "Be consistent. Be patient. You can trim in one day, two days, three days, but you can't change a Poodle's brain in one day or two days. With Poodles, it takes months and even years of work to get it right."

In fact, with any dog and even people, it takes time to change a mindset. Kaz believes that with Poodles, there is no easy way.

He says, "A lot of handlers don't like showing Poodle specials against me because, after all these years of showing top Poodles, judges have an idea of how they expect a Poodle should look and show."

Judges and spectators alike have certain images in their minds because they have become accustomed to seeing the level of time and attention Kaz puts into his Poodles. The bar has been raised and is now a new set point.

Kaz makes his observation as a statement of fact, not arrogance. A lot of handlers won't show against Kaz.

Kaz says, "This becomes true in many breeds. Certain handlers tend to dominate certain breeds. You often see the same handler winning with different dogs year after year. The dogs change. The common denominator is the handler. It would appear judges are favoring a certain handler."

Kaz explains, "The same handler tends to win because they are really great with that breed. They have a great understanding of that breed and know what it needs to excel, both mentally and physically."

Kaz concludes, "I don't think I'm special or I am better than anybody else. I just won't accept that shit happens! I want to be prepared for everything. I am always thinking about possible scenarios I might encounter, and what can I do?"

I just love the empowering messages handed down from a dog show icon, Mrs. Clark, to Kaz and future generations. At all times, focus on being your best, doing your best, and getting everything right. Conduct yourself honorably and respectfully. Always examine your mistakes, take ownership of them, and use these mistakes to help guide you along your journey toward perfection. Ready to learn more about the relationship between Mrs. Clark and Kaz and the importance of mentorship in the industry? Me too.

CHAPTER 8

Andy Linton:
Building Confidence and Establishing Trust

As a kid, I grew up watching Andy Linton show Dobermans. He had a certain confidence and dignity about him. In the ring, he appeared unflappable. I lived and showed in the North East, where the handling style in Dobermans was primarily hard stacking, meaning the handler physically places the dogs' legs in the exact position they want them to stand. This very hands-on approach gives the handler more control of the dog's body and movements and allows the handler to mold a dog into a certain shape. We knew exactly how to stack a dog with a roaching topline or a bad neck set or croup and make those faults disappear. We were illusionists, magicians of the hard stack.

One of the handlers best known for this style of handling is Gwen DeMilta, whom I discuss at length in Chapter 11. Although Andy was capable of a hard stack, his style was more open and free-flowing, which reflects his true nature. He is lithe in appearance, with a quiet demeanor. A few times, when Andy flew to show on the East Coast, he helped me out by showing one of my dogs when I had two dogs that needed to be in the ring at the same time. On several occasions, Andy took an untrained class dog and had it out at the end of a lead, standing freely on its own as if it were a seasoned special. He accomplished this after working with a dog for only a couple of minutes. The way he could quickly transform an insecure dog without using his hands seemed like another kind of magic.

Over the years, I watched Andy show Dobermans of varying temperaments. One of the things that left me in awe of Andy is his masterfulness in building trust with his dogs. He could take a dog that was insecure–crawling around on its belly, submissive peeing, completely scared and nervous–and provide that dog with a sense of confidence. The dog would be transformed, walking into the show ring with its wits together, standing freely on its own. Andy could step back five feet, eight feet, ten feet, or more while the dog held solid at its core. And then he'd sometimes drop the lead, appearing to break all connection to his dog and demonstrate complete faith that the dog would maintain composure in the middle of the ring as the judge walked around making their selection. How does he do that? If you've been in the show ring, you know the tension that it holds when a judge is making their final selection. The dog must feel it, right? How does Andy trust the unstable dog won't crack under pressure? His dog must feel the pressure. Andy must feel it too. Or do they?

Whether Andy feels the tension or not, he always looks the same: cool and collected, almost detached when he is in the ring. He is confident and relaxed yet focused. His energy is different from other Doberman handlers, who appear extremely intense, sometimes bordering on uptight and overly controlled. Many other Doberman handlers, myself included, get our dogs pumped up to help them perform and project their energy. You can observe the handler becoming extremely excited with their voice or their body movements and facial expressions.

Many Doberman handlers do this right before they are asked to move their dog or perform a free stack on their own. They start generating a lot of energy toward their dog with the intent that the dog then scoops this energy up and projects it outward, filling up the entire ring, hopefully pulling in the judge and spectators with its stellar performance. In fact, you'll notice Doberman handlers often walk like performers in the ring, standing tall, emanating a commanding presence as they project their energy outward.

Even though Andy doesn't manage his personal energy in this way, he achieves the same result. He appears calm and relaxed, while his Doberman is bursting at the seams with enthusiasm. How does Andy do this? How did he achieve and perfect this style of dog handling?

"Obedience training is a fundamental part of making a great show dog," says Andy.

This is not a universal belief among handlers. There are many handlers who discourage obedience training for various reasons. I, however, agree with Andy and have always encouraged my clients to do obedience training with their dogs.

Andy states, "Weak-minded dogs especially thrive from obedience. When a dog is given a command, and it follows through with the command, the dog learns they are going to be okay if they follow instructions. In fact, they become stronger-minded if they learn to follow the instructions they are given, and are then rewarded.

"Trust develops as the dog learns that a command leads to a reward. They feel safe and sure in the world because the rules are clear and consistent. They know what to expect. In obedience, they understand sit, stay, come, heal, wait, etc. Dogs learn all these things, and they learn to trust your specific order or request. Then later, when you give them another request, like stand for the judge, they trust you enough to do as you ask."

This is how even an insecure dog eventually has faith and trust when they work with Andy. Andy's four basic tenets are: show love, show consistency, create boundaries, and trust develops.

He says, "Once trust develops, you are good to go."

His training approach is gentle and kind. There is a certain grace and faith in how he walks through the world.

He says, "I relate an insecure dog to having a child with problematic behavior. That child's behavior will never get better if you berate him or her, are tough on them, or try to force them to change to make them who you want them to be. They need you to encourage them. They need you to trust them. You have to earn their trust, and you have to trust them in return. It is essential that a handler establish a relationship of earning trust and giving trust."

In Andy's mind, training dogs is a lot like raising children. He says, "When a kid is acting out, you act like they are normal when they are not. You treat a dog just like you would a kid with problems. Again, they need love, they need consistency, and they need clear boundaries."

He says working with an insecure dog requires a tremendous amount of patience. He gives his dogs the time and space they need to come around. And when that dog is ready to let go of their fear, Andy supports and guides them, until they are ready to freestyle stand on their own.

This trust-building is integrated into almost everything Andy does. Even as he moves about his home or yard, he continually seeks opportunities to make requests of the dogs and allow them to follow through.

Andy says, "That is what I do. It's not really difficult. It doesn't take much time. It is consistency over time that builds trust."

This explains how Andy builds trust. But how about his calm, cool demeanor? How does he maintain that? Andy is a competitor. He is highly focused, and he likes to win. How does he not get nervous or worried when he has an unsteady dog out there on the end of the lead? Andy's answer is surprising.

"I have this mindset that when I am showing, it's like I am in the kitchen making a sandwich."

He employs this technique both literally and figuratively. Much of his show dog training literally takes place in his kitchen.

He explains, "Dogs are most relaxed in the kitchen. Dogs think they are just playing, having fun baiting, and standing four-square for treats."

Yet for Andy, important work is taking place. He says, "Every dog baits like the greatest show dog on the planet when they are in the kitchen."

Andy's approach is quite brilliant. He's not in the ring trying to get their neck arched or force them into position. As he says, he is simply making a sandwich. No intensity at all.

He adds, "I mean, I am intense, but it is all controlled and managed because, in my mind, I am just making a sandwich at home and my dog is waiting for a bite."

He has essentially programmed himself and his dogs with the fun and playful memory of baiting in the kitchen and transferred it to the show ring.

He adds, "Every dog is relaxed in the kitchen. They are at home. They are at peace."

That is how Andy appears so relaxed. When he is in the ring, showing the dog and asking for the win, there is no pressure; he and his dog are just in the kitchen having fun.

I loved hearing about this unique method. It's a clever way to ensure a dog doesn't pick up any excess tension in the ring. The only vibe a dog feels from Andy is relaxation: there is nothing to worry about.

This explains Andy's outwardly calm appearance. Yet, I keep coming back to the fact that, for me, it would feel too risky to stand five feet away from an unsteady dog.

I ask, "Do you ever have a moment where you lose faith or worry that an insecure dog might break its stance?"

Andy says, "I always try to show for the long term, not the moment. I can stand one loss, but I can't stand to lose a dog for its career. One loss, that is going to happen anyway. That's why I don't panic over one loss. "

Andy Envisions His Greatest Win

I feel such a sense of conviction in Andy, which prompts me to ask, "Do you ever visualize a certain behavior or outcome while showing a dog?"

Andy follows that up with a question, asking, "Do you want to hear about my greatest win of all time?"

"Of course," I reply, nodding my head and leaning forward in my seat.

He says, "It was Serenghetti."

Andy fills me in on the backstory of how he came to handle Ch. ToleDobes Serenghetti, or "Sera" for short. He received a phone call asking if he could show Sera in Best of Breed and Futurity at the Doberman Pinscher National Convention. He agreed.

Andy admits that for him, at the time, Sera was just another dog. He had never seen her before and didn't know much about her. Her breeders, Pat and Judy Doniere, flew out with her and delivered her to

Andy. The next day, after working with her for just a few minutes, he said to his kennel assistant, "I think I can make this dog a big winner."

He called up the breeders and proposed campaigning her for the next two years.

Based on her physical attributes, Andy felt Sera had the potential to be a record-breaker. After looking at the upcoming dog show schedule, he noticed Anne Rogers Clark was slated to judge Best in Show at one of the country's largest dog shows, the Louisville Kennel Club, hosted in Kentucky. At the time, the number of dogs entered at this event usually totaled around 3500. Although he felt very confident that Sera would be a big winner, he determined the deciding factor of Sera's ultimate potential would be if judge Anne Clark deemed her outstanding.

Everything he did from that point forward was to prepare Sera to receive the opinion of Anne Clark. He spent months preparing her, building rapport, and establishing trust.

Andy says, "I had laser focus from September until March." Every day, he would dream about how he was going to win Best in Show with Sera under Anne Clark.

"I never did anything like that before," admits Andy.

He shares in vivid detail how he showed this in his mind's eye.

"I knew at that time the Best in Show judge would come from behind a curtain."

That was the procedure at the time for Best in Show judging at the Louisville Dog Show.

"I'm getting chills just thinking about this because it happened EXACTLY the way I envisioned it. I saw Anne Clark walking in from behind the black curtain. I saw her walking in the way Anne Clark walks, you know, so stately, and supremely confident. I imagined when she walked in, I would be standing as far away from Sera as possible and Sera would be standing there on her own, looking magnificent."

"I will never forget that moment," says Andy. "Anne Clark walked in, looked at Sera and stopped. She didn't stop for any other dog. It went down exactly the way I dreamt it. Sera won Best in Show that day.

"That is my greatest memory of a win ever. Not winning Best in Show at the Garden, not any national, not any of the 350 or maybe 400 bests I've won on dogs. I don't even know how many I've won. But that still goes down as my greatest win, because I dreamt about it for so long and I put in a daily regime. I had never planned something out in my mind in such detail before nor have I done it since then," said Andy.

It's interesting to hear this, since the outside world deems a Best in Show win at Westminster to be one of the greatest moments in a handler's life. Andy is one of the few who holds that distinction, having won Best in Show at Westminster in 1989 on a Doberman named Indy, Ch. Royal Tudor's Wild as the Wind. Although, in theory, Westminster is just one show in a lineup of many that handlers aspire to win, it is a very famous event that carries a certain amount of prestige, and most handlers would love to be able to list it in their personal bragging rights!

I'm dead silent, in awe of this powerful story. Then I wonder why he didn't ever try that again.

QUALITY, CONDITIONING, PRESENTATION, AND CONSISTENCY WINS DOGS SHOWS

Even in the way Andy describes Sera's career, there was no force, only flow. Andy wasn't going to make Sera a top winner, he was going to allow for the possibility. Where some handlers fight for the win, orchestrate and plan, or criticize and scrutinize, Andy believes in himself and his dog. He trusts the dog, he trusts himself, and he trusts their relationship.

He believes if he has a good dog, trains, presents, and conditions it well, judges will reward that dog. It is as simple as that.

In fact, Andy says, "If dog shows were half as political as people say they are, I would quit tomorrow."

Andy believes quality, conditioning, and presentation are what is rewarded at dog shows, not politics.

"You can't win the race without the horse," says Andy.

Although many handlers experience extreme frustration in terms of politics and dog shows, this doesn't seem to be much of a challenge for Andy. When he loses, he doesn't get angry or blame a judge. It is something I have always respected about him. Yes, he cares about the outcome. Yes, he wants to win. All great handlers have a burning desire to win. Andy, too, has this burning desire, but he doesn't allow it to cloud his judgment. He doesn't accuse others of foul play. He consistently prepares his dog the best he can, he presents his dog to the best of his ability, and he accepts the decisions of the judges.

Andy says, "I examine the qualities of my dog versus the qualities of the dogs my competitors are showing. I compare the physical condition of my dog versus that of my competitors. I analyze my presentation against the presentations of my competition. If any one of my three components are less than my competition, I don't blame the judge. This makes me a better handler." (The teachings of Anne Rogers Clark are parroted in both Andy's words and his deeds.)

Andy focuses on what he can change and makes necessary adjustments rather than wrestling with things beyond his control. Managing how you win and lose is a challenging aspect in the sport of showing purebred dogs. Andy moves through it with ease and grace—something I would hope all handlers (including myself) aspire to.

Focusing on the Long Term Goal

Andy's awareness and focus on the long-term goal brings to mind an incident when a client got upset with me. The client asked me to show her dog. When the owner asked me to handle the dog, I said I needed to meet him before I would make my decision. Physically, he was a nice dog, worthy of being in the Top Twenty, which was a goal of hers. The primary question for me was, "Is this a dog I want to be working with for the next year of my life?"

The dog had a preexisting condition. I had seen the dog struggling in the ring with other handlers. He shied away from judges during the individual exam. He would tuck and pull away from judges and even spin around out of his stack. He worried and became nervous and anxious if a judge stood on his side or behind him. This is unacceptable behavior in the Doberman Pinscher standard.

Yet, I was curious. I wanted to figure out what was going on with him. He appeared vacant and detached. I wanted to see if I could reach into his soul and pull him back into his body. He felt disconnected, and I wanted to help him with that. Yes, being a rescuer has been part of my nature, and it does get me into trouble at times!

I agreed to show the dog. I didn't feel the dog was generally afraid of things. I felt something else causing this dog to break on his exam, but at that point in time, I didn't know what was triggering it.

In my first show with him, I could feel him tensing up. When he did this, I threw chicken on the floor and encouraged him to chase after it and eat it. After he did, I would tell him he was a really good boy! I was giving him a small task that he would be excited to do, so he could be successful at something simple, which would both help build his confidence and distract him from his worry and fear. On that particular day, the judge was considering me and that dog, but the more the judge looked at my dog, the more nervous and tense he became. In the final decision-making process, the judge asked handlers to gait the dogs around a circle. I threw some bait into the air to get his attention and help him relax. Unfortunately, my dog broke his gait and dove on the floor for the chicken just as the judge began to look at us.

The dog made a mistake. He dove for the chicken when he was told to simply watch it. He didn't completely understand the game I was teaching him.

I play a game with my dogs that is similar to Simon Says. In this game, I throw bait on the ground. When I throw bait on the ground, it is followed by several different commands, such as watch, wait, get it, or okay. My dogs need to listen for my cue. He didn't understand the rules of the game yet. When I threw the bait on the ground and told him to watch, he dove for it instead.

The picture I hoped to present to the judge was that of an upbeat, proud, confident dog, gaiting smoothly around the ring. Instead, the judge saw my dog diving on the floor after a piece of chicken. Oops!

It was disappointing for me. I knew what I was aiming for, but it didn't work. From outside the ring, this may have appeared as a major mistake on my part. Essentially in a clutch moment, I blew it by not having control of my dog. However, I–like Andy–was working toward the long-term goal of getting the dog to be relaxed in the ring around judges. Yes, I wanted to win that day, but more importantly, I wanted this dog to learn that it was okay to relax around me, and I wouldn't get angry at him if he made a mistake, which he did. I was working on building his confidence, the rest would come in time.

When I came out of the ring, the owner took the dog and angrily walked away with him shaking her head.

She came up to me and said, "You blew it!"

She then said a lot of things, which I mostly tuned out.

At one point, she said, "Do you find me offensive?"

My response was, "Your behavior is offensive, although I am not taking offense to it. I know you wanted to win and you are angry. I did what I felt I had to do for the dog and it didn't result in the win you wanted. I wanted to win too."

She was mad and frustrated.

I took a deep breath, forgiving myself for my own lack of perfection and the dog for not getting it right. He and I were learning how to work together. It was going to take time.

I knew it was the right approach for the long-term benefit of the dog. I was working toward something. The owner didn't understand it because all she cared about was the short-term win. That type of attitude can ruin a show dog. That type of attitude ruins a lot of things. It was that attitude and the pressure to win that was hurting her dog. It took time for me to see this dynamic and how much it was hurting her dog and even my ability to handle him when someone was applying that type of pressure.

The owner herself was more fixated on wins. We had a disagreement, and she placed the dog with another handler. Immediately the dog reverted to the behavior I had worked so hard to overcome. He was fearful of the new handler and shied away from two different judges. I really cared about the dog, and it was painful to watch what he was being put through because his owner was consumed with the win. I felt really hurt and powerless to do anything for the dog. There were important lessons for me here in terms of my need to rescue.

Handlers are agents. We get hired to do a job. Often, we get emotionally attached to these dogs, but in the end, it is our job. All handlers, at one point or another, will have their heart broken over their emotional attachment to a dog they were hired to show. For me, that has been one of the biggest challenges. How do you put your heart and soul into an animal, and then, when a client chooses to hire someone else, just release those feelings and let them go on their way? It can be really tough.

I can see Andy's wisdom and even ways I have applied it in my own life of showing dogs, but I never really thought about it in those terms. If I allowed myself to worry over all the ways the dog might fail, I would be creating too much pressure in an already tense situation. Although we want to win them all, we don't.

Ultimately, it was that attitude and pressure to win that was hurting her dog, but it took me a bit of time to discover that. I was unable to help her dog because I was unable to change her angry disposition. Ultimately it was her dog, and there was nothing I could do to protect him and shield him from her anger and disappointment.

I feel a unique bond with Andy and how he appreciates long-term gains over short-term wins. It is better for the dog and ultimately creates a win-win for both the dog and the owner. There are so many decisions we make as handlers in the ring. Although we may look calm, cool, and collected, we are making a lot of quick decisions, including weighing short-term and long-term consequences in a split second.

Andy always sees the big picture. He doesn't sweat the small stuff. He accepts that sometimes you may lose a battle, and that's okay; it happens. If a dog breaks or you lose, you've simply lost a moment, not the entire campaign. There is grace and acceptance in how Andy approaches wins and losses, as well as the expectations he places on his dogs as they enter the show ring. Andy takes the pressure off his dogs in that he doesn't expect them to be perfect from the start. No wonder his dogs can stand out on the end of a long lead. They know that even if they mess up, Andy will love them anyway. It will be okay.

Andy believes in his dogs. That is powerful.

"I'm a Christian. I have faith," says Andy.

When Andy told me this, we weren't talking about dogs, but I can see his faith is present in everything he does, including showing dogs. He has faith in them and himself. I believe this ultimately gives his dogs the confidence they need to stand up in the ring and be rock stars. Andy's faith is unconditional and unwavering.

He says, "I find 99.9 percent of dog show people are really nice! That's all I go by. I love being around dog show people. Of course, the dogs are fun. They give unconditional love and provide great therapy. I love my job. I make my own schedule. I can show as much or as little as I decide. I can bring my daughter to work on any given weekend. I get to travel all over the place. I have been to all fifty states as well as Brazil, Japan, and more. Since I like people, competition, dogs, travel, and making my own schedule, my job is the best job I could imagine."

A Man Focused on Family and Faith

A repeating theme with Andy is children and raising them with love and understanding. He delights in his daughter Ava, who at the time of this writing was eleven years old. As a dad, he appears fun and playful yet structured and patient. There seem to be many similarities between how he raises and trains his dogs and how he raises his children. He is nurturing, patient, loving, kind, and a natural teacher.

A new arena he's enjoying is 4-H. He admits he didn't even know what 4-H was until roughly a year ago. Every Monday night, his assistant Nikki would inform him that she had to go to 4-H to work.

Finally, one day, Andy asked, "What do you do when you go to 4-H?"

She explained to him that she worked with kids and dogs and helped teach the kids about canine welfare, charity work, and learning how to support one another as a team.

Then he asked, "How come you never invite Ava to join you?"

Nikki said she didn't want to be pushy about it. Soon after, Ava joined Nikki and was hooked immediately, as was Andy.

Now Andy is involved in teaching kids in 4-H. "4-H teaches character building. They teach the kids about integrity, honesty, and supporting each other. It's not just about dogs. They do charity work. They go to food banks. They volunteer. They learn about public speaking. People involved in 4-H really care about how people treat people."

Andy says, "They teach the kind of stuff I want my daughter to learn. So anyway, I'm a big 4-H fan!"

GRATITUDE: A DEFINING CHARACTERISTIC

Andy is a man of faith. It not only shows up in his love of kids and dogs, but he walks his faith in everyday life too. For Andy, there is always a silver lining.

He says, "If I lose my arm, I am going to be grateful for it. There is a reason."

He explains that if he were to have cancer, he would try to view it as an opportunity to help someone else through it. He is not blowing smoke when he says this. Many years ago, his sister was in need of a kidney, and without hesitation, Andy gave her his kidney.

Andy says, "If you can be grateful for all things, you will always be happy. Life is so simple. The more grateful you are, the happier you are. If you are grateful for all things, you will always be happy." He laughs and says, "Keep it that simple, and nobody needs a shrink!

CHAPTER 9

Taffe McFadden:
A Spiritual Approach to Handling

My first memory of Taffe McFadden handling was on the East Coast in 2009. She was showing a Giant Schnauzer bitch named Spirit. What stood out in my memory was that she and Spirit had a unique bond that appeared almost magical. In the ring, they seemed to move as one.

Many years later, when I first had the idea for this book, an image of Taffe and Spirit dropped into my head. I was confused about why this image was so dominant. I had never spoken with Taffe; therefore, I had no idea who she was on a personal basis. However, it felt like my book hinged on this interview. I knew where I wanted to go with Taffe in regard to our interview, and I wanted to hear her story about Spirit. For me, there was something mystical I wanted to explore. I wondered, will she see and be willing to discuss her handling as a spiritual experience?

Would she be open to this? My fear and reservations were cast aside the moment I sat down to interview Taffe.

She owns her spirituality with dogs. She talks of her faith, work, and communication with dogs as not just a figment of her imagination but as a fact of life. Talking with Taffe, there is no doubt that what might sound surreal to some is very real to her.

When I first reached out to Taffe, her energy felt unique to me. It felt soft and willowy, yet strong and capable. It was an interesting contrast. We met officially for the first time in Pennsylvania, where she flew from California. She was campaigning a Havanese who was ranked the Number One Dog in All Systems. This is no easy feat. I must admit, I felt a sense of pride in a woman handler holding the number one seat. However, if you met her and started up a conversation with her, you would have no idea Taffe was pioneering the top seat. Her energy is warm, patient, loving, and down to earth. When you sit with Taffe, it's like being with a long-lost friend. Her presence is comforting. She is open and available. It is apparent she cares for the greater good of both humans and animals.

Despite her highly acclaimed position, Taffe admits to constant feelings of doubt. Did she make the right decision? Will the judges recognize and acknowledge her and her dog?

Taffe doesn't shame these feelings; rather, she makes friends with them. When I hear this, I see her humility, I see her humanity. I see that regardless of all her successes, she still struggles. It's just part of the human experience. It doesn't define who Taffe is, but it is a part of her—a part that may even lead to much of her beauty.

Taffe is a woman who, despite a very demanding show schedule, is dedicated to giving back to the world. She loves teaching others, holding handling classes, and watching individuals grow as handlers and in the joy they take in themselves as they become better at their craft. Watching people and dogs grow and become more confident in the ring is something Taffe loves. She loves encouraging this and sharing the success of her students and her dogs as well.

Sometimes a Calling Becomes a Profession

While some kids struggle with knowing what they want to do when they grow up, Taffe always knew. Her sister bred English and Irish Setters. Taffe remembers being six years old and enjoying going to shows with her but knew she didn't want to just be the one to help set up crates. Around the age of ten, Taffe knew that she wanted to show dogs professionally. She showed dogs in Canada and started competing in junior showmanship as soon as she met the minimum age requirement.

What she loves most about her job may seem too obvious, but it's true. She truly loves working with the dogs.

She says, "I don't mean for that to sound syrupy, but I really enjoy the connection with certain animals. Not all of them. It's like some people. We don't all mesh perfectly together. Some mesh better with other handlers. For instance, I might not feel a strong connection with a certain animal, but my husband does. I've been really fortunate to have worked with some dogs that really hold a special nugget of my heart. They know what I need or I know what they need prior to any kind of discussion. That is definitely my favorite part–the connection I have with the dogs. For me, showing dogs is a spiritual experience."

THE PARTNERSHIP IS BIGGER THAN THE DOG AND THE HANDLER

Taffe explains her relationship with Spirit, who was one of her first top specials. She states that Spirit was probably one of the first dogs that didn't need Taffe as much as Taffe needed her.

She explains, "Prior to working with Spirit, the majority of the dogs I tended to work with on a national level were a little timid or needed a little bit of gentle guidance to come out of their shells. That was what I was known for. Spirit was given to my husband first as a special. They worked well together, but then over time, it became apparent that I had a special bond with her and she didn't need me for anything except as an armband holder!"

She continues, "She kept me in line. She knew exactly what she needed and I just sort of went along for the ride. She brought things out in me that I didn't know I had, like a competitive edge. I wasn't competitive. I could do my job. I was good at it. But she was the one that brought that out of me. She just would flip a switch and it suddenly became the most important moment in the ring. You could see her go from doing a beautiful job and doing what was necessary and then all of a sudden, she would accelerate her ears, her tail, her neck, her carriage. It was like stardust that just happened. You could see it in her eyes. She was amazing. She was truly not just a dog, but an amazing partner."

Taffe states that not everyone saw Spirit's potential to be a big winner. She says, "I believed in her right from the very beginning. It was hard at first. The first six or seven months, it was hard getting out of the breed. I couldn't understand it. To me, she was just beautiful. I always believed in her. I remember saying to my husband one day, 'I think she is going to go Best in Show.' He said, 'You are having a hard time getting out of the breed.' I said, 'I know but this lineup feels good.' He said, 'Well, alright, we'll see.' And she did! She won Best in Show. I believed in her and I had to wait for the rest of the world to come around, and when they did, she was unstoppable. She went from zero to sixty so quickly."

Taffe admits, "I worked with an animal communicator that probably helped me more than she helped Spirit. She helped me understand different idiosyncrasies with the dog. She always told me that Spirit could read judges that didn't appreciate her and she would misbehave a little bit. She taught me how to have Spirit rely on me for confidence, to trust me and get through it. It was funny because Spirit would give me the side eye and I'd think, 'Oh no! This is one of those judges that she thinks doesn't appreciate her!' I would have to make eye contact with her and she would look me in the eye and just settle into it. She wasn't one that you could rack up (hand stack her legs into place). You couldn't touch her on the self-exam. She wanted to do it her way, and the animal communicator helped me figure that out too. Spirit would buckle under her front if I was holding the choke chain or wracking her ears. Jess, the communicator, said, 'You just have to believe in the dog. You just have to step back and let her do it herself.' She was completely transformed from 'I don't think I like this judge' to 'I'm going to deal with it because I love you.' She tolerated it for me.

"Spirit changed who I was as a handler. I've always had a knack for showing dogs. I usually got the timid ones, the ones that needed a lot of love, care, and attention to help get them showing confidently. Spirit was the first one who was a force. I had no idea that she could do as well as she was going to do. She won 100 Bests in Show. She was definitely the highlight of my career from age seven to now. She was my dance partner. She was amazing.

"Working with Spirit put me on a different level. In working with Jess, though, in regards to Spirit, I didn't feel Spirit was the problem, it was me. I felt I was blocking our progress because I didn't understand what Spirit needed me to do for her."

The animal communicator provided guidance on how Taffe could better respond to, support, and have faith in Spirit.

SEEKING COUNSEL FROM AN ANIMAL COMMUNICATOR

Since I believe Taffe is able to sense what her dogs need in order to thrive, I was curious to learn when she seeks outside counsel in terms of animal communication. When or how does she determine their needs go beyond her scope or ability to sense what they need? When does she determine she needs to consult with an animal communicator?

Taffe explained that prior to Spirit, she would seek the advice of an animal communicator if she encountered a situation in which a dog didn't want to do something she needed them to do.

Questions she might have for an animal communicator would be:

- Why is the dog not feeling like they want to show?
- Is there an underlying problem?
- Why doesn't the dog like outdoor dog shows?
- Why doesn't the dog like being in its crate?

For instance, she was hired to handle a Bichon Frise who was beautiful but didn't want to show. Prior to seeking Jess's counsel, Taffe had taken her to a vet and a chiropractor, but they couldn't find anything wrong with her.

"Jess tuned into her energy and recommended we do a urine analysis. The test results indicated a low-grade bladder infection. This was throwing her hormones off, and she just didn't feel good. After treatment, she turned out to be a great show dog."

Tragedy with Spirit Leads to a Deeper Bond

While flying to the Giant Schnauzer National Specialty Show, tragedy struck. Most any handler or owner who has flown with a dog knows the fear of flying with a dog that cannot fly in the cabin. You hope the dog will make it safely and uneventfully to the desired destination. However, there are so many risk factors, such as the weather conditions out on the tarmac as the animal waits to be loaded. How will the animal be transitioned (especially a large animal that needs to be lifted by two people)? Will the people handling the crate be gentle and attentive? What will it be like when the crate is loaded into the cargo area of the plane? What will happen when the crate is unloaded? Even, will the dog be put on the right flight?

Whenever I had to fly commercially with a dog, there was a tremendous relief when I received them at our destination and I knew they were okay. Fortunately, I never had the experience of suffering tragedy while flying.

Unfortunately for Taffe, when she and Spirit flew to nationals, something went terribly wrong. Taffe choked up as she described the event to me.

On that day, she flew with her husband, Bill. Bill offered to get Spirit and the luggage, and Taffe went to collect the rental vehicle. However, once she got the car, she had to keep circling the airport. Bill wasn't picking up his phone.

Finally, she got Bill on the phone and said, "What is going on?"

He informed her that he had the luggage, but he didn't have Spirit. He said, "They can't find her."

Somehow, she got loose and ran onto the tarmac. It was a super-hot day. Perhaps someone opened her crate to pet her or give her water.

Taffe never found out how Spirit got out of her crate, but eventually, the airport workers captured her.

"When we got her out of her crate, there was no skin left on the pads of her feet. Her crate was a bloody mess. It was horrible," says Taffe. She still remembers Spirit wagging her tail when she saw her and coming out of her crate.

As soon as Taffe and Bill got to their hotel, they began the task of doing everything they could to get Spirit comfortable and begin healing. In the midst of attending to her immediate well being, they also needed to consider whether it would be possible to get her healthy and comfortable enough to compete at the national competition.

A national specialty is a big deal. It has a similar quality to Westminster in that it only takes place once a year, so each dog only has a few chances at earning this distinction in their lifetime. Again, similar to Westminster, dogs travel from all over the country and even all over the world to compete in this prestigious event. While competition at Westminster is open to all breeds, a national club is only open to that particular breed. For those who love a particular breed, a national specialty show is a very exciting opportunity to witness so many dogs of that breed coming together to compete. For a breeder, owner, or handler, it is always an extreme honor to win a national specialty.

At most nationals, there is a regional show or shows that lead up to the grand finale. For Taffe and Spirit, the initial regional event would begin the following day. Taffe and Bill knew they would have to skip the regionals. However, it was their hope that they could get Spirit healthy and comfortable enough to compete in the national.

They had three days to prepare and attend to her wounds. In addition to the time limitations, another big factor was that the show was being held on grass. This definitely complicated matters. Having to show on grass would offer more irritation to Spirit's already sensitive pads. A show indoors on mats would have been more conducive to her being comfortable competing in the ring while her paws were still healing.

On that third day, the day of the national breed competition, Taffe remembers Spirit bounding out of her crate as if to say, "I've got this!"

Seeing her enthusiasm and willingness to show, Taffe decided to let her compete. However, as Spirit's handler, Taffe knew she needed to have a plan or oversee Spirit's performance and make sure Spirit didn't overdo it. Taffe's plan was to move her as little as possible to help save her from hurting her feet.

She explains, "She made it around the first go-around. She did the down and back. She was fabulous on the exam!"

Spirit was in contention for the win. However, on the final go-around, she just couldn't do it.

Taffe cries, "She tried so damn hard. She wanted to do it for me. I knew at that moment how much of a partner she was."

Although Spirit didn't win on that day, it is a moment Taffe will never forget.

"From that moment on, we were linked," explains Taffe. "I knew that no matter what the situation was, she would do anything she could for me. That was such a huge turning point for her and for me in my life. I never had anyone try that hard for me… not even a human. She was just so amazing."

TAFFE OVERCOMES HER OWN PERSONAL BATTLE

Spirit's episode out on the tarmac wasn't the only challenge these two were forced to endure. In fact, a much more daunting obstacle blindsided Taffe. After the scare at the airport, Taffe didn't want to ever put Spirit on a plane again. Their team was now required to put in more hours on the road. For the remainder of Spirit's campaign, the team would be driving all over the country.

Unless a handler/owner has participated in a national campaign, it's hard to comprehend how incredibly taxing it is. A handler's mental and physical limits are pushed to the extreme, and this endurance run usually lasts at least a year, sometimes longer. When the finish line was in sight, the team kept pushing through exhaustion.

"I was not feeling well and I was tired all the time. I was having seizures and they misdiagnosed it as epilepsy. It was not epilepsy." Taffe's body was giving out and yet she still pressed on.

Spirit's campaign ended in April 2009 when Spirit won her 100th Best in Show. Taffe was thrilled with Spirit's accomplishments, however, she admits, "I was also very tired and not feeling well."

She remembers the sheer exhaustion and thinking, "I'm so tired. I don't want to show dogs anymore." Three months later, Taffe was diagnosed with cancer.

Her doctor informed her that she might never be able to handle dogs again. Despite what she felt at the end of her campaign, she thought, you wait and see. I will be doing this again. She then proceeded to go through the whole cancer recovery process. Sure enough, she came back.

Taffe says, "I did it and I got to the point where I felt healthy, strong, and ready."

Soon, she was showing every weekend. She was doing great.

However, a follow-up test soon revealed that the cancer was back, and it was even more dire. The treatment this time would be much more invasive. Taffe was shocked and confused because she was feeling so good.

This time, Taffe would require surgery. She admits, "It was much worse. The recovery was grueling. It was just plain horrible!"

This time, she was restricted from contact with animals of any kind. Dirt and dander were forbidden. She must remain in a sterile environment. She was informed recovery would require one and a half years of her life. The prognosis was that she would never run again. She would never show another dog. According to doctors, her career and joy as a dog show handler were over.

Like a Hallmark movie, Taffe's story did not end that way. Not only did she run again, but less than ten years later, she earned the top seat handling a Havanese named Bono, MBIS MBISS GCHP Oeste's in the Name of Love, to the ranking of Number One Dog among All-Breeds. Few handlers have the distinction of this title once in their careers, let alone twice. Taffe's story is such an inspiration to so many.

"Because of the illness, every day is a gift. There are days that I think I am the luckiest person in the world because I get to do what I love. I get to walk around with animals I love, showing dogs for people I love."

Dogs Offer Strength, a Mutual Reliance

Despite all her success in the show ring, Taffe admits to sometimes waking up doubting herself and hoping people take her seriously. She's able to laugh at foolish thoughts that still taunt her, such as times she steps out from behind the wheel of a rental vehicle, walks onto the show grounds on the first day, worrying, did I make the right decision? Can I win here? Will these people see right through me? Will they overlook me and my dog, thinking I'm nobody?

When good results take place, she feels relief and gratitude for having made the right decision.

"Even now, I am so insecure. I hide behind my dogs. I have second thoughts about lots of things… yet with a dog in my hand, I feel strong," she asserts. And then laughingly admits once again, "But I'm always a wimp on the first day of the dog show!"

I actually have to pause to absorb the impact of what Taffe just said. Listening to Taffe and hearing her story, I find that there is a common thread among many of the highly accomplished handlers, myself included. There are sometimes feelings of self doubt that seem to magically slip away with a certain dog in hand.

This awareness brought me back in time to an interview I did in 2003 for the Eukanuba Dog Show held in California that year. If my memory serves me, all handlers with breed winners were required to participate in an interview. The show was being televised, and the producers wanted material to pull from during the show. Raisin, my most top-winning Doberman, and I sat in the hallway, awaiting our turn to be interviewed.

Suddenly, the interviewer opened the door, saw me with Raisin, and kindly stated that my dog was not permitted in the interview. I immediately informed this person that I wouldn't be there at that show if it weren't for my dog, and the only way I would agree to be interviewed was if my dog was allowed to accompany me. They acquiesced. Thank goodness, because the moment I was informed Raisin couldn't join me, I felt panic. Luckily, my false bravado ensured I had what I needed to get through the interview... my dog.

On that day, I realized I felt stronger, braver, and more confident with Raisin. Looking back now, I think Raisin was a lot like Spirit. She didn't need me; I needed her. From the outside looking in, it may appear that the handlers are the ones commanding the dogs. Yet things are not always as they appear. Sometimes a dog takes on the role of master for just enough time that you are able to see your own strength. Katie and Ty seemed to have shared this same dynamic as well.

During my interviews with Taffe, Michelle Scott, and Greg Strong, they all referred to their dogs as dance partners. Sometimes one leads, and sometimes one follows. I'd never heard dog handling referred to in this manner. I find this to be a profound statement that beautifully describes the essence of dog handling. There is such beauty to behold when a dog and handler surrender to the rhythm of each other and become one. When this happens, in that moment, there is nothing else.

From my perspective, some dogs come into this world with a mission to light up the world. They are magnetic. They are light bearers of strength and beauty. Spirit and Raisin were such animals, as are many other dogs featured throughout this book. For those of us handlers who sometimes struggle with self doubt and question ourselves and our abilities, these dogs show us how to believe in ourselves in a way that might never have been possible otherwise. These dogs hold that energy.

As Taffe said, "If you are lucky enough to be the person they connect with, they light you up. It is such a gift to connect with an animal like that on such a deep level."

A True Ambassador of the Sport of Purebred Dogs

When I ask Taffe about her purpose and the legacy she would like to leave behind, she tells me a story of when she was a little girl showing a Golden Retriever for the first time. She still recalls the name of the judge, Forrest Hall. She laughs, "He was the meanest man ever in dogs!"

She makes a pouty face and continues, "A mean, mean, mean old man. I took my Golden Retriever in the ring, and he said, 'This dog is hideous. You should take it out in the field and shoot it.'"

When young Taffe walked out of the ring and looked at her mom, tears were streaming down her face. She told her mom what the judge said.

Her mom replied, "You have your choice. You can either run scared or stand tall. What are you going to do?"

Taffe said, "I'm coming back tomorrow."

She laughs and says, "I'm sure my mom wanted to go into the ring and punch him."

Proud of her daughter's decision, her mom encouraged, "Good. You can't let that define you. You need to figure this out."

And figure it out, she did!

It made me wonder if this negative childhood event led to the depth of compassion she holds for newcomers to the sport. Despite their very demanding show schedule, Taffe and her husband Bill still teach handling classes. She says a part of her is always on the lookout for a child with their parents, attending a dog show for the first time, thinking, "This could be fun." Or she's eyeing a new owner wanting to explore whether or not they have what it takes to handle their own dog, or even a more experienced handler that wants to take their handling to a different level.

Encouraging and teaching people, as well as dogs, is one of her many passions. She enjoys helping aspiring handlers become the handlers they want to be someday. Taffe is delighted when her students spot her at a show and share their latest achievements.

She says, "It's so fun to see them encouraged, achieve milestones, and set new goals. It feels good to be a part of their transformation."

She also enjoys hearing breeders discuss the next great dog they are going to breed, or hearing how much a certain judge is looking forward to judging the next great dog, or even that a kennel club member wants to run the next great show. It's not just about dogs. Taffe enjoys encouraging people in all genres of dog showing. Similar to her dog Spirit, Taffe's message is often, "I believe in you. You can do it!"

Taffe is that voice for others, encouraging them to be more than they ever thought they could be.

PART THREE

Achieving the Pinnacle

CHAPTER 10

Anne Rogers Clark and Kaz Hosaka:
The Importance of Mentorship

We met Kaz Hosaka in an earlier chapter, but his story isn't quite complete. As you saw in our introduction to Kaz in Chapter 7, he has become a master dog show handler. What you may not know is where he began and what it took for him to become a top handler. You see, Kaz's story is not only about transformation with dogs but also about his own personal transformation from novice to expert, which was only made possible through his relationship with Anne Rogers Clark, his mentor.

As he tells it, what started off as an exciting, scary, once-in-a-lifetime mentorship opportunity quickly and abruptly became a descent into hell. That mentorship opportunity and the trials it would bring came to Kaz out of the blue, instigated by the renowned Annie Clark, a trailblazer in the industry and an iconic Poodle breeder, handler, and later judge. This opportunity and the unforeseen challenges it would present, along with Kaz's fortitude in facing them, is what molded him into the master he is today. Still, well before Annie Clark appeared, Kaz was no stranger to adversity, and this is where Kaz's story begins...

Tragedy Leads to Destiny

One of Kaz's first experiences with hardship hit when his mother died. He was just ten years old and an only child—and was often left home alone when his dad went to work. Loneliness, on top of grief, is hard for an adult to bear, never mind a child. Eventually, however, a benevolent uncle stepped in.

Kaz's uncle was a professional handler in Japan who specialized in showing working and sporting breeds. He also operated a fifty-dog boarding kennel, mostly consisting of Dobermans. Since Kaz was so often left home alone, his uncle invited him to come over to help take care of the kennel. His uncle knew Kaz loved dogs—especially Dobermans.

I was both shocked and delighted to discover that Kaz began with Dobermans! Soon I discovered that wasn't the only childhood interest we shared. He excelled in his youth as a soccer player. I enthusiastically shared with him that I was a goalie and broke my high school's record of the most shutouts by a goalie in a season.

Kaz was extremely competitive. He played soccer for eleven years in school, was captain of his high school team, and anticipated playing in college. Unfortunately, a leg injury shattered this dream.

Without soccer, Kaz felt lost. His uncle asked, "Why don't you come over to the kennel and take some time to sit back and think about your future? Don't hurry. Just come over to the kennel and give yourself time."

Kaz did as his uncle recommended.

In Japan at the time, it was very hard to get into college. You had to pass a test to qualify for admittance. After giving it much consideration, Kaz decided he wanted to go back to college. He informed his uncle of his decision.

His uncle instructed, "Of course–that is your decision, but in the meantime, I have a Doberman puppy I want you to train."

Kaz didn't know how to train a dog, but he trained it. Then his uncle asked him several times, "Why don't you show this puppy?"

Kaz repeatedly said, "No."

His uncle persisted, "Just show the puppy one time."

Kaz acquiesced. He won Best Puppy in Show at his first dog show.

Kaz was excited about his first big win, yet he was reluctant about dog showing. His heart was still yearning to be in college, where he could play soccer.

His uncle persisted, asking, "Kaz, why not show the puppy again? He is entered next weekend too. Just one more time, and then you can stop showing if you want."

Kaz showed a second time and won Best Puppy in Show again!

Kaz confesses, "I won seven Best Puppy in Shows in a row! I thought, 'Forget it! I don't need to go to school! I'll stay in the kennel.'"

That's how he got his start in showing dogs.

When Kaz was twenty years old, two iconic American judges–Mrs. Anne Rogers Clark and Mr. James Edward Clark–came to Japan. Kaz considered it an honor and privilege to exhibit dogs to them, especially Mrs. Clark, a three-time Westminster Best in Show winner, who was considered one of the most prestigious handlers in the world.

Kaz showed seven dogs to the Clarks. He laughs, "I won nothing! Zero!"

However, Mrs. Clark did award his uncle Best in Show with a Doberman. Two days after that show, a Poodle specialty was being held in Tokyo. Although Kaz's uncle primarily showed working and sporting dogs, his hobby was working with Standard Poodles. This hobby developed because he admired the handling abilities of Frank Sabella, a well-known professional Poodle handler from the United States. He wanted to show a Poodle like Frank, so he bought a Standard Poodle from America.

Kaz's uncle entered two Standard Poodles in the Tokyo show. A groomer at the show prepared the Standard Poodles for Kaz and his uncle to handle, since they didn't know how to groom Poodles. Mr. Clark was judging Standard Poodles. There were only two Standard Poodles entered. Kaz showed one, and his uncle showed the other one. Kaz won.

Since it was a Poodle specialty, that Best of Breed win qualified him to compete for Best Poodle in Show. The Best in Show judge was Mrs. Clark. Kaz remembers his time in the ring when Mrs. Clark was judging.

"I walked in the ring with the Standard Poodle, and I could see Mr. Clark sitting outside the ring watching me. I looked at him. He gave me a hand signal indicating that I had stacked the front legs too wide apart, and I needed to narrow the distance between the front legs."

Kaz made the correction. Then Mr. Clark gestured that Kaz had made too much of an adjustment.

Kaz says, "I was so excited... I didn't speak English, but I understood body language. I didn't win, but Mr. Clark taught me something. It was very exciting because the Clarks were very famous people and Mr Clark took the time to instruct. It was an honor."

Opportunity Rings

Three days later, the kennel phone rang. Kaz answered. It was Mr. and Mrs. Clark's interpreter. Kaz said, "Hold on, I'll go find my uncle."

The interpreter said, "No! No! Mr and Mrs. Clark want me to give this message to you."

Kaz laughed, incredulous. He was shocked they remembered him, let alone wanted to reach out to him. The interpreter continued, "Young man, if you want to become a professional dog handler in the United States, Mr. and Mrs. Clark will teach you how to show dogs."

Kaz was dumbfounded. He couldn't believe it. It felt surreal, like a dream, and one he wasn't sure if he was ready for.

Kaz explains that, at the time, being just twenty years old, he felt afraid of everything, especially going to America. He talked the decision over with his uncle, who explained that the dog shows in the United States were not like the dog shows in Japan. For one, there were a lot more dog shows in the United States, and the competition was intense. Kaz's Uncle wanted to help prepare Kaz, not only for the culture shock of being in a new country, but also for the culture of dog shows in the United States. In order for Kaz to experience this first hand–prior to agreeing to work for the Clarks in America–his uncle offered to pay for Kaz to experience a dog show tour in the United States.

Kaz ventured off to America for the sole purpose of watching dog shows. I was deeply drawn in as he shared his story with boyhood wonder. While at the Santa Barbara Ventura dog shows, Kaz spotted a handler with a Doberman that captivated his attention.

He confesses, "Kelly, you would not believe how excited I was. I didn't watch any breed except Dobermans all three days!"

Since Kaz knows my love of Dobermans, he asks, "Do you know who I saw? Moe Miyagawa with Mary Hartman! They won Best in Show!"

I laughed out loud. Of course, I knew this team. As a little girl, I heard stories and saw pictures of this famous duo. Moe, also Japanese, was one of the top Doberman handlers, and Mary Hartman was the number one Doberman at the time.

Kaz explains, "I snuck behind Moe to watch. I watched to see everything Moe was doing. Moe put Mary Hartman on a grooming table. I thought, 'What?' I had never seen a Doberman put on a grooming table! You understand, in my country forty or fifty years ago, we didn't groom Dobermans on a grooming table!"

Kaz laughs and then adds, "We cut whiskers, and that's about it. Moe used clippers to trim the hair on the tuck-up and inside her ears. He used thinning shears on her neck to create a smoother appearance. He had a special leash and collar for showing. I had never seen that before!"

Kaz admits, "I was shocked! Everything he did, I found amazing!"

Kaz applied his newly discovered knowledge and bought a special tack box (a box designed to store tack/grooming supplies) and a pair of clippers. He enthusiastically recalls, "I couldn't wait to go home to show my uncle everything I learned about grooming a Doberman!"

In fact, when he returned, he started grooming Dobermans for everyone in Japan!

Poodles? No Way!

Although Kaz was honored that Mr. and Mrs. Clark wanted him to move to America, live with them, work for them, and learn how to show dogs, he had a major concern. The concern had a name. It was spelled P-O-O-D-L-E!

Kaz was a Doberman handler. Mr. and Mrs. Clark wanted to teach him how to show Poodles, but he had never groomed a Poodle in his life! Grooming and showing Poodles felt outlandish to him. Not only was grooming Poodles way beyond his skill set but there was also a certain stigma associated with Poodles. At that time in Japan, people were not very accepting of gay men, and Poodles were not considered a "real" man's breed. The prevailing perception in Japan at the time was that only gay people showed Poodles. "Real" men were supposed to show Dobermans and Boxers. Kaz worried about what others might think about him handling Poodles. Kaz explained his worries to his uncle.

Yet his uncle declared, "This is a once-in-a-lifetime opportunity. You have no choice. You go. There is no choice. If you don't go, you will be sorry."

A GRUELING START

I can only imagine how overwhelmed Kaz must have felt having such a limited background in grooming and being unable to communicate verbally. The only English words he knew were yes and no. (Well, there is another phrase he knew, but I'll save that for later.)

Mrs. Clark used hand signals to teach Kaz how to hand wash and dry a Standard Poodle. It is standard practice for groomers to put oil in a Poodle's coat so the coat doesn't need to be groomed on a daily basis. In fact, this process was instituted by Mrs. Clark herself, who was very innovative in her grooming techniques.

Even now, groomers often leave Poodles' coats in oil for up to three months. The oil helps protect the hair from getting damaged and breaking during a non-grooming phase. However, when it comes time to begin grooming a dog whose coat has been set in oil, it is a long, tedious process. The groomer must wash, de-mat, and dry the entire coat. The first time Kaz attempted this process, it took him eleven hours to completely wash out, de-mat, and dry just one dog.

Kaz thought, "I can't do this."

The next day, Mrs. Clark came into the kennel, looked at Kaz, pointed to the same dog he had washed the day before, and commanded, "Wash again!"

Kaz was shocked at the thought of repeating the process again so soon, but this time, it only took him seven hours. On the third day, the Clarks placed an English cocker on the grooming table. Kaz was instructed on new grooming techniques: grooming stones, stripping knives, and how to pull hair. It was hard work. Kaz's fingers were bleeding by the end from working the coat.

Again, he thought, "This is not working. I want to go home."

Yet, he couldn't go home. He promised to stay with the Clarks for three years. Kaz began counting down the days. People back home said to Kaz, "You are strong. You are in America, all alone, in the middle of a cornfield, with no one else who speaks Japanese, plus you are working with Poodles!"

Kaz recalls people declaring, "You are amazing! You made it! You got through it."

Yet Kaz readily admits, "No. I was not strong. I was afraid to go home."

From his perspective, if he didn't make it through his agreed-upon 1000-plus days and returned home, he would feel humiliated. He admits, "I was afraid of what people would say about me. I didn't want to go back to Japan and have people laughing at me. No. My staying in the United States had nothing to do with being strong and brave. I simply stayed because I didn't want to be laughed at and feel humiliated."

One thing I must say about many dog show handlers, myself included, is that we know how it feels to have our backs up against a wall. At that moment, we know there is no turning back. There is no retreat. We enjoy testing our limits and pushing the extremes. Knowing we might not succeed—for some, this is even part of the excitement.

The fear itself can become a spark that propels us forward. Successful dog show handlers are a unique breed. Our mindset is, if there is something we seek and we do not try, then we have failed ourselves. For most of us, competition inspires, motivates, and invigorates us. Although many of us may question our own self-worth, for some of us, this is how we find it–by digging deeper than we thought we could. At dog shows, we test our limits, and we prove to ourselves our own worth. At least, that is how it worked for me when I was starting out. Kaz may not have set out to test his self-worth in this manner. However, his pursuit to become a dog show handler certainly gave him quite the education as to his true nature and his capabilities as a human being.

LESSONS LEARNED

A couple of weeks after he arrived in America, Mrs. Clark asked Kaz, "What is your dream?"

Kaz understood the question and was overjoyed because he knew the words to respond. He excitedly pronounced, "Best in Show!"

Although his understanding of the English language was limited, he thinks Mrs. Clark replied, "If you try, and you work very hard, you will get it."

That first year Kaz remained home alone, grooming and caring for Mr. and Mrs. Clark's dogs while the pair ventured from home most weekends due to their demanding schedules as AKC licensed judges. When Mr. Clark was home, he would spend every night talking to Kaz in English. Mr. Clark bought two dictionaries so he and Kaz could communicate back and forth each night.

"A ten-second conversation would take an hour to understand. Mr. Clark always had a lot of patience with me. He became my father. He taught me how to live in this country," Kaz explains.

Although Kaz describes both Mr. and Mrs. Clark as his teachers, he says they each taught him very different things. Whereas Mr. Clark taught Kaz about life in the US, Mrs. Clark taught him everything he needed to know about the dog show life, and she took her role as teacher and guide very seriously. Once she set her mind to something, she saw it through to completion. Kaz was no exception.

Kaz spent about a year and a half diligently working in the kennel, and at that point, the Clarks decided he would exhibit a dog at the Poodle Club of America dog show. Mrs. Clark assigned Kaz a Standard Poodle to handle in the open dog class. Kaz admits, "I was big-time nervous!"

According to Kaz, Mrs. Clark told him to go first in line. Kaz immediately rejected her notion. He still didn't understand English very well and didn't feel confident he would be capable of comprehending what the judge would be requesting of him. He tried to express his concern to Mrs. Clark, yet she was adamant that he be first in line. Kaz said, "No."

Mrs. Clark said, "Yes."

Kaz laughs and says, "She kicked my ass! She made me do it! She commanded, 'Go in there!'"

Kaz thought, "This is the end of me!"

He was so upset that she forced him to the front of the line. He says, "I was in a panic!"

In fact, when the judge came to examine his dog and asked him to move his dog straight down and back, his dog galloped the whole way down and the whole way back.

Kaz says, "It was terrible. I was not happy. I will never forget the ride home. I told Mrs. Clark I wanted to quit. I am not good. I cannot do this. I am not good enough."

Any guesses as to Mrs. Clark's reaction?

Kaz says, "She smacked my head so hard! She said, 'You are here with me for three years! You have a year and a half left. If in a year and a half you want to quit and not be a dog handler, you can quit, but I am not going to give up on you!'"

It seems odd that Mrs. Clark's harsh, demonstrative action toward Kaz tugged on my heartstrings, yet that is how I felt when he relayed this story to me. Mrs. Clark believed in Kaz when he lost hope in himself. Mrs. Clark was a force of nature; when she set something in motion, she would not be deterred. To fail or to quit were not words in her repertoire.

"I didn't work for a handler, I worked for Mrs. Clark. A lot of people work for a dog handler to gain experience and go to dog shows every weekend. But for me, I learned so much more than that."

In addition to grooming and handling techniques, the Clarks also taught Kaz dog anatomy and how to evaluate litters. If someone brought a litter of puppies to be evaluated by Mrs. Clark, she would call Kaz over and have him examine each puppy. She would then instruct him to rank them first, second, third, fourth, and fifth pick, and he would have to tell her why. Then she would grill him with questions.

He says, "I learned from her how to pick the right dog and all the reasons why."

Her teachings extended beyond handling and grooming. He also learned about breeding and whelping and so much more.

Kaz Describes Mrs. Clark as a Handler

Kaz says, "I think Mrs. Clark and Mrs. Jane Forsyth (another icon in the sport… more on her in Chapter 12) were the best dog handlers I've ever seen. They were absolutely amazing!"

Mrs. Clark retired early, at the age of thirty-six after marrying her husband, James, who was an AKC licensed judge. At one point, she needed to choose to either remain a professional dog handler or become an AKC judge. AKC considers it a conflict of interest for members living in the same household to both exhibit dogs for a fee (professional handler) and get paid to judge dogs. Consequently, Mrs. Clark chose to become a judge. As a judge, she was not allowed to show dogs for a fee. However, it was still permissible for her to exhibit her own dogs.

Kaz recalls the many times he went with her to dog shows, and she was showing her own Norfolk Terrier or one of her Poodles. Kaz says, "Every night before the dog show, we would be in the hotel, and she couldn't sleep. She would be throwing up in the hotel bathroom. She was so worried and nervous about it! I hated going to dog shows with her because she wouldn't even let me go to the bathroom! No eating either! She had that much focus! No one could talk to her when she was grooming her dogs."

Mrs. Clark often became so consumed with dogs that she simply forgot to eat.

She noticed every detail and every nuance of a dog and a dog show. Kaz says, "She would even pick all the grass out around her dog's feet so the judge could clearly see the feet. Winning was everything to her. I could feel how intense she was."

ADVICE ON WINNING AND LOSING GRACEFULLY

Mrs. Clark took winning very seriously and would often get upset when she lost. Kaz recalls Jane Forsyth, who was a close friend of Mrs. Clark and another fierce competitor, saying to him, "Annie is the worst loser! She screams and gets so upset!"

Although Mrs. Clark sometimes lost her cool, she believed it was important to be respectful and demonstrate good sportsmanship. She passed these ideals on to Kaz, teaching him to always be a good sport, have patience, and focus on being the best and doing everything right within his power.

When Kaz was making his debut, there were very few people from Japan or other Asian countries showing dogs in the United States, and this was challenging. Kaz says, "I had a really hard time and often felt like I was being ignored."

I can relate to Kaz's frustration. I remember being a young teenager and competing against ten to fifteen top professional handlers in the Doberman ring. Often, more than one hundred Dobermans would be competing. I remember feeling so frustrated by all the times I was ignored by a judge, or a judge would look over or away from me when it was my dog's turn to be evaluated. I felt like I needed to stand on my head and do cartwheels to get a judge's attention. I must confess there were times in my life when I engaged in attention-seeking activities. I'm not sure how Kaz managed his frustrations, but I can certainly relate to feeling powerless and invisible.

When Kaz would express his frustration at being ignored by judges to Mrs. Clark, she emphatically responded, "There is nothing that you can change about judges that ignore you. You are the only one that can change their idea about you."

I loved hearing such wise counsel, which teaches empowerment. Kaz further explains Mrs. Clark's instructions, "Aim to get a judge's attention, not because you scream and demand attention, but because you are always a gentleman and you always do a perfect job. Your focus should always be on presenting dogs perfectly."

She continued, "Do NOT ever try to bribe a judge or offer a judge money as a reward for putting you up. Furthermore, do not ever accept money to show a sub-par dog–that will hurt you. Don't get upset in front of judges. Be polite. Be respectful. Be patient."

Such sound advice of patience and fortitude.

Kaz says that Mrs. Clark explained to him that if he grooms a dog perfectly and handles a great dog perfectly with great showmanship, then maybe he will be equal to Richard Bauer (a highly esteemed Poodle handler and breeder, and later, AKC judge) with a terrible dog, who isn't groomed as well, or in as good of condition as Kaz's dog. It is only at that point that Kaz should ever consider himself equal to Richard Bauer. She emphasized that only at that point would Kaz be on an even playing field and stand a chance at winning. She continually warned Kaz that if he showed bad dogs, he would never beat a well-established and respected handler like Richard Bauer.

Kaz says, "This is why when I was first starting out on my own as a professional handler, I only agreed to handle great dogs."

I really love hearing this advice. When I first started as a handler, I would feel so frustrated when other – much more established – handlers would beat me with an inferior dog! I would get really down on myself. Years later, I can acknowledge the wisdom of Mrs. Clark's mentoring words because I found this to be true as well. Sometimes, a new handler or an owner-handler can show a great dog, and a judge may still favor the more established handler in the ring. This means the dogs you are showing need to be twice as good and shown perfectly in order to beat an established handler. Yes, this is frustrating, but it is a fact and takes place in most areas of life. It can take time to get judges to shift into something unknown, yes, even an unknown dog or handler. Be patient. Over time, good, hard, quality work will eventually be recognized.

As a handler who has experienced much success and is on the other side of this dynamic, I'm known and liked by many judges. They respect my work with my dogs, how I present them, and my professionalism in the ring. I am often awarded with lesser dogs. Sometimes, this is because I am highly skilled at handling. Like many great handlers, I can make a lesser dog look magnificent despite its faults. Sometimes, my showmanship is so good that it is hard for the judge to see my dog's faults. I'm not bragging, just stating facts. I am good at my job. Many judges have come to know me over the years. I have an advantage, and I've earned it, just as Kaz has.

No one likes it when they are the one paying the dues. I can feel how angry and resentful some owner-handlers (and yes, this applies to other professionals, myself included) feel when a lesser dog is awarded over theirs. My sympathy goes to those struggling against the professional handlers who tend to do all the winning. My message to them would be, I've walked in your shoes. I understand your frustration more than you know. Stay the course. Focus on being the best you can be in every moment. That mindset will get you where you want to go.

A Successful Outcome Arrives: Kaz Is Excited, but What of Mrs. Clark?

I often laugh thinking about the vision of Mrs. Clark smacking Kaz in the head when he declared that he wanted to quit. What would cause a dignified woman to react in such an undignified manner? From where I sit, a ridiculous statement warranted a ridiculous response.

When Mrs. and Mr. Clark traveled to Japan on a judging assignment and saw Kaz as a young, developing handler, they saw raw talent and had a vision for how his talents might come to fruition with proper mentorship. I guess that they believed that, with time and applied effort, they could help Kaz cultivate his skills and strengths to become a talented, accomplished handler. From everything I've heard about Mrs. Clark, she was a very wise, well-respected woman. She was revered not just for her talents as a handler but also for her wise intellect. There were many facets to her. She was not just a handler, she was a breeder, groomer, trainer, and judge. She could view dog shows, breeding, and handling from a variety of perspectives. When she and Mr. Clark offered Kaz a work visa, my feeling is that it came about from careful thought and deliberation. For it appears nothing this woman did was happenstance.

Two months shy of his three-year agreement, on May 16, 1982, at the Lancaster Kennel Club dog show, Kaz was awarded Best in Show with a Miniature Poodle! Kaz recalls this day in vivid detail.

The first standout moment of the day occurred, winning the group for the first time in the United States! Winning the group was exciting in and of itself, and to top it off, he beat Richard Bauer, showing Raising Cane, the top Poodle at the time! Kaz was beyond excited. Unfortunately, sometime during the excitement of the win, he lost sight of his group ribbon. He was afraid someone had stolen it. He began fretting over the ribbon. He was so upset and didn't know what to do.

When he told Mr. Clark, Mr. Clark simply said, "Don't worry."

Kaz was so upset, but he needed to simply focus on preparing and showing his dog in Best in Show. The Clarks watched as Kaz competed against top handlers such as Richard Bauer, Bobby Fisher (a very successful Terrier handler), and Lina Basquette (a Great Dane handler well-known for her high degree of drama) for Best in Show.

When Kaz went on to win Best in Show, he admits, "Nobody thought I was going to win!"

After hearing Kaz's story, I found myself wishing Mrs. Clark was still alive so I could ask her what she was thinking when she watched her protege win his first all-breed Best in Show two months prior to the end of their agreement. I wondered, was she feeling a sense of completion or pride or perhaps some other emotions while witnessing Kaz achieve this milestone accomplishment?

BIG ACCOMPLISHMENTS LEADING TO SHARED DREAMS

The Best in Show win at Lancaster was the beginning of more winning to come. Although he had spent much of his time counting down the days until he could return to Japan, when he satisfied his commitment to the Clarks and was free to return, Kaz chose to remain in America. In 1991, after eleven years of handling in the US, he won his first Best of Breed at the highly prestigious Westminster Kennel Club.

Although Kaz's path to success was bumpy and full of challenges, through persistence and hard work he paved the way to a well-established career that yielded consistent results. Several more years transpired before he won his first group placement in 1994, winning a group four. The following year, he won the group on Spice Girl's mother, Ch. Surrey Sweet Capsicum. This set the stage for more to come, and he was ready for the challenge.

The uphill climb to Westminster holds significant relevance in Kaz's life script. For it would appear there was an unwritten understanding between him and Mrs. Clark. Remember when she asked him about his goal all of those years ago? He said Best in Show, but Mrs. Clark must have known Kaz's sights weren't set on winning Best in Show at any old dog show. No. He was aiming for the most highly coveted win in the dog show industry. He looked into the eyes of Mrs. Clark, three-time winner of Best in Show at Westminster, and said Best in Show at "the show." The first time Kaz officially staked his claim at the top of that mountain (winning Best in Show at Westminster), he arrived with a Poodle named Spice Girl at the end of his lead.

In a rush of words, Kaz admits, "Spice Girl was the most difficult dog I had ever shown. Mrs. Clark bred her and we all loved her, but we had temperament issues. In the beginning, when I first worked for Mrs. Clark, her Miniature Poodles had great temperaments."

According to Kaz, these Poodles were very sound and stable in body and mind. You could pick them up into the air, and when you placed them down on the floor, their feet were perfect. Their fronts were placed perfectly, their legs were straight. The side picture was nice, too.

However, as all great breeders know, there is no perfect dog, and one is always working to improve their breeding stock. Mrs. Clark and Kaz both acknowledged that, although their breeding program was incredibly sound, their dogs' heads weren't very pretty, and their backs were a little long.

He states, "We decided we wanted to breed and show prettier Poodles."

This breeding tactic was successful in many ways yet presented new challenges. Kaz says, "We bred Poodles that were shorter back with a prettier face and overall head structure, but we lost the brain!"

Most great handlers know the incredible challenge of showing a dog that is not of sound mind.

As he tells his tale of the challenges he experienced with Spice, it is clear that "difficult to show" was putting it mildly. Some handlers do their best to avoid temperaments like this and only select specials with rock-solid dispositions. Since I am one of those handlers who chooses to take on difficult temperaments for a variety of reasons, I can completely relate to the angst Kaz describes when he explains her temperament. If something is going wrong or is less than perfect with a dog, it's our job to correct it or, at the very least, minimize the damage a dog may be doing to itself. It takes a special person with a certain mindset to take on a dog such as this because each time you walk into the ring, there is a chance your dog may leave you feeling like a fool. Not every handler can withstand the public shaming you feel when your dog buckles under pressure or, even worse, loses their composure for no logical reason.

According to Kaz, the first time he showed Spice in the group ring, she galloped around the ring, barking at everybody! The whole way around, she dropped her tail. (She would drop her tail if the wind was blowing or there were leaves blowing on the ground.) Kaz laughs, "I had a lot of patience with that one!"

Then in 2001, he won the Variety with Spice at Westminster and took Group Three. Again, this was no easy feat. In the group ring, there was a flower arrangement by the breed names. Spice spooked because of the flower arrangement and wouldn't walk by it. While most handlers stand up in front of the breed sign, Kaz couldn't do that. He needed to position himself further up and away from the flowers. According to Kaz, it was a nightmare. Not only did she hate the flowers, but she also hated the automatic camera that came up in front of the grooming table during the individual exam. She hated everything. Kaz admits they were lucky to be awarded a Group Three.

Kaz was committed to showing Spice another year as a special. He knew he had a lot of training to do in order to have her better prepared to show at Westminster the following year. In an effort to desensitize her, he placed a similar flower arrangement in his kennel next to where he worked and groomed his dogs so she could get used to seeing something like that on a daily basis.

That following year, Kaz not only worked on desensitizing Spice to possible areas of concern, but he also came to the show with a tactical plan to address each stressor Spice would encounter while showing at Westminster.

He says, "In the breed, she showed excellent. We won the breed. In the group, I never let her see the flower arrangement!"

Kaz strategically always kept his body in between the flowers and Spice so she could not see them. When he put her on the grooming table for the judge's examination, he covered her eyes with his hand.

He explains, "I put my hand over her eyes until the judge stepped in front of Spice and blocked the camera. Once the judge was between Spice and the camera, I removed my hand from over her eyes. Everything went perfect! I did everything I needed to do to address her idiosyncrasies. She showed excellent in the group!"

In fact, she won.

While Kaz was thrilled with how smoothly things went in both the breed and the group, he had just one more event to get through: Best in Show!

Some people dream of grandeur, but Kaz admits he had frequent nightmares of Spice dropping her tail or spooking in the Best in Show ring. With his typical self-deprecating humor, Kaz says, "Although I did a flawless job navigating each one of her challenges perfectly in both Best of Breed and the Non-Sporting group, I blew it in Best in Show! I was one second too late covering her eyes on the table and she spotted the camera."

Kaz laughs and recalls, "Mr. Everett Dean was the Best in Show judge. Spice saw the camera and started backing up from the judge on the table. Mr. Dean looked at me as if to say, 'Hold on to her!'"

Kaz did indeed hold on to her and kept her together. He was so upset. Then it was time for the individual gaiting pattern, he knew her well. He expected she was going to drop her tail. He put her down, moved away from the judge, and her tail dropped below ideal. When Spice came back to free bait in front of the judge, she started to drop her tail again, but then it came back up to an acceptable height.

As he was trotting her around the ring to the end of the line to complete his individual exam, he mentally began going through all the scenarios. Her tail wasn't where he wanted it to be, and he missed covering her eyes. He was so upset about all the things that went wrong that he forgot about another obstacle… the flower arrangement. Kaz says, "Spice spotted the flower arrangement and boom! She spooked and dropped her tail. I thought, 'Oh my God! This is a nightmare!'"

As a fellow handler, I can relate to Kaz's story. When I am at my best as a handler, my energy is highly focused and controlled during my individual exams. When I circle around to the end, I know my turn is complete. The judge is no longer looking, so I tend to let down my guard just a bit because that level of energy is hard to maintain for long periods of time. I take a deep breath, let myself settle a bit, and tell my dog "okay" so they know they can relax for a second as well. Then I will quickly regroup and determine my next plan of action.

When a handler has a dog that is spooky, though, the handler must practice constant vigilance. It's exhausting and very difficult to maintain that kind of energy for long periods of time. It puts a tremendous amount of pressure on the handler and requires a high degree of energy to maintain. Handlers, in a sense, are dancers or actors on stage, and the show must go on.

As Kaz sees his house of cards beginning to crumble, he still needs to plan his next move. He quickly assessed his situation and how much time he had to get Spice back mentally. Two dogs remained in need of an individual exam. One of them, an Affenpinscher named Cosmo, was the crowd favorite. There was so much applause and noise that

Kaz could barely hold onto Spice. She was coming undone. He needed to think fast and get her under control and connected back to him. He didn't have much time. As Kaz describes it, he got lucky.

Once again, I sense Kaz's self-deprecating humor and how he often doesn't give himself credit for things. From my perspective, what transpired was more than happenstance. In fact, Deepak Chopra, author of *The Seven Spiritual Laws of Success*, writes, "Good luck is opportunity and preparedness coming together."

And this is how the story unfolds.

Once all the dogs were individually examined, Mr. Dean could have asked all the dogs to move around the ring together. If the judge had given that order, Kaz was convinced he would have been unable to get Spice to recover. She would have, in all likelihood, gaited around the ring with her tail down, which would have been viewed as unacceptable Poodle showmanship and would have left a lasting impression on the judge as he made his final decision.

However, as I said, Kaz believes he got lucky and caught a break. Mr. Dean instructed each handler to move their dogs around the ring individually. Kaz had four dogs ahead of him, which gave him a little extra time. He had to think quickly.

He had placed a little squeaky toy in his pocket prior to showing in Best in Show. He used to play with this toy with Spice almost every day at home but he had never brought that toy to a dog show before. Since he had so many nightmares about what might go wrong at Westminster with Spice, Kaz decided to take that toy to Westminster… just in case.

He took out the toy, picked Spice up, and put her under his arm. Normally he wouldn't carry one of his Poodles this way because of the way their hair is sprayed up.

He says, "I was holding her like a baby in the Best in Show ring! I was desperate. I prayed to God, 'Have mercy on me.' I had her on her back like a baby, and I thought, 'I don't care if I ruin her top knot and her hair. I don't care… just please, God, get me through this!'"

He was desperate to do something different, something unexpected to shock her out of her overwhelm. He says, "I had only one more dog ahead, and I put her down on the floor and had her look at the squeak toy. She looked at the toy like, 'Oh my God!'"

Kaz could see she was up and excited about the toy. Then he gave her a piece of chicken. He explains, "Normally when she is nervous, she won't eat bait. Yet this time, she ate it!"

He knew that was a good sign that Spice had refocused her energy. Kaz says when she went around the ring, her tail was up and she was perfect!

"When I got to the end of the line and our turn was over, I just started laughing. Anyone watching me would have thought, 'Is that guy crazy? Why is he laughing like that?' That moment was so special to me. I was so excited! I didn't even care about Best in Show. She had her tail up. That's all I cared about."

I can relate to Kaz's elation at that moment. The fear and the pressure to get that dog together and to deliver a good performance is incredible. Not only does the handler want to do a good job, but there is also an awareness that we have owners paying us a lot of money to come through for them. We want to deliver. We don't want to disappoint. Every ounce of energy Kaz had at that moment was focused on that very difficult dog, and he nailed it! While owners may be wishing for Best in Show, for us handlers, these are the moments we cherish. Facing an incredible obstacle and overcoming it with great execution is quite the adrenaline rush! You know you made a difference with that dog.

Because of your resourcefulness as a handler, you brought out the very best in your dog, and you made it happen!

Kaz says, "Nobody saw what happened between me and Spice, (or so he thought at the time) but that moment meant everything!"

Spice had her head up, and her tail was perfect. Kaz just didn't care about anything else. He says, "I didn't care if Spice went Best in Show, it didn't matter. I was already happy."

And from that place of satisfaction of a job well done, Kaz and Spice were awarded Best in Show!

On that night, a long-held dream came true. Kaz had made it to the summit of the mountain, and his mentor was there.

He said, "Mrs. Clark was watching me. She watched everything I had to go through with that dog."

As a handler, she understood what Kaz had to overcome to achieve that win. After witnessing his performance, she congratulated him, stating, "You did a great job!"

This may seem a little lackluster, but to Kaz, it was more than he could ever have hoped for. Kaz says, "After twenty-three years, that was the first time she said, 'You did a great job!'"

Mrs. Clark's acknowledgment of this win brought Kaz's thoughts back in time to when he first arrived in the US, and she asked him what he wanted. He explained, "When I said, 'Best in Show' to Mrs. Clark, that meant Westminster, but I couldn't pronounce or say Westminster!"

Kaz's voice lights up as he recalls, "She knew what I meant. Winning Westminster was my dream."

Being the first female professional handler to win Best in Show at Westminster and having won it three times, Anne Clark well understood Kaz's desire and had practical knowledge of what it takes to turn that dream into a reality.

Kaz admits, "I dreamed and dreamed of winning Best in Show at Westminster, but I didn't think I could get there."

I wish Mrs. Clark was still alive so I could ask her if she herself ever had any doubt.

Magazine articles following the event reported that Mrs Clark's protege won Best in Show. This is what dreams are made of. Not only did Kaz earn that designation, but that designation also put Mrs. Clark in the Westminster record books once again, as a breeder and owner of the 2002 Westminster Best in Show Winner.

Never Make an Excuse that Excuses You of Responsibility

According to Kaz, while working for Mrs. Clark, her motto was: prepare for everything. In her mind, a handler must never fall victim to the belief that something happened beyond their control and, therefore, the end result was not their fault. This is probably one of the reasons she was so pleased with Kaz's performance in the ring at Westminster with Spice Girl. He was prepared—even for things that were extremely unlikely!

It is a handler's job to be in control at all times, regardless of the external circumstances. If you are frustrated with a dog over how it is behaving and reacting, it is your job as the handler to figure out the problem, manage it, and overcome it. A guiding principle for me was, if all dogs showed perfectly, owners wouldn't need handlers. (Although this is not exactly true, it did keep me focused on solving problems versus wishing there weren't any.) It is a handler's job to assess how to best navigate how their dog reacts in all circumstances. I do not allow myself to blame the dog or make an excuse about why the dog didn't behave better, and neither does Kaz. Yes, sometimes we all become frustrated, especially when there is a recurring problem. Yet, I see it as my job to figure out how to maximize each dog's performance based on the ingredients I am given. I learned some of these lessons–just as Kaz did–by watching great handlers.

Kaz is a great handler because he has dedicated his life and career to becoming the best he can be. He has put into practice all of the lessons Annie Clark instilled in him. Great handlers like Kaz with Spice overcome obstacles and guide their dogs through the challenges presented. This goes beyond mere skill. A person becomes a master and the best of the best when they are able to create a masterpiece with limited resources.

A master, according to Merriam-Webster, is someone of great learning, skill, or ability; an original form from which copies can be made. There are those of you aspiring handlers reading this book, seeking to copy and follow the path of the masters I share with you. It is my hope that by emulating the attitudes, skills, and techniques laid out for you in this book, you, too, will achieve and experience your own mastery!

Prior to their time in the Best in Show ring at Westminster, Kaz extensively and meticulously prepared himself and Spice to the best of his ability. In addition to great preparedness, he remained open and allowed his instincts and experience to guide him through those challenging moments. That is a great handler. That also makes for a great chef, basketball player, accountant, or even barista.

Spice didn't win Best in Show by herself. Kaz made that happen. As a handler, that is the best feeling, knowing you are what made the difference. In a clutch moment, Kaz knew what to do to secure a win! He took inspired action to get Spice to connect back to him, allowing her to be more than she may have felt capable of because Kaz was there to guide her through her own uncertainty. Kaz's decisions and actions are what beat the odds.

On that night, Kaz achieved his own mastery with Spice. He became the best of the best. With someone else, that might not have happened. He says, "It is important what goes on between just me and my dog. I trust them, and they trust me. I think Spice was very worried, but she did it for me."

Kaz's relationship with Spice lasted long after her career ended. They spent a lifetime together. She died with Kaz. Kaz laughs, "She was an asshole to show, but I did love her, and she had a great life."

I ask Kaz, "If you could do it all over again, what would you change?"

Emphatically, Kaz replies, "Not a thing. I wouldn't want to have done it any other way. There is no easy way. It needed to happen the way it did."

In twenty-nine years (from 1991 through 2020), Kaz has won roughly twenty-five breeds at Westminster! He sees the underlying potential. He finds this process deeply fulfilling, and it's what keeps him engaged and passionate about his work day after day, year after year. And it all started when he said yes to his uncle and yes to Annie Clark.

CHAPTER 11

Gwen DeMilta:
A Force to Behold

If there were ever a dog show God of War, HER name would be Gwen DeMilta. When it comes to gods, mere human words cannot capture their grandeur and the larger-than-life feelings they elicit. Although I did not interview Gwen for this chapter (she passed in 2022), I knew her for most of my life, and she played an influential role in how I approach handling—as she did for many in the industry. Gwen's unique, powerful presence is difficult to convey.

Her power was visceral. She stood proud and moved as if she was floating. As she walked around a dog show venue, it was as if she was cloaked in a cool, dark mist. She evoked fear in people, deep-seated fear. Owners, judges, breeders, and spectators alike did their best to get out of Gwen's way or join forces with her. She was the most intense dog show handler I have ever witnessed. Words can't fully express the depths of her talent when a dog's lead was placed in her hands. It was otherworldly. Her passion, presence, and, yes, even her fury were captivating.

Her mastery in the ring elevated her status among humans, giving her great power. Dog owners wanted access to that power to promote their dogs (and their own ego/status). Others envied her strength and power, and some offered her their loyalty to avoid her wrath. Gwen utilized everything at her disposal to serve her quest—WIN EVERYTHING!

Although she was greedy and domineering in her thirst for wins, showing dogs was her happy place. I think for Gwen, having a great dog in hand and being up against a worthy opponent made her feel alive, whole, and complete. She lived for dog shows.

She was a polarizing presence in the dog show world. There were those who idolized her and those who abhorred her. I fluctuated between both extremes, often feeling both simultaneously. Gwen made you feel emotions deeply and intensely. I wanted to love her, yet I often hated her, and when I hated her, I hated that there were aspects of her that I wished I were better able to embody. I wanted to be like her, and yet I absolutely didn't want to be like her. One of the great gifts of being exposed to such an intense person, if you have the right mindset, is that you will be forced to dig deep and overcome (or die!). She was an absolute force to be reckoned with.

Many of us, myself included, want to classify someone as "good" or "bad." But life isn't always simple. Sometimes it's messy, and it challenges us to grow and see things differently. Everyone contains both light and dark. If people were all good or all bad, that would be simple. But that isn't how life goes. No one is all good or all bad. In fact, when it comes to people, we all have preferences of what we like and who we like, and our preferences tend to lead us to designate people as good or bad.

What was "good" about Gwen and what was "bad" about Gwen was right there on the surface for all to see.

She was a layered and complex person, even for those of us who knew her well. I am honored to share my perspective of my mentor/arch enemy, friend/foe, and absolutely one of the most challenging individuals I have ever loved. She leaves a profound mark in the dog show industry, but for me, her biggest legacy is that she showed us that no matter how messy we are and how much we struggle, we all have gifts to bear.

When I began watching Gwen handle Dobermans, I was just a girl. I idolized her abilities as a handler. I studied how she showed dogs and strove to emulate her.

Gwen was from the Northeast, as am I, and as I grew into my abilities as a handler, she was a constant opponent of mine. Although, on the one hand, it was a great opportunity to be exposed to such a talented master, it also meant that if I wanted to establish myself as the best, I needed to best her. In a sense, she was the primary person who stood between me and all that I wanted to attain in my career.

Because of this dynamic, our intense exposure to one another, and our combative history, I think it's important to note that this chapter is unlike other chapters. My observations and insights are based on my own highly personal experiences with Gwen. Other chapters carry more objectivity, as they are based primarily on interviews with peers that I have come to know and understand more deeply through the writing of this book. My relationship with Gwen was difficult, complex, and spanned roughly forty years.

The Making of a Dominant Force

This domineering dog-handling savant ruled the Doberman ring from an early age. At the age of sixteen, she won Winners Bitch from the Bred-by-Exhibitor class (a class that designates the handler as also being a breeder and owner), at the highly prestigious Doberman Pinscher Annual National Convention in 1973. Her Doberman, a lovely red bitch named Kinderwick, was owned and bred by Gwen and her mom, Joann Satalino.

Gwen had a passion for her most beloved breed, Dobermans, and an even stronger passion for winning. Although some handlers love training, nurturing confidence in an insecure dog, strategizing, and politicking, Gwen's true love was winning. Her thirst for winning was insatiable. For her, winning not only signaled that she and her dog were the best, but also that the integrity of her favorite breed (Doberman) remained intact.

Gwen stood out in the crowd. It wasn't because of her looks or how she dressed. In fact, she had little regard for outward appearances. Instead, it was her intense energy that made people take notice. She was like a lion in a den of lambs. With strong square shoulders and slim hips, standing proudly at five foot ten, Gwen's power was visceral, emanating outward for even the most unobservant individual. Despite her strong, aggressive temperament, she had calm hands and moved with quiet grace.

Growing up, I was in awe of Gwen. When it came to Doberman handlers, she was in a league all her own. No one was a close second. She won everything in her breed. No matter how much she won, she always wanted more. Gwen strove for total domination at all times. Her drive to win and her passion for Dobermans was all-consuming.

Gwen wanted it all, had to win it all, and often did win everything, and I mean everything. If Gwen showed twelve Dobermans, she would often win every single class. It was unusual for a judge to award every single win in a particular breed to a certain handler when breed entries were large. (To give perspective, back in Gwen's heyday, Doberman entries were much larger than entries in 2023. In the eighties or nineties, if my memory serves me, in order for a Doberman bitch to win a three-point major, she needed to defeat a minimum of thirty-six bitches. I remember competing in classes where there were thirty-six bitches entered in the Open AOAC class alone. Just winning a class that size is a major victory, let alone winning several.) The chances that a single handler has all the best dogs against that many contenders all the time are rare.

It was often infuriating for myself and others who competed against the impenetrable force known as Gwen DeMilta. She controlled her dogs, she controlled her clients, and she often controlled the ring. If a judge wasn't strong and assertive enough running their ring, Gwen would sense their weakness and use it to her advantage.

Contrary and rebellious, Gwen made her own rules. Because she was such a domineering force, judges, spectators, and competitors alike complied. Her commanding presence made people really, really uncomfortable. People who didn't adhere to her rules were often yelled at, glared at, ostracized, bullied, or demeaned either verbally or through her confrontational, non-verbal body language. To put it bluntly, most people found Gwen downright scary. On at least one occasion, a judge left the ring crying.

Before stepping into the ring with Gwen DeMilta, you needed to prepare for war... the war for your life. And the very hostile, combative nature of war brings forth both the light and the dark within each of us. When we wrestle with these opposing forces, we often bump up against our own values and beliefs. Competing against Gwen did that. It would test a person's limits, not just as a handler, but a person's personal ethics as well. Gwen would work every angle, and anyone who competed against her would be tested.

Despite her hard shell and aggressive nature, certain people gravitated toward Gwen. She didn't often seek people's friendship, they sought hers. She had a very protective nature for those who occupied her inner circle. She hated to see those she cared about get taken advantage of. If someone attacked or mistreated one of her friends, she took it personally.

She might say to her friend Debbie, "You are too nice! You shouldn't take that from those clients. They don't deserve you!"

And depending on the slight, if someone did something to Debbie that Gwen deemed wrong, the offending person would be dead to her. And by this, I mean Gwen would literally say to that person, "You are dead to me."

Once you were deemed dead, Gwen wouldn't look at you or say hello; it truly was as if you didn't exist. I think this protective quality led many people to seek refuge with Gwen. If you were one of her people, she would fight to the death for you, and if she trusted you, she trusted you with every ounce of her being.

Understandably, many were intimidated by her and afraid to approach her. However, even if you were in her close circle, you still might get stung. Gwen didn't coddle anyone. She rarely apologized. Gwen spoke her truth with unflinching directness. What she said didn't always make the recipient feel good. However, you always knew where you stood with Gwen. Those of us who loved her really valued and admired her forthrightness. If you were offended by Gwen's truth, then it was your job to sort that out for yourself. She respected people with a backbone, and if you were lacking in that area and she offended you, that was your problem, not hers.

Gwen reminds me of the Dennis Rodmans of basketball or the John McEnroes of tennis: incredibly talented athletes who were not called to be role models or to lead by example. They assumed no part of that responsibility once they stepped out onto the court. They were unapologetically themselves, regardless of what individuals or society at large had to say about them. Their passion for the game trumped all other desires.

A Competitive Streak Plus Talent Makes Room for Magic

Gwen's excessively competitive nature was not the only component pushing her to win in the ring. She had talent as a handler. When Gwen placed her hands on a dog, it was like an artist with clay. The way she manipulated bone and flesh was truly magical. She had an uncanny way of making every dog look like the ideal Doberman. To the inexperienced, this may not seem like a big deal, but let me tell you, it's a rare talent.

No one could compare to Gwen's ability to manipulate a dog in the hard stack. Similar to Jane Forsyth, an icon I discuss in Chapter 12, Gwen rarely trained or practiced with her dogs. Instead, she had incredible focus and an unwavering vision of the ideal Doberman in her head. And from that vision, she molded and willed her dogs into form.

It's in the DNA of dogs to respect the alpha, and Gwen was pure alpha. Gwen's alpha energy, paired with her inner vision of the ideal Doberman, was a powerful combination. When she took the lead, the dog simply fell into place.

Based on my observations, Gwen didn't think about how to show a dog, she just did it. She was one hundred percent in the moment, allowing her instincts to guide her. She didn't beg, plead, or sweet talk a dog into showing. She commanded it. She didn't beat a dog into submission. She didn't overpower them. Instead, like an alpha, she just took charge.

A leader such as Gwen, who is clear, sharp, and decisive, brings a sense of order and peace to the follower, be it a dog or a person. When you are the follower and a leader like Gwen is in charge, you don't have to think; all you need to do is put one hundred percent of your effort into doing what you are told. When dogs did that for Gwen, she rewarded them. She often gave them a hard slap on their side or chest, similar to athletes giving a high five. Translation: awesome job!

When she acknowledged their performance, it meant something to them. She held the line and got them to step up. One could see them stand a bit taller, puff out their chests, and lift their heads high. Gwen was pleased with them, they knew it and, therefore, felt good about themselves.

Gwen loved to get the best out of a dog. When a handler with great hands places those hands on a dog's body, there is an energy transfer. Gwen not only manipulated a dog's physical structure, but she manipulated a dog's energy as well. Gwen could calm and channel an exuberant dog's energy as well as invigorate and inspire a laid-back, lazy dog.

Not only that, when Gwen was into a dog and truly believed in its conformation, it was like watching a seasoned race car driver get behind the wheel of a well-engineered sports car. She couldn't wait to get her hands on it. She wanted to feel it, to test it, to show it. Gwen's whole body–from her face to her hands to her stance and her posture—responded to a dog when she believed in it. It was exciting... like a little kid playing with a new toy. Gwen would come alive. It was an awesome sight to behold.

One such magical moment for me personally was when Gwen handled a bitch of mine named Tali. Through the years, I asked Gwen to show several dogs I had bred for various reasons. In this case, my bitch Tali wasn't showing well for me. I was frustrated by the lack of effort she gave when I attempted to show her. Because she was my dog, I began reacting personally to Tali's resistance. Reacting to a dog's behavior personally doesn't often yield good results. I acknowledged that this dynamic wasn't serving me or Tali, so I asked Gwen if she would show her for me.

Tali had a significant forechest (a quality hard to come by and lacking in many Dobermans) with a nice layback of shoulder and a lovely neck set. Tali's biggest fault was a poor topline in which she had a slight break after the withers with a steep croup. The Doberman standard calls for a level topline with a slightly rounded croup. When Tali didn't show well, these faults were more apparent.

Gwen loved Tali's front and shoulders, and when she put her hands on Tali, Tali transformed. It took my breath away. I was a great handler at the time, yet I was in awe. Tali looked taller and more confident than I had ever seen her. I barely recognized this majestic bitch. Tali looked proud of herself, and Gwen looked proud to have her hands on Tali. Every part of Gwen's energy shouted—this Doberman is magnificent!

Gwen stood proud, puffed her chest out, and glared at the judge, energetically demanding, "This is the best damn dog in the ring, and if you don't point to me, you are an idiot, and I will kill you."

Although Gwen was an ass to compete against, when she put her hands on Tali, I was so proud, and I thought, "Damn! That's my handler, and that's my dog."

When Tali walked out of the ring a winner, she looked at me as if to say, "See, I am magnificent."

She even had an air of arrogance as she walked past, barely acknowledging me. She was proud to be with Gwen. She was proud of how Gwen made her feel. On that day, I witnessed magic.

MASTER OF ILLUSION

Magic. What do we deem magical? Magic is something we witness, yet can't explain. Gwen had this ability to transform dogs' physical appearances completely. She knew how to make the most of Tali as well as hundreds of other dogs. Not only was she able to mechanically manipulate Tali's physical structure, but she was able to manipulate Tali's internal demeanor and physical presence as well. These two abilities—being able to influence both internal and external characteristics of the dogs she handled—led Gwen to be a master of illusion. She seemed to magically change the physical appearance of a dog when she placed her hands on them.

What made her a master magician is the manner and degree to which she was able to minimize a dog's faults and maximize their virtues by how she positioned the dog's body and her own in the hard stack. For instance, with Tali, Gwen overstretched her rear legs (the general rule of thumb is to stack a dog's rear legs with the hocks at a perpendicular angle to the ground). Overstretching the rear legs tends to flatten the croup area, making the croup appear less steep.

In addition, Gwen used bait to direct Tali's weight and center of gravity high up on top of her toes and then positioned the bait downward while holding her collar high, creating a beautiful arch on her neck. This action further helped to smooth out Tali's topline as well as create a beautiful silhouette of a well-arched neck into shoulders. This method maximized and called attention to Tali's beautiful arch of neck and smooth transition into shoulders, as well as minimized her steep croup. These adjustments made Tali look more ideal and better than her true physical structure.

Gwen employed these tactics with all her dogs. She always focused on maximizing her dogs' strengths and minimizing their faults. Another dog that Gwen did this with was Edna, Ch. Deco's Hot Fudge, also referred to as Deco.

Edna was a nice moving bitch with substantial bone and substance, nice feet, and a nice transition of neck into shoulders. Her biggest detracting flaws were her head, a dip after her withers, and her body proportions, which were slightly longer than tall. Similar to the way she worked with Tali, Gwen guided Edna to stand as tall as possible, using bait, causing Edna to stand several inches taller than she would naturally.

This increase in height made Edna's body, which was naturally longer than tall, appear square. In addition, positioning Edna's head downward made the faults in the shape of her head less apparent. The mechanics of this are difficult to master, yet Gwen made it look smooth and effortless.

In regards to Edna's break in topline, Gwen generally wore dark-colored pants to help camouflage the dip following Edna's withers. The dark color positioned behind Edna's black coat made Edna's fault less apparent while in the stack and even while moving, as long as Gwen kept her body positioned behind Edna's withers.

When Gwen brought Edna back to the judge to pose for the free stack, she would let out Edna's lead and kneel down in front, creating a dramatic picture. This dramatic act served two purposes. One, by kneeling in front of Edna, Edna would lean forward over her front and arch her neck downward toward where Gwen held the bait. Secondly, Gwen created drama and flair, drawing attention to herself and the picture she was selling, making Edna look more captivating than she would have on her own.

Similar to a talented actor on a stage, Gwen was very skilled at projection. Actors, as well as many dog show handlers, have a highly developed ability to project their energy outward to fill a room, a stage, or an entire auditorium. (Side note: for those young girls and boys who are shy and quiet, showing dogs can be a great way to develop this skill because they are developing and cultivating it for the dog, not themselves!)

Secondly, great handlers (like Gwen) know how to build confidence in their dogs and teach them how to project their energy as well. Handlers, especially those with lesser dogs, must have the ability to get and hold a judge's attention. That is what every handler in the ring is vying for: the judge's attention.

The majority of Doberman handlers are fabulous at this. For dogs that are confident, showy, and upbeat, this comes quite naturally. They are often fun to watch in the show ring and are natural entertainers, born to win, be a star, and take center stage. As you may remember from reading Michael Scott's chapter, he looks for this natural quality in the dogs he is considering campaigning. However, the majority of dogs aren't born with this innate confidence in the show ring.

For dogs that are insecure and don't naturally project their energy outward, it is important for the handler to help create that confidence and energy. The chapter on Kaz Hosaka goes into this dynamic as well. He, too, knows how to create, nurture, and expand this energy for his dogs. Often, a confident handler's energy alone can enhance a dog's confidence in the ring. Dogs sense a handler's confidence, feel safe with them, and are therefore more confident in themselves. A great coach brings out the best in their athletes; the same is true of a great handler.

This talent and skill cannot be overestimated. I've always believed anyone can show a great dog. Great dogs stand out. They are easy winners. However, it takes an extremely talented handler, such as Gwen, to be able to win with a less-than-optimal dog.

Gwen won with many substandard dogs. She was so well known for this that spectators practically smirked and elbowed one another when a dog that Gwen had been handling was handed off to another handler. Suddenly, one could see all the dog's faults that were practically nonexistent in the hands of Gwen. It became so glaringly obvious it was almost laughable. I'm sure many judges were shocked to see the dog they had earlier deemed to be the best completely fall from grace in the hands of a different handler. I often wondered if they felt duped.

Having witnessed this so often with Gwen, I came to believe that if I wanted to be truly great, then winning with lesser dogs was not only a testament to greatness, it was essential. After all, anyone can win with a great dog. It takes a master to win with an inferior dog. Thanks to this unintended lesson from Gwen, from early in my career, I considered it my responsibility to win with a dog regardless of its attributes and developed my own form of mastery in this regard. I enjoyed the challenge of figuring out how to get a less-than-optimal dog to look beautiful.

To me, mastery is being able to maintain excellence under myriad challenging circumstances. Give me a recipe with all the right ingredients and a proper list of instructions, and I can make a great meal. However, this does not make me a master chef. A master chef can create magnificent meals with subpar ingredients in subpar conditions. Gwen's ability to win with inferior dogs on a consistent basis is a testament to her mastery of skills, strategy, and talent.

ILLUSION AND INTIMIDATION: A POWERFUL COMBINATION IN THE SHOW RING

Not only did Gwen manipulate her dogs' physical and emotional attributes, but she also manipulated her environment. She excelled at intimidating judges in the ring to rule in her favor. She often viewed herself as the underdog and walked around the dog show with an angry chip on her shoulder. In many ways, that anger served her.

Her anger provided her with a feeling of power, and people responded to the way she emanated that power. Often people found her so intimidating they were afraid to confront or even simply approach her. Many people feared Gwen, and rightly so. She would regularly lash out at, bully, and intimidate judges, peers, clients, and spectators alike.

Gwen's need to dominate was so intense that no one was safe—even those she considered to be part of her inner circle. I vividly remember competing with her and her daughter Carissa at shows in West Springfield, Massachusetts. The judge had signaled Gwen out as the likely winner. Gwen rushed up to the front of the line, looking confident and smug that she had pulled off the win she had been pushing for. However, just before making his final decision, he paused, looked toward the back of the line, and asked the rest of us handlers to take the dogs around the ring again. Then, despite the fact that he had positioned Gwen in the lead, he pointed to Carissa as the winner.

In an instant, Gwen's physical demeanor went from satisfaction to angry disbelief. She stopped running and turned her head around to discover that the victor was her daughter. Carissa quietly scooted past

Gwen into the winner's position as her mother shot her an angry look of disdain. Gwen walked to the position for second place and belligerently snatched the ribbon out of the judge's hand with an air of defiance.

Gwen was pissed. She didn't see that coming. None of us did. Unbeknownst to us, while Gwen and I were duking it out for first place, Carissa was in the back of the line watching Gwen's antics. Carissa watched her mother posturing and gesticulating. She saw her mom's chest getting puffier and puffier, growing bigger and bigger as she glared at the judge, demanding with her presence, trying to intimidate him for the win.

An infuriated Carissa watched as her mom took center stage by using intimidation to secure her win. Carissa was angry that the judge had dismissed her and her dog in favor of her mom once again. Taking a page out of her mom's book, Carissa began staring down the judge, every ounce of her demanding the judge pick her instead of her mother. Carissa stared at the judge, repeatedly rubbing her hands along her dog's rock-hard topline and—in a sense—calling attention to the poor topline of the bitch her mother was showing. Carissa's behavior influenced the judge to change his mind, and she was rewarded for it.

Many years later, after Gwen's passing, I was conversing with Carissa, recollecting my own memory of the event. I was surprised to hear Carissa quietly state that, rather than being proud of her daughter for being a chip off the old block, Gwen gave Carissa the cold shoulder for weeks, and that wasn't an isolated incident.

This power dynamic played out with them for many years. Carissa still sounded hurt and torn, trying to sort out her own conflicting feelings about the mother she loved and whose absence she was still grieving.

I felt Carissa's pain and mine as well. So many times, I had taken Gwen's behavior personally in and out of the show ring. I thought she hated me. I thought she was angry at me. Gwen was always angry when she didn't win, but perhaps it wasn't out of a lack of respect for me. She hated losing, and she especially hated being outmaneuvered. Gwen loved her daughter, so if that's how she reacted to her daughter beating her, then I guess I couldn't expect her to react any more gently toward me!

The above scenario is one of hundreds in which Gwen used her body language to intimidate and influence a judge's decision. It was remarkable how often she garnered a win by glaring, posturing, and gesticulating. Sometimes, she would even point her left hand toward her dog while her eyes looked specifically at where on the dog she wanted the judge to look, then she'd stare back at the judge boldly demanding, "Pick this dog. It is clearly the best one in the ring!"

She used every ounce of her power and presence to command a win from every judge she ever encountered.

And yet, Gwen guided and directed those of us in her inner circle. We felt the light that lived inside her. We knew she cared for us and wanted us to do well. She was a huge proponent of the underdog and didn't like to see her friends taken advantage of. However, she didn't want you using your power against her.

Control Inside and Outside the Ring

Not only did she work to influence judges using body language, but she also influenced her clients, peers, and spectators to clap the instant a judge pulled her out of the line and up into first place. She used this tactic to make the judge believe her dog was the crowd's favorite. She also seemed to glean a modicum of satisfaction if a competitor beat her and the room was dead silent. To her, that conveyed the crowd's lack of approval for the judge's selection.

We could see her glare at her friends and clients from within the ring, visually signaling when they should clap and when they shouldn't. She watched the crowd and knew who clapped and who didn't. She watched everything and always knew what was going on both inside and outside the ring. Those who didn't clap appropriately were chastised.

Her clapping tactics infuriated me. I felt they were highly manipulative and completely unprofessional. Most handlers competing against Gwen had to determine how far they were willing to go to influence wins. Bumping up against the darker forces of Gwen often put me face to face with my own personal beliefs and values regarding competition and showing dogs. I came to learn very quickly just how far I was or wasn't willing to stretch my personal ethics and integrity. In the big scheme of things, clapping was relatively harmless, and while I didn't agree with it, I too engaged in it. I *asked* my clients and friends to clap because experience showed me it was a necessary tactic to employ under certain judges if I wanted to win.

If you wanted to win, you needed to get on board with Gwen's rules and beat her at her own game. Everything stemmed and grew from her need to control all things, even her clients. Gwen didn't show dogs for the money. Money was a by-product.

Occasionally, Gwen worked with (not for) clients with money and power who would try to control, dominate, or dictate how Gwen ran her business, and felt they had a right to do so because of their money. They felt they owned her. They assumed (wrongly) that they could control Gwen and how she approached handling, because they paid her. They were disavowed of these notions early, and if they didn't bend to Gwen's will, she let them walk. Gwen could not be influenced to submit to another's control. She did things her way, and if someone didn't like it, they could leave. In fact, Gwen would often say she fired a client.

The majority of us would laugh at Gwen's high-handedness and think to ourselves, and even say to her, "You can't fire a client. They are paying you, not the other way around!"

However, Gwen didn't care about formalities or appropriateness or even about being smart or professional... She would have said, "F*** 'em!"

Although the callous way she often went about firing clients was completely unprofessional, there is great value in her instinctive removal of anyone not in alignment with her way of doing things. In fact, I admire her for this keen survival instinct that she cultivated in her life. It's beneficial to know when a client isn't a good fit and release them from an agreement. Gwen knew where she was strong, and she knew her limits and worked within them. She knew what worked and what didn't. This strategy, whether conscious or not, kept her in her power and in control in many ways.

Using Her Strengths to Navigate the Politics of the Dog Show Industry

The way Gwen navigated the dog show political arena clearly displays her knowledge of her strengths and limitations, and how to work within them. Gwen was NOT a people pleaser. She used her power to intimidate so that she could ultimately get what she wanted–wins. This gave Gwen a reputation for invulnerability, and she used this and her strategic mind–inside and outside the ring–to garner support and win at all costs.

When it came to strategy, not surprisingly, everything in Gwen's playbook started with control. Gwen wanted to be in control of all things because control meant strength. Strength meant power. Power meant being invincible. In order to be invincible, you must never lose.

She would research judges, know their preferences, and study their behaviors. In order to be most closely in alignment with judges' physical preferences for dog flesh in the ring, Gwen would often show different dogs on different days of a show circuit, depending on who was judging on which day. Most handlers pick one class dog to show throughout a show circuit because it's easier and keeps things simple and more consistent for the handler. If they have several dogs to choose from, they often will pick one dog that best meets the preferences of the majority of the judges.

However, Gwen had a plethora of client dogs to choose from and the willingness to put forth the extra effort to get the results she wanted–the most wins possible. Therefore, she would choose the right dog for the right judge, even if that meant being responsible for caring for twice as many dogs during a show circuit as she would have if she'd picked just one for each class and showed that same dog throughout. Gwen would strategically pull together a lineup of dogs each day that she felt would best appeal to each judge's preferences. She studied her judges, took note of their preferences and their tendencies, and used this knowledge to generate more wins for herself and her clients.

In addition to researching and studying judges' physical preferences when judging dogs, Gwen would also determine their ability to be swayed and influenced. If she felt this would benefit her, she would work to influence them in the ring.

Gwen also sought to determine if judges could be influenced outside the ring. However, influencing judges outside the ring was NOT one of her areas of expertise. As I have already clearly established, Gwen was NOT a people pleaser. However, even though she was not good at befriending people or making them feel comfortable and safe in her presence, she found other ways to get the job done.

Gwen had an instinct for reading people. I believe she could walk into a room and, without even thinking about it, be able to assess someone's nature as trustworthy or not, influenceable or not. If Gwen felt a judge's decision could be swayed outside the ring, she would seek out people she could call upon to do her politicking for her. Gwen even did this once with me. It is important to acknowledge that her behavior, this politicking, is not unusual in the dog show industry.

When I was a very young professional, Gwen came to me asking for help with a judge with whom I was familiar. I still remember the feeling in the pit of my stomach as I pondered what to do. At the time, Gwen was competing against another dog for number one Doberman in breed points. They were neck and neck. It was a tight race. The judge she would be showing to had already awarded several breed wins to the dog Gwen was competing against. He was a big advocate of her competitor's dog and made it known that he felt the dog had outstanding merits.

Gwen asked me if I could talk to the judge. She said she really needed my help; otherwise, she was afraid that she would lose her number one position.

At that point in time, Gwen was yet to have campaigned a Doberman to the number one national ranking. She explained that the other handler was being unfair and arranging wins. I felt so conflicted. Here was Gwen, someone whose handling abilities I idolized, coming to me for help. Although I knew wins at dog shows were often arranged in advance and behind the scenes, it was something I hated about the dog show industry. I felt it was unethical and went against my own personal integrity. At the time, I had an idealistic view of dog shows and believed that a dog should win based solely on its merits. Even though I am no longer a novice in the industry, I still hold this viewpoint. I didn't like it when judges allowed themselves to be influenced like this or when handlers went about the business of arranging wins ahead of time. It's a behavior I knew was part of the business, but I chose not to engage in it because I believed it wasn't right and it was unfair.

That being said, I wanted to help Gwen, and so I did. My sympathies, my desire to help, and my idolization of Gwen led me to make a decision that I ultimately felt ashamed of. I still do. For me, it was a learning experience regarding how far I would go to do something for someone else I care about. In this case, I committed an act for someone else that I wouldn't even have engaged in on my own behalf.

Gwen continually challenged my personal integrity. She stretched how far I was willing to go. Through competing against her, I found my edges. I learned what I was willing to sacrifice and what guiding principles resided deep within my core that were non-negotiable.

Values Influence Behaviors and Outcomes

Gwen is no longer in this world. I can't ask her what she valued most. What I did witness was that Gwen loved Dobermans and saw herself as a protector and an authority of the breed. Gwen's greatest joys were her beloved Dobermans and being able to step into the ring and compete with them.

I can only speculate as to what drove her to compete in the way she did. Who we are and the things we've been exposed to in life affect how we compete and what we bring forth into the world. Our personal values undoubtedly affect the manner in which we are willing to pursue a win and how we treat others.

Gwen is a poignant example of this, helping us to see that we are all driven by both known and unknown forces—both light and dark—constantly influencing our behavior and responses. Generally, with age, many of us become more aware of the forces driving us and adjust our behavior so that we can remain in alignment with our values.

This happened with Gwen, too. As Gwen grew older and was faced with a variety of health conditions, she changed as a competitor. She became more human, more compassionate, and less divisive. In time, her priorities expanded beyond dogs to include the people she came to care for who shared her interests.

Gwen identified herself first as a breeder of Dobermans and second as a handler. And although she was a professional handler by trade, she didn't define herself as a businesswoman. In fact, she openly admitted that she wasn't good with business matters.

She got angry when judges didn't understand her breed and didn't adjudicate it properly. She didn't care much about being kind, fair, or appropriate. Her competitive nature governed her behavior and took precedence over all matters. Her masterful skills in the ring, along with her strong ability to control others and manipulate situations and outcomes, resulted in a plethora of wins.

Gwen had great instincts and acted on them. Ideally, as civilized humans, we use our instinctive natures to help guide and protect us while discerning the most appropriate actions to take based on each individual situation and how our actions impact the whole. Although we may strive for this, it is often a quite challenging balance to strike. But it is even more difficult when our drive to win takes over. I think Gwen struggled with this, like so many of us do at times. Although her passionate, reactive nature did serve her in many ways, at times, it came back to haunt her. Gwen did a lot of winning, but big prestigious wins, like Best of Breed at the Doberman National Convention or Westminster Kennel Club, eluded her.

Like Gwen, we all have gifts to share and struggles to overcome. Gwen and I valued different things, but that doesn't mean her values were less than mine. It just means they were different. Sometimes relating to people who have differing values can create friction—we've all experienced this. This friction, although frustrating, can help us see that there is more than just one perspective.

Although competing against Gwen's passionate nature was challenging to say the least, I am grateful to have had the opportunity to not only witness but compete with a living legend. Her larger-than-life presence in the ring left a void for all of us who enjoyed watching the godlike DeMilta come to life when a dog's lead was placed in her hands.

A Legacy in the Breed

In 2014, Gwen and her daughter Carissa of Alisaton Dobermans were designated breeders of the year. This was an incredible, heartfelt moment for Gwen as her work with family and friends and her beloved Dobermans was recognized. This brought her life's work full circle. Alisaton Dobermans was conceived in 1972 when Gwen and her mother (Joanne Satalino) bred their first litter of Dobermans. In 2018, Gwen and her mom were awarded the Doberman Pinscher Club of America Lifetime Achievement award.

Gwen lives on in the dogs she bred, produced, finished, and campaigned, as well as the breeders and handlers she mentored. Her presence leaves an indelible mark on the sport of purebred dogs, and her performances inside the ring will forever be etched into the hearts and minds of those she touched.

In 2022, Gwen proudly stated that Alisaton Dobermans and their extended family of co-breeders had produced over 220 champions. And that number continues to grow. In Gwen's final message, taken from a section in the October 2022 *Doberman Network Magazine*'s tribute to Gwen, she wrote, "This sport and specifically the Doberman breed has given me the truest gift… it has given my life's purpose but more than that it has given me friends that have become family and the gift of combining my family and my passion. I would love for this passion to live on in all of you dear friends."

CHAPTER 12

Jane Forsyth: The Mother Who Inspired an Industry

Taking Professionalism to New Heights

I hadn't yet drawn my first breath when the iconic force known as Jane Forsyth was setting the dog show world on fire with her competitive spirit and passion for showing dogs. Back in her heyday, Jane stood about five foot nine inches tall, with short brown (later blond, then silver) hair, broad shoulders, and big square hands along a hardy physique—a commanding woman who exuded strength, determination, and a no-nonsense approach to life. Like a commander in chief, her presence couldn't be missed.

Jane, a pioneer in her trade and a woman ahead of her time, did things no woman or man had done before. Similar to the way McDonalds set a whole new standard for the fast-food industry, Jane changed the dog show industry. In this case, she took a great service–her talent–and created a practical business model that, decades later, industry leaders still emulate. Not only did she earn a decent living by monetizing her passion, but she made exponentially more money than anyone in the industry had ever done before.

In Jane's case, the money she banked reflects the degree to which her talent, skill, and presence were valued within the dog show community. To assume that money flowed into Jane's hands simply because she was extraordinarily talented in her handling abilities or a great businesswoman would be to miss her true significance.

It's important to note that Jane was not alone in her business endeavor. At the age of thirty-seven, she married long-time professional dog show handler Robert S. Forsyth. Prior to teaming up, each was successful in their own right. However, after joining forces, they went on to become the most successful handling team in the history of purebred dogs. They each handled Westminster Best in Show winners, and as of 2023, they were still the only married couple to do so. They co-authored the award-winning book, *A Guide to Successful Dog Showing*.

Despite Bob's outstanding talents as a handler, Jane is almost universally revered as the best handler of all time. What Gwen DeMilta achieved in the Doberman breed, Jane Forsyth achieved across all breeds. Jane was named Kennel Review Handler of the Year three times, which earned her a place in the publication's Hall of Fame. She won three Gaines Awards, including Woman of the Year, and was inducted into the American Boxer Club Hall of Fame in 2001.

After forty-three years of handling, Jane retired in 1981 to become a judge. As an all-rounder judge for FCI (Federation Cynologique Internationale–a foreign dog registry) and AKC breeds (a rare and difficult designation to achieve among US individuals, deeming one competent to judge all breeds in the US). She judged at every prestigious US dog show event, as well as internationally.

Jane was ahead of my time, so I was not able to interview her for this book before her death in 2018 at eighty-six. However, I interviewed several key people within the dog show industry who were close to her. These individuals knew Jane not only as a dog show handler and a businesswoman but also as a human being. I used the information gathered from these individuals to tell Jane's story. They are as follows: Sioux Forsyth-Green, Jane's daughter, former handler, and current AKC licensed judge; Mark Threlfall, former employee/apprentice and Janie's right-hand man, currently an AKC licensed judge; and Wayne Cavanaugh, former employee/apprentice, third generation dog fancier, AKC Vice-President, United Kennel Club President/founder, World Congress Leader for various kennel clubs, Charter Board Member of the AKC Canine Health Foundation, AKC licensed judge, breeder, exhibitor, with twenty-seven years in television, many years in radio, and life-long friend/advisor to both Jane and Bob.

Although Sioux is Jane's only biological offspring, there are many within the industry that Jane referred to as a son. Mark and Wayne are two such people.

Before we get into what made Jane so dynamic, I'd like to share a little background to help set the stage for who she became. Jane was born at the onset of the Great Depression, the worst economic crisis in modern history. Businesses went under, people's fortunes plummeted instantaneously, and most never recovered.

Her daughter Sioux says, "Nowadays, people sometimes think if a person is money driven, that is a bad thing. Not if you were raised during the Great Depression. If you were raised during that time frame, you never wanted to have to worry where your next meal was coming from, whether you would be able to pay your electric bill, or could afford to put gas in your car. Growing up in the Depression made you want to earn money."

And even those who recovered and prospered over time lived with an underlying fear that it might disappear overnight.

Jane was also raised during a time and within a culture that didn't cater to emotions. The majority of people could barely make ends meet and were just trying to survive. Emotions and feelings were not given much significance. There was no time for that.

Jane's communication style was often abrupt, sometimes abrasive, and lacked sensitivity. Although her forthright nature led many outsiders to think she lacked heart, it kept her focused on her goals. There was so much to admire about Jane that most people simply overlooked or accepted these characteristics.

I believe that a critical turning point in her life occurred when she chose to walk away from a traditional education. According to Sioux, Jane dropped out of high school–walked out and never looked back–because she didn't like how a nun evaluated her performance. Life became her master teacher.

STRONG CONNECTION LEADS TO A SOLID FOUNDATION

Jane was competitive, talented, driven, and extremely focused. Her passion led the way, and life seemed to bend to her willful, stubborn nature. Throughout her life, she remained steadfast in her intention to provide for herself and her family. She aligned herself with like-minded people who supported or shared her mission and passion for dogs. One of her first significant relationships was with Anne Hone Rogers (who later married and took on the surname Clark). Jane met up with

Anne when she was sixteen, and they quickly became best friends and eventually business partners.

In 1956, Anne became the first woman to win Best in Show at the highly prestigious Westminster Kennel Club. (She is featured in Chapter 10 and mentioned throughout the book.) Fourteen years later, Jane became the second woman to do so. Their friendship lasted a lifetime.

In the beginning, they set up their crates together and frequently traveled together. They became known as "The Sisters" and would often refer to each other that way.

Mark Threlfall shares a story, "One year on the old Tar Heel Circuit, where it was necessary to drive at least a couple of hours every night to get to the next show site, Annie had trouble with the transmission of her international travelall. (At the time, the travelall was the de rigueur for dog show transportation.) Because there was no time to get the transmission fixed between shows, Janie pushed Annie's vehicle with her own throughout the circuit!"

According to Wayne Cavanaugh, they would often play off one another. Wayne says, "Their motto was, 'We're gonna beat the boys!' They didn't play dirty. However, they did whatever it took to beat the boys. They won, and they had fun doing it."

People admired the ingenious ways these two young women brought in the wins. Sioux remembers being told a story of a show in which her mom was competing for Best in Show.

Jane was handling a dog with beautiful feet. She got the idea to pull out the grass around the area of the dog's feet to help call attention to this great attribute. This was back in the '40s or '50s and had never been thought of before. According to Sioux, it worked, and Jane's dog won Best in Show. (There are stories of Anne utilizing this technique as well.)

Another well-known Jane story took place early in her career. Before the prevalence of motorhomes, trailers, vans, and big rigs led to handlers camping on the dog show grounds the night before the show, handlers would show up to a dog show early in the morning with a vehicle full of dogs. Handlers would often put ALL their dogs in an exercise pen together to relieve themselves.

One day, Jane did that, and a fight broke out among her dogs. Bob Forsyth, a young handler at the time who worked for Henry Stecker, stepped in, broke up the fight, and walked away. Later, while Bob was standing with Henry, Jane walked up and said, "I don't like you," and walked away.

Bob looked at Henry and asked, "Who was that?"

In time, Bob would come to know this woman quite well and eventually develop a deep love and respect for her, but that didn't happen overnight. Jane was busy making a name for herself. She and Anne were a force to be reckoned with.

Bob, a man who was a product of his time, was known to say, "Get those women out of here!"

Wayne laughingly admits that if Bob had had his way, there would be no women in the sport. It would be all men–male judges and male handlers. Bob's views were typical views shared by many men at that point in time.

Needless to say, the two women would not be run out of town. They were tough, determined, and undeterred. Their work was their passion. Together and each in her own way, Janie and Annie were glass ceiling breakers. The Sisters had no sympathy for whiners, victim mentalities, or people who wanted success yet allowed excuses to stand in their way. Janie and Annie made it okay for women to go Best in Show against the big boys. They did it every weekend and with great glee.

Wayne jests, "I always wondered if Bob married her because he was tired of getting beat by her!"

THE SUBTLE ART OF SHOWMANSHIP AND PERSUASION

I remember hearing about Jane Forsyth as a kid. People said she was a machine. I interpreted that to mean that she was robotic, showing every dog the same. As I have come to know Jane more deeply through these key people, I now understand this couldn't be further from the truth. Jane may have appeared to be machine-like in her precise execution, handling dog after dog, breed after breed, yet despite this systematic approach and efficiency, there was a subtle art that took place every time she took the lead of a different dog.

While moving a dog, she may have appeared strong and rigid and similar in stature as she did with the dog before. Yet what may not have been apparent to the uninformed observer were the minute adjustments she made in the lead, or perhaps a slight shift in the tone of her voice, the exact angle she presented a dog's head.

For someone who never had the pleasure of witnessing Jane in action in the ring, it may be hard to comprehend the level of reverence her handling skills garnered. The mastery she displayed every time she walked into the ring inspired and captivated people, leaving them in awe. When someone is that good, whatever the skill may be, we as humans tend to bow down to them as gods. We know we have just witnessed greatness. That's how good Jane was.

There were so many nuances to Jane's handling that if someone weren't an astute observer, it would be missed. She knew the exact angle a dog's head should be arched or the exact speed a dog needed to gait in order for it to appear its best. Jane believed that the handler should fade into the background and that the dog should take center stage at all times. However, just because a handler should not take center stage does not mean they should be absent. In fact, Jane's presence in a ring couldn't be missed. She had an aura about her, a certain mystique in how she made every dog she put her hands on look its best.

When an extra push was necessary to get the win, Jane would find a way to make her dog look better than anyone else's. Every time Jane walked into a ring with a dog in hand, she was mentally prepared to do whatever it took to win. She didn't do this in an underhanded manner, yet she did capitalize on another's weakness, such as lack of decisiveness, attention, or skill, when the opportunity presented itself.

Mark Threlfall shares, "One of Jane's oldest tricks was getting right behind the dog she wanted to beat, and while waiting in line she would strike up a conversation with the handler of the dog. She'd talk and laugh and then, suddenly in mid-sentence, pose with her dog. All the time while talking to the handler she had been pulling her dog together and keeping an eye on the judge. When she snapped the dog together, many handlers found themselves staring at the judge with their dog a mess and Janie's looking like a million bucks!"

I can't speak for other competitors, but I can say that if I had encountered this type of competitiveness in another handler, it would inspire me to be better. It would be fun to compete in that way… to be electrified, on guard, and pretty much on fire, thinking of all the fun creative ways to oust her. You better believe that the next time I stepped into the ring with her, I would be more deeply engaged, I would pay closer attention. It would be unlikely that I would ever let down my guard around her again. That type of competitive intensity levels up everyone's game!

Jane was always looking for an edge, but she wasn't malicious in her intent. She wasn't a cheater. She would never fix a win. She believed in honoring the integrity of the sport of purebred dogs, and that extended to all members of the community.

Jane was often resourceful in the way she pulled off wins. Wayne shares a story of Jane's resourcefulness. He says, "Jane had started handling a new Irish Setter special owned by Mrs. Porter. This dog looked very different than the previous Irish Setter Jane showed. Many of us wondered how she was going to catch on with this one. She began showing the dog on the fly circuit, a group of shows held in Ballston Spa, New York, (located on a fairgrounds, well known for the disturbing presence of flies and bees) during the month of August. The first day she won the breed, but she didn't win the group. She got a group three, which didn't go over well with Jane! Jane was used to winning.

"The next day, an older woman who was well known at the time, but is since long gone, began making a cut in the Sporting Group, with the intention of pulling out a number of dogs for further selection. Her mannerisms indicated to the rest of us that she hadn't yet made a decision; she was just preparing to pull out a selection of dogs for further consideration. She started at the front of the line.

"Janie was in the front, so when she got pulled out for the cut, Janie ran right over to the group one sign and said, 'Yah!' And the judge was just like, 'It's Janie, it's okay. I guess I'll allow her to be first.' So, she got that win that way... whatever it took. And then the judge had to go find her second, third, and fourth place winners."

Another way that Janie garnered wins was with the subtle use of her hands. Not only did she use her hands to steady or mold a dog, but also she used them as guides. Jane is credited as being one of the creators of this great, subtle way of pointing out an asset on a dog. She would use her hands to softly draw attention to a quality that her dog had and the other didn't. Her mannerisms were so smooth that the judge often didn't even know Jane was "selling" her dog.

Jane was respectful in her persuasiveness. She believed in good manners and respectful conduct, and she believed it was essential to the betterment of the sport of purebred dogs. Judges, in turn, respected the skillful way she presented her dogs. This fine art of handling is still instilled in our young handlers learning the techniques of greatness.

Jane's ability to dominate among all breeds has not been replicated since her departure from handling. It was common for Jane to dominate not only one or two breeds, but an entire group. She, Bob, and their assistants would often win all four placements in a group... and not just one but all groups! That is practically unheard of.

THE ABILITY TO TRANSCEND: READ, ADAPT, AND RESPOND

Jane is remembered by many for her uncanny ability to read a dog and quickly get it to respond to her commands. Her daughter, Sioux, believes one of her mom's biggest gifts as a handler was adaptability. Jane had tremendous competence in her ability to read a dog and adapt to that dog. Part of Jane's brilliance was knowing what each dog needed to perform its best, and demanding that they do so.

Jane put expectations on her dogs, and they knew what was expected of them. Yes, the dogs are pets when they retire, but while they are on the road campaigning or working toward their championship, they need to do their job.

Sioux explains, "You don't want to work today... okay, then you don't get to play."

The dogs Jane handled were rewarded for good behavior, and likewise, they were not rewarded for bad behavior.

Although I never had the honor of working alongside Jane or knowing her in an intimate way, I feel a connection with her. When a client hires me to handle a dog for them, it is my job to win. It is my job to get every ounce of enthusiasm and showmanship I can muster out of my dogs. Some dogs give you everything they have, but often, a handler needs to encourage, guide, nurture, and–at times–demand the dog to engage. If a dog won't engage, a handler needs to find the way in, make that dog receptive, and get that dog to show. I have had times that I have had to nip, pinch, growl, play, or even ignore a dog to get its attention. This isn't done in an abusive way... it is done to get the dog to engage when they are tuning out their handler and are unreceptive. Different dogs need different things. Jane knew this on a very deep level.

Life Experience Melds with Acquired Knowledge

Jane was always seeking ways to optimize her performance and give herself an edge against her competitors. She had natural talent that she applied and developed, and she armed herself with knowledge.

Part of Jane's knowledge came from reading and understanding the AKC standards of every dog she handled (roughly 147, back in her day). She believed all great handlers should have a thorough understanding of every breed they handle.

Another part of her knowledge base, although less identifiable, came from the vast experience she had interacting with a multitude of different dogs of all breeds.

She sensed the basic needs and inner drives of the dogs in her care. She knew them intimately because she lived and breathed dogs. According to Wayne, she averaged boarding sixty or more dogs at her kennel upon returning from a dog show and had three shifts of workers providing round-the-clock care and supervision. Her entire life revolved around dogs. Dogs and her work were often the sole focus of her life. If left to her own devices, Jane would have worked 24/7.

Through her deep knowledge of breed standards and her constant interaction with dogs, Jane knew what dogs in her charge needed. She knew what to feed them. She knew what worked and what didn't. Jane was so tuned into her surroundings that it could be described as a sixth sense. Like a mother who tells her children, "I have eyes in the back of my head," Jane always knew what was going on around her.

She could be preparing a dog standing on a grooming table for the ring, and then there would be a row of exercise pens at her back, and she'd say, "You better take care of that Boxer in the last pen, it looks like he is going to get into an argument with the one next to him."

She didn't miss a trick.

Jane would somehow know exactly what a dog needed, and even so, she often couldn't explain how she knew what she knew. This dynamic was a common occurrence in the manner in which Jane attended to her dogs.

Wayne Cavanaugh gives an example. He says, "We had a giant paddock called Porter's Acres that Mrs. Porter had bought. (Mrs. Porter was a well-known dog owner of considerable means and influence, for whom Jane handled dogs.) Porter's Acres contained enormous paddocks for dogs to exercise and play. We had other big areas as well with beautiful kennels and runs… all kinds of stuff for dogs. Every once in a while, Janie would come back from a show and say, 'Take Duke and put him in Porter's acres for a while.'"

Wayne might inquire, "You mean you want him to socialize with other dogs?"

Jane might shrug and respond, "Yah, exercise."

She knew what they needed and what worked. Sometimes, she just wouldn't be able to explain it.

Being tuned into the needs of her dogs was an essential ingredient in Jane's success in the ring. Her dogs came to know and trust her, and she knew what to expect from them. This resulted in a solid relationship in which she knew her dogs' edges, how far they could be pushed, and when she needed to ease up. This type of skill develops over time, and it develops due to a handler's connection to their animals.

Jane and Bob weren't big into training. You didn't see them running up and down their driveway, training dogs at home in their care. Yet when dogs went home with Jane, they often came back better show-dogs, because their relationship with Jane often deepened while in her care. Again, she knew what they needed.

Jane's dogs were happy because she let them be dogs.

Sioux says, "Dogs got to be dogs. They had huge runs and paddocks. If you came to the kennel unannounced, lord knows what those dogs looked like because if it was raining out, those dogs were outside running. If it was snowing outside, they went out. In Connecticut, there might be twelve inches of snow, and those dogs were outside every single day— Boxers, Smooth Fox Terriers, out in the weather every single day. Dogs were treated like dogs, not people, and they knew how to act like dogs."

Sioux relays the story of another handler's conversations with her mother. The handler complained that his dog didn't like showing in the rain. Her mother's response was, "If you are not going to put your special out in the rain, then don't bother bringing her to the dog show when it's raining."

Sioux explains her mother's thought process, "When it's raining, the cows don't care, the horses don't care, the livestock don't care. Weather is a natural part of life. Animals accept that. If the human doesn't make a big deal out of the weather, the animals won't either."

Too many people personify their pets. They don't understand their dogs' needs. Not Jane; she loved her dogs, and she let them be dogs. She knew what a dog needed to feed its soul to flourish. Jane also knew more basic concepts, such as proper nutrition and exercise. Her dogs were fed the proper diet for their breed, they were given the proper type and amount of exercise for their breed. Jane believed in doing things properly and NEVER cutting corners. Other handlers might pass an exit and choose not to set up exercise pens, but not Jane and Bob. They believed in taking great care of their dogs, they saw to every detail in terms of proper care, conditioning, and mental well-being.

Proper care also meant ALWAYS presenting dogs that are impeccably clean and well-mannered at shows. Their coats were clean, and the ears, teeth, and eyes were bright, clear, and clean. No eye boogers ever! Dog show people know what that means!

Often, people want to know the secret to someone's success or to a successful life. Most of the time, it's not about doing one big thing right, it's about doing 100 small things with intention. With Jane, no detail was too small.

WINNING IS GREAT FUN!

Jane had a passion for dogs, and a passion for competing. Wayne Cavanaugh reminisces, "Jane enjoyed winning every single time. She especially loved beating Bob! She just thought it was great fun."

He laughs as he adds, "But boy, you didn't want to mess with Jane on her way to great fun!"

People felt intimidated by Jane, not because she tried to overpower them, but simply because she was that good! Wayne Cavanaugh explains,

"I know there are people that have to win because they have feelings of deep insecurity or need to be in control or better than others. They feed on winning like it is a drug. It was never like that for Jane. She was confident in her abilities."

Jane's competitive nature, her passion for competing, and her love of winning raised her up, and also raised those around her. Her competitive nature kept her continually striving to better herself and those around her.

Sioux says, "My mother did not hold others down to serve herself. No. Not ever! My mom lifted up everyone around her."

Although not a common term back in her time, Jane was growth-oriented. She was always seeking opportunities to do better and be better. Life was a game, full of obstacles and opportunities to better yourself. She not only accepted that about life, she embraced it.

As a healthy competitor, even though she loved the win, she also loved the thrill of the pursuit. A competitor like Jane works from the heart and loves the feeling of the adrenaline rush. When you are in this zone, you feel alive, focused, connected, and consumed. This single-minded pursuit can move mountains. Her passion not only transformed dogs and people but also inspired an industry.

A Mother Is Born: A Reluctant Teacher and Role Model Who Inspired an Industry

An interesting dichotomy is that many who came under Jane's tutelage refer to her as Mother, yet Jane's very own daughter states, "My mom was not nurturing. That was probably her biggest downfall."

Perhaps that shouldn't come as a surprise, considering that Jane was raised during a time within a culture that didn't hold space for emotions. Life was hard. Emotions and feelings were not dwelled upon, they were handled.

Jane was all business, even in the raising of her own daughter, and she hired a nanny. Sioux, who carries her mom's same frank truth-telling tongue, says, "My mom must have really loved me based on the amount of money she paid that nanny!"

We both laugh, knowing Sioux's meaning. She was making reference to her mom's frugality. Everyone knew how cheap Jane was, yet she paid that nanny well. And as it turns out, Sioux developed a deep love for her childhood caretakers. In fact, their relationships remained strong throughout the years, and when they died, it felt like the loss of a parent. Sioux received a softness from them that was not in Jane's nature.

Although this way of being appears cold and detached, Jane did the best she could with the skills she had. Despite her hard exterior, abrupt manners, and emotional detachment, she did serve as a mother figure to many people in the dog show community.

And if we think about the most basic need a mother fulfills for her offspring, it is to teach them how to survive all the challenges life will throw at them. Many of us carry idealistic versions of how a mother should care for her children. Yet, each mother must find her own way. Speaking as a mother myself, each of us must find balance between what we learn along the way and what feels right in the situation or circumstance. The majority of moms want what is best for their children and strive to improve upon the mothering they received as a child. Jane was doing her best with what she experienced in her own life and what her own mother modeled to her.

Jane learned to take care of herself at a very young age. She left high school early and began working on her own in a kennel. If she didn't know something, she would ask questions and put those answers to work. I don't think Jane set out to be a mother figure, yet her strong, competent, resourceful nature led people to seek her company and willingly offer her their loyalty.

Mark explains the high level of regard Jane's assistants felt toward her.

"We had great respect for her because we knew she had started at the bottom of the sport as a young person and had risen to the top through hard work and being frugal."

Mark started working with Jane at the ground level, performing the most basic tasks. Jane had an eye for talent. Seeing potential in his abilities, over time she assigned him more weighted responsibilities. Eventually, he became Janie's right-hand man. Mark was in charge of organizing the daily schedule, which was a monumental task.

"In the early days at my position, Janie was prone to double-check my directions. She always wanted to show every dog she was supposed to. She grew to trust me, and I grew more proficient and confident in my role."

Marks says, "I admired her drive and her wish to get to every single dog in her string. Every single day she showed up, ready to work and show as many dogs as she could. She had days when she didn't feel good, was tired, or whatever, but she always gave 110 percent."

Jane knew how each dog needed to be presented, but she often couldn't explain the how or why of something. Mark states, "Jane didn't teach. She expected you to learn by watching her. If you asked her, she would simply say, 'Watch me.' So, we did. And while at first Janie's answer seemed like no answer at all, it was the best answer."

Jane led by example. Wayne Cavanaugh explains Jane's teaching style, stating, "She was really good at teaching if you were good enough to learn."

When she offered instructions, it was always in small pieces. Wayne states, "I covered (a term that refers to when a handler that is hired to show a dog has a conflict and another handler fills in during their absence) a lot of dogs for them. Sometimes when Janie showed up too late to take over, she would watch me handle. Then she would tell me one thing that I needed to do differently while handling that particular dog."

Or she might tell Wayne, "I've got a new Pointer special, and I want you to watch."

Wayne might wonder what she wanted him to watch. When she was done, she would ask him, "What did you see?"

He'd reply, "Nice Pointer."

She'd say, "Watch again."

The next time he watched Jane handle that dog, he observed that her Pointer did not have a great head, but he had a great neck and shoulders. He saw how Jane gracefully drew the judge's eye toward those attributes. It was fascinating to sit or stand ringside and simply watch Jane handle dogs.

Wayne says, "Those of us who worked for her learned to really listen to the smallest of instructions."

When Jane took the time to instruct someone, if they were smart, they listened closely and took it to heart. She didn't waste her time teaching those who were incapable of learning from what she had to share. She kept things simple. She wouldn't give an assistant too many instructions at once, which might get jumbled in their head. She explained things in parts.

Wayne adds, "I'm not even sure that she was conscious of it."

Assistants had to learn quickly how to ensure that every detail was covered. That was expected.

Mark states, "Janie got angry when things weren't done properly. She was serious about the business, and she expected everyone else to be as dedicated and single-minded toward it as she was. She expected everyone to do their job."

Those who were eager learned a lot about business just by watching her. If you wanted to watch and learn, the opportunity was there. Jane was good at helping others fine-tune their handling, figure out how to take themselves to another level. However, she didn't sit anyone down for an hour and teach them a lesson.

Wayne clarifies, "That just wasn't in her DNA."

There were many other things that could be learned simply by watching Jane in action. You could learn the power and respect that is generated by interacting with others in a forthright manner. When Jane or one of her assistants made a decision, clients were expected to respect them. Jane didn't waste her valuable time placating disruptive behavior among her clients or her staff.

Clients didn't get far if they complained. Jane or Bob would simply say, "You got beat by a better dog. It's a dog show. You can win tomorrow," or, "You paid for an opinion and you got it."

That was their response. End of discussion. They might add, "If you are going to whine about losing, you are probably in the wrong sport."

Sioux takes great pride in her parents' sportsmanship. She says, "They were always kind. You never saw them tear off an armband and throw it down or give people dirty looks. Instead, they would congratulate people. That doesn't mean they didn't get upset behind the scenes, but they were always kind to people."

Sioux relays a story that Mary Dukes, a former handler and current AKC representative, shared with her. Mary reminisced about the year she handled a Whippet against Sioux's dad at Westminster. Mary won. Bob turned to her and said, "Congratulations, kid."

He never made a scene or a negative remark. Mary said she will never forget his kindness and professionalism. He accepted the judge's decision, even though he lost the breed at a highly prestigious event.

Sioux, an AKC-licensed judge herself, states, "I see some exhibitors turn away and not show a judge an armband number because they are mad, or they will walk to the other end of the ring, or not say congratulations."

She finds that behavior disrespectful and lacking professionalism, adding, "The two of them in the ring together competing against one another, they were both out for blood. But once a judge made his or her decision, it was over. This was back in the day when all the handlers went to dinner together and they were all friends. And if you broke down on the side of the highway, there was someone there to stop and help you."

That's the type of people they were. They were truly great dog show ambassadors.

STAFF AS FAMILY

It has been well established that Jane took her business seriously, handled her dogs to perfection, that her dogs received the best of care, and that she conducted herself in a professional manner. Yet a quality that may fall under the radar was Jane's commitment to her staff.

She demanded a lot, but Jane also cultivated greatness in her staff. She taught them how to become better handlers, run a successful business, and at the same time, she took good care of them.

Sioux states, "The staff sat at the dinner table with the family. They weren't taken to McDonalds. They were well provided for. They were not treated like second-class citizens. They were treated like family."

Everyone sat at the dinner table after a dog show or a full day of work, and they all had a full meal. During the day, however, the main focus was on the dogs. The dogs' needs were always the first priority. Staff had to earn their keep.

Jane ran a tight ship, and she always kept an eye on the bottom line. She was thrifty in all she did. This taught workers a healthy respect for money management. You could see the value of making money, but also the benefit of learning how to be resourceful and save money, especially in creative ways.

Jane and Bob were teaching life lessons if you were smart enough to pay attention to all they were demonstrating.

Wayne explains, "It was really hard to get all your work done because there were a lot of dogs, and they required extraordinary care for those dogs, which is a great way to learn to do it right. You were going to learn how to go out to dinner with clients, and you were going to learn how to use your fork and knife, and what to order. Jane and Bob didn't always explain what to do, some things were learned the hard way, through trial and error."

Wayne explains one such incident. He was out to dinner with Jane and Bob when he was eighteen. He felt honored to be with Bob, yet also felt somewhat intimidated. Although he and Bob eventually became great friends, at the time, Bob was a strong authority figure that he admired, and Wayne was just a kid.

Bob ordered Dewars on the rocks and then asked Wayne, "What will you have, son?"

Wayne said, "I'll have Dewars on the rocks."

Wayne had never tasted whiskey in his life. He remembers it tasting like gasoline to him at the time. However, he drank it and shared a bonding moment with Bob.

Bob could see that Wayne was suffering through it. His response was to tell the waiter to "Bring me and the kid another one!"

Wayne laughs, reminiscing, "That's one of the ways you learned while working with Jane and Bob."

Sometimes, they would let you make your own mistakes. Those who were smart and able learned real quick what not to do! Wayne says, "They did it in their own way. You weren't going to read it in an etiquette book. You learned it the hard way."

Staff was exposed to a lot of situations that led to learning how to navigate a variety of life circumstances by jumping in, doing their best, sometimes succeeding, sometimes failing. Either way, they had gained valuable knowledge.

Wayne says, "Jane was a caring human being who, if you wanted to work hard and learn and keep your mouth shut, you were under her wing and you were there forever."

He adds, "There is a saying that the day you stop working for the Forsyths is the day you die. Because you worked for them forever."

Even though Wayne hadn't worked for them in more than fifty years, Bob would often reach out to him to talk when Janie's health was declining. Janie would call, too, just wanting to connect and talk about life.

Wayne says, "I cherish those personal, private moments with Janie and Bob. Even fifty years after being employed with them, if Janie needed something, I saw to it that she got it. I was dead loyal to her, and she was to me as well."

As I hear Wayne's story, I begin to think of my own relationships with the assistants I have worked with over the years. Many came from troubled homes. Perhaps some of the loyalty shown by the assistants who worked for the Forsyths is similar to what I've seen in my own experience. I found that, when these kids were consistently given tasks, structure, rules, and meals, they actually thrived within the structure.

The rare occasions that I had a serious talk about my expectations regarding their behavior, or showed them that I had certain boundaries that needed to be respected regarding the care of my dogs, what I needed, and how I expected them to conduct themselves, always resulted in a positive experience. Rather than rebel against the rules, they showed up to do their work with a greater sense of purpose. This is proof that stating your needs and expectations clearly and consistently and expecting everyone to pull their weight leads to a safe environment in which everyone can thrive. I believe Jane must have created this type of environment. Everyone felt a certain level of safety because they knew what was expected of them, and these expectations were consistent.

Safety is a huge component often overlooked in our relationships. When people don't feel safe and their basic needs aren't being met, they can't thrive. Jane was actively teaching skills that would empower each individual under her care. Although her demeanor was not what we would classically define as the ideal feminine mother, Jane's approach was highly effective. When her employees ventured off into the world, they had all the necessary skills to thrive. And even after they flew the nest, many felt they always had a home to come back to.

Meanwhile, at times, Jane's daughter Sioux may have felt alone as her mom traveled off to dog shows or spent endless hours working in the kennel. Yet Jane was known by others as Mother because of the profound impact she had on their lives. Jane was teaching life principles, helping others take care of themselves, and she did the same for her daughter, but in a different way. Sioux is at peace with her relationship with her mother, knowing in her heart that the biggest lesson she learned from her mom was to take care of herself.

Treat the Sport as a Business

Success can be defined in many ways. In business, success is often measured by financial gains, leadership, innovation, and the ability to have a positive impact on your chosen industry. Jane hit the ball out of the park in every category.

From the outside looking in, it might appear that Jane's success in business was a matter of basic accounting, yet it wasn't just about numbers. Jane's success was nuanced.

When Jane came onto the dog show scene in the 1940s, dog showing was seen as a gentleman's sport. It was an enjoyable pastime that allowed professional dog handlers to earn a decent living. Janie's strong work ethic and business acumen revolutionized the sport. Her motto, *treat the sport as a business*, is a mantra that continues to guide several generations of professionals.

Jane had the numbers that conveyed her financial success. From all accounts, her wealth far surpassed your average professional handler. In fact, it's hard to even make a comparison. It would be like comparing the income of a minor league athlete to that of a major league ball player–not even in the same ballpark.

This is staggering to think about for a dog show handler. For any new professional looking to enter the dog show arena, these figures may elicit excitement for the financial opportunities available. However, the reality is that a large percentage of handlers aren't able to capitalize on these opportunities.

Although history shows that such revenue is, in fact, possible, it is NOT the norm. A large percentage of professionals make high volumes of money yet tend to have poor money management skills and end up broke. That is the sad reality for many. They may be talented as dog show handlers and have great stats, yet they fall short in business matters.

Jane approached business with a strategic mindset. She not only focused on making money, she also focused on saving money. The creative ways she went about penny-pinching are part of her lore. In fact, upon her retirement, she received a value pack of toilet paper because Jane required her staff to steal toilet paper each time they stayed in a hotel for use back at the kennel. This philosophy of hers was a constant joke among her staff.

Employees knew Janie hated anyone wasting anything. For example, she refused to buy paper towels. Her staff was expected to use a cloth that could be washed, dried, and used again. In addition, she insisted that the clear plastic bags used for group placement ribbons be repurposed as ear and topknot wrappers for coated breeds.

Yes, Jane's over-the-top obsession with saving money was often laughable. Yet to Jane, it was no laughing matter. She inherently understood the need to plan for the ups and downs of a fluctuating economy or clientele. When the money is pouring in, it's hard to believe it will ever stop. Yet all of life has its ups and downs. Economies experience recessions, clients' dogs finish or retire, the breeders who flood a handler with dogs have bitches that aren't producing, and at times the money that was once flowing dries up. Even worse, an accident or physical ailment strikes, and a handler is unable to perform their own physically demanding job.

Jane didn't have a mentor to help her learn how to run a profitable business. Instead, she set about running a business in the same fashion she approached other life matters. She observed. She took what she deemed relevant and necessary based on her observations and added her own perspective and style into the mix.

Even though Jane did not have the benefit of many years of education, she had common sense and an intelligence beyond book learning. She applied her knowledge, thoughts, and ideas. Increase the bottom line by increasing revenue as much as possible while minimizing spending to the highest degree. The ability to practically apply ideas is an ability that is often underestimated in our society today. At this point in time, much of American society identifies individuals who have the ability to remember concepts and ideas and regurgitate them as intelligent. By these standards, Jane would have fallen short, yet her practical intelligence and application of details led to success that far surpassed others in her industry.

As far back as 1975, Janie and her husband were showing an estimated forty-plus dogs a day at any given show. Very few handlers manage a caseload of dogs this high on an intermittent basis, let alone on a continual basis. The fact that Jane maintained a business that was consistently in high demand speaks volumes about the level of service provided. And if forty dogs per day, every day, among two people, isn't hard enough to comprehend, try wrapping your head around Sioux's figure of an estimated 120 dogs shown one year at Westminster!

That is a staggering amount of responsibility for two people to take on. Not only were there the physical demands of managing the ring schedules and coordinating all the details of such a large caseload of dogs to show, but there were also the demands of managing the needs of the dogs and maintaining client satisfaction. It would seem they would be spread too thin to manage so much responsibility on a daily basis, yet somehow, they maintained high standards of care with excellent results and high client satisfaction.

I believe one of the reasons they were able to maintain these high standards is due to the high level of integrity they applied in business matters. Integrity is an essential building block to any strong foundation.

Life coach and author Martha Beck writes, "The moment we deny our truth, we're like an airplane that's lost structural integrity."

The New Oxford American Dictionary defines integrity as

1. the quality of being honest and having strong moral principles; moral uprightness

2. the state of being whole and undivided

It has been well established that Jane and Bob had strong beliefs regarding right and wrong and proper business conduct. They were walking examples of good sportsmanship. They set the bar high in this category. Equally so, Jane was whole and undivided in her single-minded approach to running a business.

This single-minded approach kept Jane in alignment with her vision. She didn't waste her energy on those that didn't share her vision. When Jane received that poor grade from a nun, she made the decision to walk away from her education and never look back. According to Sioux, a nun gave Jane a B on one of her assignments. Jane's response was, "I am not a B student." That was a defining moment. She knew her worth, and wasn't going to waste her valuable time and energy with anyone that did not recognize her value. I've seen many handlers over the years tolerate a client's complaints or abusive behavior (myself included), but Jane would have none of that.

Jane knew her strengths, and she worked with them. She didn't beat herself up personally over areas where she may have been lacking. Instead, she surrounded herself with the right people. Her husband Bob was talented in ways that complimented Jane. He had a different style of handling. He was masterful in his ability to handle breeds such as Whippets and other sighthounds that don't like to be controlled. He was a master trimmer and groomer, which was not Jane's forte. In addition, the talented employees and apprentices she took under her wing gave her the capacity to serve a larger clientele and serve them well.

Staff members took on a tremendous amount of responsibility. She expected a lot out of her staff. Assistants knew that they must remain aligned with Jane's principles: work hard, don't waste time or money, and think of the dogs first.

Jane's confidence, focused mindset, and stubborn nature kept her surrounded by people who were in alignment with her mission. This mission was also deeply guided by Jane's strong values and principles. She applied these principles: work hard, pay attention, do your best, be prepared, conduct yourself appropriately, be respectful, take responsibility for your life and your actions. The application of these strong values led to a reputation above reproach, one that often became her advantage.

Jane's hard-won reputation snowballed. Judges, handlers, breeders, spectators, superintendents, and show chairmen respected Jane. Jane won consistently, in part due to the level of respect and reverence she garnered through the years of diligent, appropriate action.

Mark says, "Janie would tell the kids of today to work hard, don't spend all your money as fast as you can make it, and learn all you can about the breeds. Watch the best handlers in specific breeds and emulate them."

Janie's business legacy of skill, competence, and appropriate action lives on through those who worked for her and continue to influence others.

CHAPTER 13

Kelly Lyn Marquis: The Fuel That Feeds Champions

Navigating Burnout in a Competitive Industry

We are all drawn to our work for a variety of reasons. For fortunate individuals, our work is an expression of our passion. It is one of the reasons why our clients hire us and why spectators gather around a ring to watch us handle dogs. We love what we do, and we have a special bond with our dogs that is palpable. We feed on challenges and thrive when competing against a worthy opponent. When piloting dogs we believe in, we not only feel inspired and filled with purpose, but we inspire others as well.

At the height of our inspiration and passion, we are on fire. Not only are we lighting the world up, we feel lit up from the inside. Yet, what happens if the fire begins to fizzle out? What happens when what fed and fulfilled us no longer sustains us?

When we are beginners and even when we are on the path to our success, we are always looking to the next milestone, the next achievement, or the next mountain to scale. It's how elite competitors are wired. The foundation of our lives is built around achievement. Although the path may be full of obstacles, the pursuit of a desired goal gives us purpose.

But what happens after we have achieved most or all of the goals we set for ourselves? For many, including myself, suddenly not having a monumental goal backed by a burning desire is disturbingly disorienting. Once I scaled the mountains I set for myself and achieved the success I desired, I wasn't prepared for what came next.

Having my talents and skills acknowledged among handlers I admired and achieving national recognition in the process fulfilled a childhood dream. However, conquering that mountain set into motion a challenge I didn't see coming. Instead of spurring me on to achieve bigger, better, and more, the fulfillment of my dream sparked what I have now come to understand was an existential crisis that eventually led to a spiritual awakening.

You may be wondering: how does success in the dog show industry cause an existential crisis? Stick with me. I believe this dynamic happens more often than we realize. My hope is that by sharing my story, I can help others when they unexpectedly find themselves in a similar place.

So what was it that I didn't see coming? Simply this: when I achieved my greatest success, instead of feeling elation, pride, or joy, I felt lost and empty inside.

What was wrong with me? I should be happy. But I wasn't, and not being happy made me question my purpose in life, my values, my identity, and generally, how I would move through the world now that I had conquered what I thought would be the pinnacle of my success.

My friends and family—those I was closest to—didn't understand what I was going through. How could they? They had not conquered a mountain like mine or accomplished nearly all their career and life goals by their early thirties.

To the outside world, it seemed I had it all. I had a handsome, intelligent husband, a lovely home, nice cars, and a successful career. What more could anyone possibly want? It appeared that I had everything the outside world says will make you happy (minus the two kids), yet I wasn't. I knew something wasn't right, but I had no idea what it was or where to begin looking for answers.

Oddly enough, reflecting on this, I recalled an incident my former brother-in-law, Bill, shared with me about their dog, Brindle. Brindle was a sweet, gentle Greyhound Bill and my sister, Natalie, adopted from a local race track. One day, shortly after adopting her, Brindle dashed out through a side door of their home, and Bill immediately went after her. In an instant, Brindle's Greyhound nature took over, and she began to run.

Quickly realizing running after a Greyhound would be a futile effort, Bill grabbed his keys and raced after her in his truck. Bill's speedometer clocked Brindle running thirty-five miles per hour. Not bad for a retired, old broad!

Out the truck window, he called her name over and over again, but she was in her own world. She ran and ran and ran until she couldn't run anymore. When she finally ran out of steam, she stopped, huffing and puffing in a daze. She ran so hard, so fast, and for so long that she wore the pads of her feet down to a bloody mess.

During her blind run, she appeared focused, yet where was she running? She had no real goal or direction. There was no rabbit to chase or food to hunt down. What was driving that behavior?

In fact, many of us dog handlers understand what is driving our dog's behavior, but do we know what is driving our own behavior?

In the beginning stages of my life and career, I was that Greyhound running with all my might. Showing dogs was all-consuming. It excited me beyond measure, and I couldn't wait to get in the ring. I wanted to explore my dogs, my abilities, and myself. I wanted to play. I wanted to learn. I wanted to grow. I wanted to put my hands on as many dogs as possible so that I could be the best handler I could be.

Handling a wide spectrum of dogs excited me. Shy and submissive dogs lacking confidence? Yes, please! Wired, neurotic, and unmanageable dogs (and people!)… sign me up! I wanted to know how to optimize a dog's performance, how to help it function to the best of its ability, and how to get into its head and give it the necessary support and guidance to perform at its highest level. That's what lit me up. I loved a challenge, and working my way through challenges offered a fascinating puzzle to solve. Showing dogs with poor conformation and figuring out how to transform bone and flesh was exhilarating! The more I watched other great handlers like Gwen DeMilta, the more I developed a belief that it was easy to win with a great dog, but it takes a great handler to win with a less-than-optimal dog.

I had a tremendous amount of respect and admiration for the talent these handlers wielded and was driven to become that same caliber of handler. Although I had a tendency to be hard on myself and my abilities, especially when I compared myself to the godlike DeMilta, my passion overrode my insecurities. I loved showing dogs and had the self-discipline to work hard, face challenges head-on, and practice to perfect my skills. I didn't know that one day, I would be viewed as a master myself. I was convinced I would never be good enough.

Figuring dogs out and making them look their best intrigued and inspired me. I was driven to be the best I could be. I was in love with my work. It fascinated, inspired, and fulfilled me. In addition, my clients valued my skills. It was a win-win situation.

Over time, that passion began to dissipate, and I found myself struggling to reignite that fire that made me feel alive and purposeful. While my clients still valued my role as a professional handler, my passion for the role I was playing for them was losing steam. While it didn't fizzle out overnight, there was a catalyst that—in hindsight, I can see—triggered the beginning of my existential crisis.

That catalyst—more than twenty years ago now—started in 2001 at the Cincinnati Doberman National. I was handling Blue Chip Purple Reign, a.k.a. Raisin, in the nine to twelve months Puppy Bitch class. Gene Haupt was judging the pre-national, and he awarded Raisin and me Winner's Bitch. I was thirty-one years old. I had a thriving clientele and was respected by my peers, but I hadn't made it big. I had shown several Dobermans that ranked nationally within the top twenty, but never had I campaigned a number one dog. All that was about to change.

FANNING THE FLAMES

A well-respected backer by the name of Jo-Ann Kusumoto approached me and asked if I would join her, her husband Roy, and her handler Moe Miyagawa for dinner. Moe was handling their Doberman, RP, Ch. Marienburg's Repo Man, who was bred by Mary Rodgers, and was ranked number one. Moe handled, while Jo-Ann and Roy owned and backed many dogs bred by Mary Rodgers, a well-respected Doberman breeder (and breeder of Mary Hartman–the Doberman Kaz was in awe of when he first visited the United States).

During dinner, Jo-Ann stated that she felt I was very talented and she wanted to work with me as well as Moe. She told me that her son-in-law's Doberman needed two majors to complete his championship, and she wanted the dog to obtain his championship by Christmas, so the dog could retire from showing and be with the family. Regretfully, I informed her that it was unlikely that I would be able to meet her Christmas deadline as I had obligations to fulfill to my existing clientele.

Although a vast majority of handlers would have moved a few lower-level clients to the back burner to accommodate this influential backer, I did not. I had several class dogs whose owners were loyal to me, and I wanted to remain loyal to them. I was honest with her that it was unlikely I would be able to finish all my current dogs since Christmas was just two months away. I told her I would do my best and that as soon as I had an opening, I would contact her immediately.

It turned out that my values didn't hold me back. I finished all my dogs, creating a last-minute opening for shows I would be attending the weekend prior to Christmas. Jo-Ann registered her dog in those shows, and I finished him in three shows, fulfilling Jo-Ann's deadline! As I look back on this experience now, it is a classic example of how, when we know what we value and live in integrity with those values, our lives fall into alignment. Things start coming together. This was the case for me, at least.

Jo-Ann wanted to continue working with me and expressed an interest in becoming a backer for Raisin. This possibility was an answer to my prayers. Raisin was an outstanding Doberman both mentally and physically, but her breeder/owner had very limited resources and could barely afford to pay her entry fees, let alone pay my handling fees, bonuses for additional winning, traveling expenses, and marketing. Without money and influence, Raisin's potential would remain unrealized.

I often wondered how other professional handlers found backers for their dogs. In fact, on several occasions prior to handling Raisin, I asked Andy Linton how I could find a backer to promote my dogs.

Andy's response was, "Don't worry, a high powered owner will find you."

I didn't like Andy's answer. It seemed like no answer at all. What did that mean? Was I actually supposed to do nothing and just trust that a great owner would magically appear? Yet, Andy was right. Jo-Ann saw my talent and sought me out to pilot her dogs and be a part of her future showing dogs. Money and influence found me.

Finally, to my surprise, I had a great dog and owners capable of going the distance. The proverbial stars aligned, and the sky was the limit. In a perfect world, this would be the perfect ending to this story. Yet life, in its infinite wisdom, had more to teach me.

Something that is important to note is that when a handler or owner makes the decision to go for number one ranking on a national level—especially on the group and all-breed level, and when it's the first time going for a win like this—their limits will be tested. There is a monumental difference between the responsibilities and challenges facing a handler that shows locally or regionally versus those orchestrating a national campaign. There is a reason why a handler as talented as Michelle Scott consciously chooses NOT to take on a national campaign. This is not for everyone. It is not a decision one makes lightly.

A national campaign means that you agree to do whatever it takes. Sacrifices will need to be made. In most cases, it will require every ounce of your strength. You will be tapped out mentally, physically, and emotionally. In all likelihood, you will have little to nothing to give to those you care about. You will be living on the road, driving, or flying all over the country. Your body will most likely pay a heavy price as well.

For instance, at one point during my campaign for number one Doberman, I was competing in the Midwest. Best in Show competition finished around 6 p.m. I needed to be in Long Island, New York, by 8 a.m. because a better panel of judges was slated to judge there versus my current dog show venue.

I exited the Best in Show ring, got in my vehicle, and drove through the night, arriving at the dog show fairgrounds at 7:00 a.m. After winning Best of Breed, I went in search of a hotel, hoping it would afford me some much-needed sleep before our next event that day. Unfortunately, I couldn't fall into a deep sleep. My body was hyper awake and humming–thanks to all the coffee I drank to keep me awake for the drive. Plus, I was afraid I might oversleep and miss group judging. It was rough, but I pushed through it, maintained a strong mindset, and did what was necessary. As Greg Strong said, mind over matter.

Running a national campaign is a complex and arduous undertaking that often leaves you feeling like you are competing in multiple events. First, you feel like you are running a never-ending marathon that requires you to be in a constant sprint. If you aren't sprinting, someone who wants it more will pass you.

Second, it also feels like a game of chess, with multiple players and a changing environment: so much strategy involved.

Finally, on top of all of that, depending on your competition, you will be exposed to guerilla warfare. In a competitive environment like dog handling, everyone is seeking an edge, and your opponents want to take you down. It is quite common for competitors to create drama, make up reasons why their dog is better or their owner is a better person. All of these stories are told to create sway and manipulate the playing field to help their dog's chances of winning. These tactics have nothing to do with a dog's physical merits in the show ring, yet judges sometimes succumb to these emotional tactics. The drama outside of the ring can tap you out mentally and emotionally, especially when people are attacking your character, your dog's merits, and your overall worthiness. While competition can bring out the best in us, it can also bring out the worst in some!

I jokingly nicknamed a promoter of one of my competitors Judas, because almost every time he said hello to me, he would offer me a big smile and a kiss on the cheek, and then I'd lose the breed or the Working Group! It felt uncanny how often this happened when he was present at a show.

The highly coveted Kennel Club of Philadelphia brings to mind another incident that took place during the campaign. It was November, and I was really feeling the pressure to close out the year strong. We had made it to number three all-breed and then fell down to number five all-breed. I wanted to stay in the top five.

There were six more weeks of shows until the rating system closed out. I was showing in Syracuse, New York, on Friday. I won the Working Group but didn't win Best in Show that day.

The following day, Jim White, a well-known and respected judge, was slated to judge Best in Show. He had already awarded my Doberman Best in Show twice. He loved her. Statistically speaking, I had a good chance of winning Best in Show for a third time.

However, I felt expecting another big win from him was asking too much. At times, handlers are accused of following a judge around for wins, or a judge is accused of favoring a particular dog or handler. Sometimes a judge needs to "spread it around" to keep entries up.

Otherwise, exhibitors won't show to a judge when chances are they have no shot at winning. Plus, the judge may like other dogs as well, and want to recognize the merits of a different dog. I had a feeling I might not get lucky a third time with Mr. White, plus I wanted to be respectful and not put him in the position to have to choose either for or against us.

Additionally, the Best in Show lineup in New York was super strong, with great dogs and great handlers. So, I made the decision to leave Syracuse and NOT show to a judge who had already proven he recognized my dog to be of outstanding quality, not just once but twice. I chose to leave Syracuse in favor of showing to an unknown judge from Mexico.

At the time, I was married. My husband Jeff had traveled to the show with me. When I told him that I didn't want to show to Mr. Jim White and instead wanted to take a shot with an unknown judge, he was outraged. He didn't understand why I was making such a seemingly stupid decision.

To top things off, it was November, and we needed to drive through a pretty bad snowstorm. Snowstorms, weather, and hours of treacherous driving were never factors I took into account. If something needed to happen, my mindset was on solutions, not problems. So I tuned out my husband's outrage, packed up the forty-foot motorhome, and drove to Philadelphia.

Yes, the drive was stressful. Plus, I couldn't logically explain to Jeff why I was leaving. I just felt it was the right call. Soon after I entered the show building, several handlers asked me what I was doing in Philly. They said everyone already knew that the Terrier was going to win Best in Show. I felt sick to my stomach. I made the wrong call. I was so disappointed in myself.

I pushed down my disappointment because there was no sense in dwelling on it. Later in the day, I heard that there would be a contest in which the viewers at home would vote for the dog they felt should win Best in Show. Since I knew that there was no way the judge was going to award Raisin and me Best in Show, I decided that my goal was going to be to win the vote of the home viewers.

At that point, I felt no pressure. I knew we couldn't win. Plus, I was upset at myself for the decision I made and the unfairness of being at a show where I had no chance of winning. In fact, I was angry. Oddly enough, I show my best when I'm angry. It focuses me and makes me feel strong and capable.

Raisin and I came charging out from behind the black curtain that Saturday evening and put on the show of our lives. The camera crews descended on us. It felt surreal. And guess what? We won!

What many may not realize is that it isn't just the losses and disappointments that deplete and tax us, it's the wins, too. A national campaign is a rollercoaster ride of ups and downs, big highs and big lows. Everyone on your team is emotionally invested.

One thing is for certain: the road to number one is full of lots of twists and turns, ups and downs, and important decisions to be made. Some are logical, others are intuitive. A handler needs not only to be tuned into their dog, but to be tuned into their environment and their inner knowing. And they need to trust and act upon these often seemingly illogical impulses.

If you are lucky, the people you are working with trust in you, and hopefully, you trust in yourself. For those who like testing their limits, it can be very exciting. It forces you to dig deep and fully explore untapped reserves of strength, talent, and focus.

Although it was a very tumultuous experience for me, I came out on top, which was very satisfying. In the aftermath, I was incredibly grateful for the accomplishment. However, what surprised me is that rather than feeling elation, I felt relief. I didn't fail. I didn't let my clients down. I did right by my dog and helped her reach her highest potential. I made my professional dreams come true. Still, a buzzing voice in my head (and the people around me) kept telling me I should feel amazing, but I didn't. Instead, I was thinking, is this really IT? Now that the campaign was over, who was I without a mountain to conquer?

The Flip Side of Passion Is Burnout

What was wrong with me? I didn't understand why I was thinking and feeling this way. Back then, I wasn't very self-aware or tuned into my feelings. In fact, I was a master of managing my emotions and stuffing them down, not feeling them. Twenty years later, I understand what those feelings were trying to tell me. Those feelings were indicative of depression and burnout.

What I know now is that these feelings are not uncommon. Back when I experienced it, no one talked about it, or at least I wasn't aware of it. Not only have I battled with burnout myself, but I've seen my peers struggle with it too. The light fades from their eyes. Their energy, and how they carry themselves reads, "I'm not happy, but I'm putting on a good face because that is what is expected of me."

Some of us are better at pretending than others. Some of us are so good, we manage to convince ourselves we are happy. But deep down, we are not. We are battling, trying to convince ourselves that we should be happy, and we chastise ourselves for not feeling grateful. That inner battle erupts eventually.

Unfortunately, the term depression still carries a certain stigma, yet truly, there is nothing to feel ashamed of. Having feelings of depression or experiencing burnout doesn't mean we are lacking. In fact, it can be quite the opposite—a sign of a very strong person who takes on too much responsibility.

When we experience these thoughts and feelings, we are actually at war with ourselves internally because we are not honoring our conflicting feelings. What once filled us with immense passion and drive suddenly no longer fuels us. Without that external goal to pursue, we don't know who we are or how to value ourselves.

We feel depleted, stressed out from our inner war, and apathetic, not knowing how to move forward other than the ways we have always operated. When we are not feeling satisfied with (or without) our work, it is often a sign. Perhaps a yellow flag if we catch it in its early stages, or a red flag if we ignore the signs for too long. If we don't heed these early warning signs, the road is going to get very bumpy. At least it did for me.

WHAT DO YOU DO WHEN YOU FEEL BURNED OUT?

I believe anyone who throws themselves all in will face burnout at some point. When you give 110 percent of your energy to something for months or years without letting up, your energy stores become depleted. When you are struggling like this, it is a sign that what you are doing is no longer working for you… and you need to make some changes. (Or continue to forsake your own happiness and well-being for a paycheck or some other reward.) When you've been highly successful navigating life one way, and now a part of you is wanting change… it can feel very uncomfortable.

Unlike my sister, who is a Gemini and takes sudden leaps into new careers and locations that surprise everyone around her but land her right where she wants to be, I am more methodical and less of a risk-taker. Big change unsettles me, as it does many people. Adhering to my Taurean nature, I take my time to process and make slow changes.

Unfortunately, back then, "slow" meant that I dragged my feet for many years, hoping my feelings or circumstances would change. Some of the smaller changes I made included taking more time off, traveling less, showing locally, and prioritizing my personal life outside of dogs. I changed how I interacted with my business.

Still, I made changes at a snail's pace, and eventually, life began intervening and causing me so much discomfort that I was forced to make bigger and bigger changes in order to stop the pain and suffering. It was not a fun time for me, but I learned a lot along the way. One of the biggest lessons was: DO NOT get into a fight with life… you will lose!

In addition to external conditions, there was a force inside me seeking change. These forces (both internal and external) were relentless. They left me feeling confused and out of sync, not knowing how to bring seemingly conflicting needs, wants, and desires into cohesion with one another. Honestly, I became detached from my own wants and needs and didn't even know where to begin. Sometimes, when you don't know what you want, it is best to start with what you know you don't want!

Through my struggles and deep self-reflection, I was able to identify that I was a big part of my own problem. I had a long-standing habit of working with difficult dogs and difficult clients. In the early days, this motivated and inspired me, but later it became draining. If I was going to survive, I had to get better at saying no. I had to get better at making my needs and well-being a priority.

I made lots and lots of adjustments, and each adjustment I made felt better and more liberating. Yet, I struggled with getting that feeling of inspiration back in a consistent manner.

While there are recognizable symptoms for burnout, like anything, it may look different for different people. I experienced anger, resentment, guilt, frustration, grief, sadness, apathy, and avoidance, as well as a physical breakdown of my body.

Despite the many changes I made, I didn't reach rock bottom until I could barely walk. The physical and emotional demands of handling and training dogs were taking their toll. I was in so much pain, yet rather than stop and take care of myself, I filled my body with high doses of Advil because, without it, I was incapable of gaiting my dogs. At night, I didn't want to put more medicine in my system, so I would lie awake shaking with pain. Then I would wake up the next morning and do it all over again—all the while shaming myself for being such a crybaby. In time, my muscles began to atrophy.

This sounds extreme, yet I know I am not an anomaly. It is the norm among handlers to show through immense physical pain, much like professional athletes.

Because I ignored the yellow flags (and the red ones for a long while), I eventually needed two total hip replacements at the age of fifty-one. This necessity was a major wake-up call, and I finally started giving myself permission to rest fully. Ironically, through all of this, my clients were not demanding I show their dogs through immense pain. I put these expectations on myself because, in my mind, that was what a hard-working, successful person does.

Although I had already begun making significant changes in my life, my hip surgery forced me to take life and business adjustments to a whole new level.

All of this points to one thing. Going too hard for too long can derail even the best of us if we don't have a strong connection to why we started in the industry or how this sense of purpose changes over time. Our sense of purpose and what we value changes and grows, just as we evolve and change throughout our lives. If we keep doing the same things and applying the same strategies we used when we began in the industry, we often find ourselves suffering and feeling unfulfilled.

When you get to a state of burnout, there is a lot going wrong. Life is out of balance. We need to make space and time for reevaluating and identifying our current values and priorities. We need to hit the pause button. Even though it is not what we are accustomed to doing, we need to step back and reexamine our lives so we don't end up like that Greyhound after it expended all its energy in a run, not knowing where it was or how it got so far off track.

SELF-REFLECTION TO GET BACK ON TRACK

When you have changed everything in your life that isn't working, and your clientele and dog-handling business are still leaving you feeling depleted, burned out, and uninspired, it may be time for a more significant change, or even a total career overhaul. Change like this can be very scary (as evidenced by my slow-moving, slow-to-change behavior). Leaving behind a role that once served you in so many ways–financially, emotionally, mentally, and physically–is not for the faint of heart.

So many of us feel stuck and without options. Many of my peers try to change perspective and find meaning in other ways. For example, handlers like Greg Strong find meaning and fulfillment in the relationships he has built with his clients; they set mutual goals, and he enjoys helping bring those goals to fruition. Taffe enjoys helping newcomers to the sport. Michelle loves working with new dogs and building their confidence.

As we have seen repeatedly in the stories gathered here from masters in the industry, professional handling is an extremely physical endeavor, especially if you work with larger breeds. Additionally, handling is mentally and emotionally taxing. Just as nurses, social workers, and other professionals that require a tremendous amount of emotional regulation tend to burn out, so do dog show handlers. It's helpful to be aware of this so you are better able to navigate these turbulent waters.

It's also helpful to stay open and explore all available options. For example, I recently began exploring obtaining a judging license. This is not a consideration to take lightly, as it would require giving up my career as a professional handler. As I was pondering this major career change, I noticed Cliff Steele, one of my peers, handling a string of dogs in a nearby ring.

Cliff is ten years my senior, and he's been handling dogs for the better part of forty years. During that time, he segued out of handling dogs to explore a career as an AKC-licensed judge, and later, as an AKC representative. This was a good opportunity to pick the brain of a peer who was further along on the path than I was when it came to exploring career opportunities after a successful handling career.

Although people have been encouraging me to get my judge's license for years, I was resistant. My body, however, was now asking me to explore other options in hopes of finding a less physically demanding job. In mulling the pros and cons, I was well aware of the benefits. I knew lots of people who loved judging, my dad included. Yet I wasn't so sure I would find it as gratifying as handling.

What I really wanted to know was why someone wouldn't like judging, so I approached Cliff because he had been a handler, then an AKC judge, then an AKC rep, and finally came back to handling. I wanted to know why.

It's interesting to note that the day I walked over to ask Cliff my question, I had lost with every single dog I handled earlier that day, and Cliff had been watching. I was in contention, but I didn't win. What I didn't see at the time is that I didn't lose because I was a terrible handler or because I lost my edge. The real issue was that I wasn't handling high-caliber dogs. This was another insight I gained from my chat with Cliff.

Sometimes, we just plain lose to a better dog, not because we are a bad handler but because the caliber of our dogs isn't great. Great dogs win. Great dogs win more with a great handler who knows how to present them to the best of their ability and who understands their competition, what they need to do to win, and how to best run and strategize a national campaign. Rarely will a great handler lose with a great dog, yet often, we are fighting to be the best with mediocrity, then chastising ourselves as failures.

When I approached Cliff, I prefaced our conversation by telling him that I was considering judging, but I had a lot of reservations. I thought perhaps he had stopped judging for financial reasons, because he couldn't generate as much income judging as he did handling dogs professionally. That was certainly a concern of mine. I shared with Cliff that I was thinking about transitioning into judging and asked him why he stopped judging and returned to handling dogs.

Cliff responded by pointing to an Old English Sheepdog lying on his grooming table and said, "I came back for her."

I wasn't expecting that response, but it made so much sense to me. Suddenly, things started to click into place. That dog, a prime specimen of its breed, helped rekindle Cliff's desire to handle.

Rekindle the Flame or Ignite a Whole New Fire?

My conversation with Cliff was an eye-opener for me and allowed me to see things from a different perspective. If you stay in a job long enough, you will enter bouts of burnout or stagnation. Burnout requires rest and space to rejuvenate. Stagnation requires space and reflection. Any job can be similar to a long-term marriage: in order to keep it fresh and thriving, you need to be able to ebb and flow and challenge yourself in new ways. Although old routines may have served you well in the past, they can, over time, leave you feeling at a crossroads.

How we address burnout and stagnation varies from handler to handler. Many handlers move away from handling yet remain in the industry, choosing to contribute to the sport in a different capacity. Perhaps if we know it is coming, we can be better prepared, or at the least have more compassion with ourselves through the transitions when they happen.

I believe people like Jane Forsyth and Anne Rogers Clark stayed ahead of these passion detractors by proactively moving in a new direction. They chose to start a new chapter. Annie made the transition from handler to writer, author, and thought leader. Her subsequent work impacted the dog show industry well beyond her career as a professional handler.

Jane transitioned out of handling as well, and her legacy is also still felt throughout the industry. I admire these two women who always stretched themselves, their abilities, and their capacity to learn and grow.

Jane's body became riddled with pain due to physical exertion, and it took a toll on her. I believe Jane knew her ability to perform the physical aspects of her job was fading and chose to take the information she had obtained all those years as a handler and apply it toward being a judge. The role of judging in dog shows is crucial to ensuring the protection and betterment of purebred dogs. As Andy Linton stated earlier, when a judge such as Annie or Jane came along, handlers rose to the occasion. Their opinions and reputations were highly regarded and valued in the industry. They took those same high-caliber standards and brought them into the judging community, where they brought a new level of reverence to judging. This is something that we are sorely missing at this time.

Some handlers are able to reframe how they run their businesses, who they work with, how they perform their job. They do this in a way that leaves them feeling satisfied and able to continue their work in their chosen profession. Handlers like Gwen DeMilta feel this passion for a lifetime. For some, it is their dream to die in the ring, going out doing what they love.

Six months before she died, Gwen's legs were full of fluid. Just walking was a painful experience, yet she willed her legs to run so she could handle her Doberman special at the national. Handlers like Gwen want to continue being a professional dog handler for as long as their body is physically capable of performing the job. Even when their body is in pain and breaking down, they still want to be in the ring. Their passion for handling remains true for a lifetime.

Others choose to remain in the industry, yet serve in a different capacity. Several areas that professional handlers move into after retirement from handling are running a boarding kennel, teaching handling seminars, working for a superintendent, becoming an AKC rep, going to work for AKC, or becoming an AKC-licensed judge.

As I hope you are starting to see, burnout doesn't have to be an ending. It can be a stepping stone to a whole new chapter and an opportunity to experience yourself in a new way.

Elliot More had the foresight to prevent burnout as a handler. At the height of a very successful career, he retired from handling in his thirties to pursue a graduate degree and become a veterinarian. He owns his own practice and still maintains ties to the dog show industry as an AKC-licensed judge.

Vicki Seiler-Cushman retired from handling in her forties and worked in public relations for various dog food companies. She later became an AKC-licensed judge and continues to expand the scope of breeds she is qualified to judge. In addition, she enjoys working with her son in his donut shop!

All handlers are part entrepreneurs. Vicki took her talents in a whole new direction, and she still remains in the dog show world. These new career paths can be exciting and can give us an opportunity to explore unexpressed or untapped parts of ourselves.

In hindsight, I see that once I accomplished all my outward goals, nothing on the outside was going to give me lasting satisfaction, fulfillment, and joy. Instead, I needed to focus more attention on what was going on inside me, seek deeper meaning, and figure out what really mattered to me.

Burnout is a sign indicating that our priorities are in need of adjustment. Depending on your degree of burnout, it can be life-changing. In fact, I think that is its intent.

For me, it was an indicator of all of the things in my life that weren't working, and there were a lot. What matters to us changes, and it will impact how we choose to invest our time. When we experience an inner conflict of this kind, we need to tune into a deeper part of us that is seeking change—something more, something different—and honor and explore it.

WHEN NEW CALLINGS EMERGE

I made more and more changes, and each time I responded to inner exploration, my world began to change. One of the most shocking changes that took place was a desire to write.

The desire to write came out of nowhere. As an elementary and high school student, my best subjects were always math and science. I found peace in logic. I liked things being in order, having a plan. This sudden desire to write felt strange and alien, but it grew so loud and incessant, it eventually became easier to give into it and write than to understand it.

That urge to write started with journaling in a notebook, which led to writing an article that was published in *Dog News*, then several more published articles on personal responsibility (accountability) in the dog show arena. It eventually led to writing this book!

Through the writing of this book (along with many other trials and tribulations), things started to make more sense and my path forward has become clearer. Just as my work as a dog handler taught me so much, my experience as a writer has forever changed me. Writing helps me process my thoughts and emotions. It helps me understand myself and others more deeply. It transforms me.

In my youth, I was very private. My dogs knew me intimately, but people did not. Writing allows me to share myself intimately with my readers in a way that feels good to me.

My message to anyone who is feeling the pangs of burnout is that you can't hear the voice that's calling because you are too busy running in the wrong direction (like that Greyhound). But what if you didn't run? What if you slowed down and started looking around you? What if you began to heed the call?

Stop and listen to what is going on within you that wants your attention. Living within this messy middle may feel foreign and may not make sense, but it is worth the discomfort. Unraveling who you were and who you are now can feel extremely uncomfortable. You may decide to make some simple changes (such as who you work for, how you work, or when and how often you work), or you might be tugged toward something totally new.

I felt alone in my journey with burnout. I was confused and felt no one had answers to my personal dilemma. I didn't like feeling confused. It was arduous and uncomfortable, and it felt like it lasted an eternity. Yet, I can now see its intention. Confusion and apathy are difficult emotions to navigate, but if you allow them their process, they can lead to an incredible gift.

When you feel burned out, there is a sense of grief. The full-on passion you once felt has burned away a part of you and an old way of navigating life. That is scary and uncomfortable because we have to give something up, while taking our chances on something new. And we are afraid that the next thing won't be as satisfying or gratifying. Yet that is part of the beauty and mystery of life: it is filled with discovery that only you have the power to unlock.

As Michael Scott said, "It just happened." Life is happening through us, and it is growing us up during the process. Anyone who sets out to become a professional dog handler, or even a highly competitive owner-handler, is signing themselves up to learn major life lessons.

If we do the soul searching it requires, burnout breaks us down so we can build ourselves back up again. The question is, will you be conscious and aware of the dynamic taking place within you? Will you have the awareness and capacity to seize the opportunities opening up to you? Will you be able to view these uncomfortable feelings, not merely as obstacles and frustrations, but as harbingers of change, valuable opportunities to serve your higher purpose and live your best life?

As you navigate burnout, it may feel as if you are lost in the dark, unable to find your way. Most master handlers have tons of grit and determination. When burnout strikes, rather than fighting it, try something counter-intuitive: light a match, look around, and see what wants to be birthed anew.

Burnout is an inward journey that's meant to bring you to your knees and reignite you as you rediscover parts of yourself that have been left unexplored. Regardless of where burnout leads you or where your explorations take you, you won't be alone. In this industry, you will always be surrounded by a group of peers, clients, judges, and friends who will stand by your side as you find your way.

AFTERWORD

A Community to Support You

The dog show community supported me through a lifetime of changes, from eager kid, dog lover, and competitive athlete to seasoned professional, mom, and writer/teacher/coach. Reflecting back, I can see how often my community supported me at various stages in my journey. As competitive as my peers were when I was a kid, and even as I grew older, there were always people who helped me. Yes, even Gwen helped me with dogs that were in competition with hers. Although we may appear strong, confident, and unapproachable, most of us are very willing to help anyone who wants to learn, even if helping may threaten our odds of winning.

We are a motley group. We can be combative, aggressive, hostile, and unreasonable. But despite all of our messiness, we show up for each other. When someone is at the top of their game, their position will be challenged, and yet, when someone is struggling, people rally for them.

When tragedy strikes, organizations like Take the Lead help dog people who are in need. This characteristic is also present in the individuals that make up our community. Sometimes they come through in small ways, and sometimes in big ways.

I have often described my dog show world to outsiders as the Land of Misfit Toys. What greater gift is there for a group of individuals with their sometimes quirky talents than to be brought together in an area where they feel a sense of belonging? For many, the dog show world is a place where they feel seen, heard, and understood in a way they've never experienced before or elsewhere.

I feel grateful that I get to decide what's next. I can remain in this industry as a handler, writer, teacher, and even judge if I so choose. For many, the dog show community becomes our family because we spend all our time immersed in the community. However, the dog show family is not like *The Waltons*... it sometimes feels more like *The Sopranos*! As with any family, there are ups and downs, there is conflict and comradery, but we weather the storm together.

Every handler I interviewed for the book simply said, "How can I help?" Not one person questioned what I was doing or even asked to see what I had written about them. They trusted me to do a good job, and overwhelmingly, they each just wanted to support me. Each interview was very, very special to me. Working with the handlers and getting to know them on a deeper level was such a gift. Unlike when I was pursuing the goal of number one with Raisin, this time, I was aware of each blessing I experienced along the road of writing and publishing a book. It wasn't about making a bunch of money or receiving accolades; it was about everything I learned and all the people I connected with along the way.

In addition, when COVID-19 shut down the dog show industry, I felt a calling to help kids through the transition. I felt they might be suffering. For many kids, dog showing is their happy place, it is something they look forward to. (I know it was for me when I was growing up in the industry.) COVID-19 and forced quarantines took that away from them.

I started a webinar series titled "Meet the Professionals" as a way to help kids feel connected to their passion and the dog show world during the COVID lockdown. Each month, I hosted a Zoom call and invited a professional handler to talk about their work, answer questions, and connect with the kids. Handlers donated their time and enthusiastically showed up to help those kids.

This type of community is what the world is craving right now. People join together to help navigate the chaos and the upheaval, each person showing up, offering what they have to help others along the way.

For many, the dog show community provides a unique environment to thrive, change, and grow through all of life's stages. It's a culture many call home. Some find their calling and stay for a season, and others remain for a lifetime. Every handler, in their own way, leaves a mark that lasts long after their presence has moved on.

Acknowledgments

Prior to writing my own book, I used to think writing a book was a solitary endeavor. It is not. As the saying goes, it takes a village, or in my case, a community of friends, family, and colleagues.

One of the most instrumental people responsible for the development of this book during its birthing and adolescent stages is my sister, Natalie Eve Marquis. Her sharp mind and extensive background in marketing and creative writing were invaluable. She encouraged me, guided me as a writer, at times showed me, and at other times stood back and simply said, "You got this."

There were days when we worked side by side (she on her art, check out NatalieMarquis.com!). Other times, she was just a phone call away, and she was a constant source of inspiration and support.

Natalie, you know and care about what truly matters to me. You always have my back and are always there to help pick me up, lend me support, or simply laugh and play with me! I admire the leaps of faith you often take that surprise us all as you follow your heart and your inner callings. No matter how busy you are, you always take time for the people you love and those that need you. You are an important person in my life in so many ways. Your talents are extraordinary. I love you.

Although I've known many of my dog show friends for more than twenty years, the writing of my book deepened all of our relationships. I will never forget walking toward our dog show set-up in Syracuse, New York, in March of 2019, and seeing my dog show friends sitting in chairs, gathered on my behalf. They didn't know why they were there. What they did know was that I needed something–that's all that mattered to them.

Their attentiveness and willingness to show up for me so completely nearly brought me to tears. Those that know me well know I'm not one to cry! Luckily, Lorrie Moreira read my body language and saved me from myself by cracking a joke. (Knowing Lorrie, it was probably a disparaging remark about my character just as I was getting ready to say something nice!). Thanks Lorrie! We all appreciate your odd sense of humor, which shocks us and then sends us into peals of laughter!

Once Lorrie redirected my emotion, I expressed my desire to write a book. Without hesitation, my friends began jumping in, offering advice and ways they could help. Carissa Shimpeno recommended several handlers that she felt would be a great fit.

Debbie Struff, who has a background in the corporate world, felt that, although I planned to begin writing about my inner circle of peers and then work my way outward, I should start outward and work my way back in. I'm not sure why Debbie made that recommendation, or if even she knew why, but it felt right to me as well. It was the right call. Carissa, who is very social, helped connect me to the right people in a comforting manner. Their support and contribution didn't end there. They read countless drafts and offered feedback. Carissa recommended areas I could develop more and even shared the draft with her husband, Eric, for comment.

Lorrie gifted me with her frankness, always encouraging me to be me, or to get to the point! I could always count on Debbie to be thorough and think things through. At one point, she read a draft I was struggling with and her constructive feedback turned into tears! Even though it was difficult for her, she wanted to support me. After witnessing Debbie's emotional response, I determined there was more work and emotional processing that needed to be done on my part in order for me to achieve the level of integrity that I expected of myself as a writer and thought leader.

Gwen DeMilta, although not as actively present during my writing process, did what Gwen often did so well: remained quiet and steadfast, in utter conviction of my abilities.

To all my dog show friends, I love you and am so grateful for how each of you uniquely "shows up" in the world. You bring richness, love, and support to my world.

And of course, this book wouldn't be possible without all its characters, the real-life characters that freely and willingly offered their time, their names, and their reputations to help me and my endeavor. Thank you to Janice Hayes, Frank Murphy, Greg Strong, Michael Scott, Michelle Scott, Katie Bernardin, Kaz Hosaka, Andy Linton, and Taffe McFadden, as well as Sioux Forsyth-Green, Wayne Cavanaugh, and Mark Threlfall for volunteering their time and allowing me to write a story to share with dog show enthusiasts.

Each of these individuals freely and willingly showed up and simply asked, "How can I help?" My time with you and the insights I gained are truly gifts that I hold in my heart.

Thank you in spirit to Gwen DeMilta, Jane Forsyth, and Anne Rogers Clark. I am grateful for the insights I was able to draw from your presence during your time on earth. You were all potent wayshowers of the power we have as individuals to impact the whole.

Patricia Proctor, who at the time was an AKC Executive Field Representative, one of the best ever, in my opinion, helped facilitate the sharing of my writing in its infancy within the industry. Pattie recognized that others may benefit from my writing and was a constant source of support whenever I reached out. She helped bridge the gap for me with the late Matt Stander at *Dog News Magazine*. I am truly grateful for Pattie's receptivity and personal commitment to be of service, not just to me, but to so many members of the dog show community. Pattie truly cares for the needs of others and aims to make a positive difference in the world.

And to Matt Stander, and by extension, Eugene Zaphiris, with *Dog News*, who always insisted that I write more articles. You made me feel worthy and recognized when I was a budding writer. Having the support of insiders from such an influential magazine was the proverbial green light from the universe, telling me to keep writing. Matt, your presence in our community is truly missed.

My deepest appreciation goes to David Frei, for supporting my endeavor to shine a light on some of the opportunities that can be explored and attained within the dog show community. David, thank you for your kindness, encouragement, and enthusiasm for my mission to help others and help our sport. It was an honor working with you. You are a true ambassador for the sport of purebred dogs.

Also, to many of my peers not mentioned here who shared their thoughts, opinions, and themselves with me throughout the writing of this book: thank you. I am grateful for your support.

On a lighter yet no less significant note, I would like to thank my friends Joe and Diane. They endured many long conversations on the phone, always willing to lend an ear, brainstorm ideas, and just simply talk things out. Although you were just being you–showing up, being a great friend–the time you generously gave me was invaluable. I am truly blessed to have such kind, loving friends, who are always there for me. I love you.

To my mom and dad for giving me life, and for the constancy they provide in my life. Mom and Dad, we live in a world where so many people are pulled in so many directions, yet you both never waiver. Family is ALWAYS your number one priority. Your presence throughout my life has made me stronger.

To my daughter Gabrielle, being a mom has been one of life's greatest gifts. You help me see life through new eyes. You are one of my best friends. You are so smart, kind, and fun. You are one of my favorite people to spend time with. You have helped me experience my softness and even discover a playfulness that I didn't know was buried deep within me. I have learned so much about life raising you, being with you, and watching you blossom into a young adult.

To all of you, my heart overflows.

Thank you to Heather Doyle Fraser with Compassionate Mind Collaborative for helping me further develop my abilities as a writer and for bringing my work forth into the world in such an articulate, well-executed, professional manner. I am so grateful for your wise, compassionate counsel in helping me create a product that I am proud of, one that is uniquely mine. Heather, you helped fulfill a childhood dream, to contribute something beneficial and worthy to the world. Your compassionate dedication to me, your work, and your mission is commendable. I am truly honored to be aligned with a person whose values and vision help empower others. You also made it possible for my work to remain mine, enabling me to maintain my independence.

Additionally, I would like to acknowledge other contributing members of the Compassionate Mind Collaborative Team: Hope Madden, for her copy editing and proofing skills; Cindy Curtis-Rivera, for cover design and interior design and layout; as well as Jesse Sussman, for helping guide, launch, and direct the book's Amazon campaign.

To Jesse and Heather, I am so grateful for your support in guiding me step-by-step through the daunting endeavor of an Amazon launch. Your guidance and know-how stretched my comfort zone and helped me reach a broader audience. Thank you for allowing me to dream big and reach for the stars!

Lastly, a big thank you goes to the dog show community. The community and its members have been an integral part of my life. I am grateful to so many of the dogs I have worked with, clients I have served, and colleagues who have taught me. My time with you is an intricate part of my being and pours through me into my writing and all I do. My exposure to and presence within the industry helped create the woman I am today. I am eternally grateful.

ABOUT THE AUTHOR
Kelly Lyn Marquis

Kelly Lyn Marquis was born into a dog lovers' den. Not only did her parents have a deep love and affinity for dogs, but for many other animals as well. Her childhood was filled with horses, cats, goats, pigs, and cows, as well as singing and talking birds! Dogs were her happy place. In fact, in her early years, she preferred the companionship of dogs above any other living creature. When not spending time with her favorite companions, she enjoyed playing sports and spending time in nature.

Her deep resonance with dogs combined with her competitive spirit, as well as her love of learning, to make handling dogs the ultimate expression of her inner nature and drive. Upon graduating from the University of New Hampshire with a Bachelor of Arts degree, she worked full time in marketing and public relations, while handling dogs professionally. After almost ten years of working two jobs, she decided to follow her heart and become a full-time professional dog show handler. Within three years of making that decision, she piloted a Doberman named Raisin, Ch. Blue Chip Purple Reign, to the position of Number One Doberman, Number One Working Dog, and Number Five All-Breeds. A couple of her career highlights were being awarded Best in Show at the nationally televised Kennel Club of Philadelphia dog show, which aired on Thanksgiving Day, and being featured in *Sports Illustrated* magazine.

After handling several dogs ranked within the top-five nationally, Kelly gradually eased back from the pursuit of top-tier national rankings to take on one of her greatest joys, being a mom. Her daughter, Gabrielle, traveled the country with her, attending dog shows in a forty-foot motorhome, until she entered school. Stepping away from the high demands of pursuing national rankings, Kelly created space for other endeavors to emerge as well.

In 2018, Kelly began writing articles on dog show dynamics and personal accountability for *Dog News*. In 2019, she began writing her first book, *Behind the Scenes of Best in Show: Intimate Moments with the Masters: Handlers and Their Show Dogs*, as a tribute to the dog show community, shining a light on the unique and varied gifts embodied by top handlers within the industry, revealing their wisdom, skills, inner workings, passion, as well as the deep connection they share with their dogs.

In 2020, during the pandemic, Kelly began hosting a monthly webinar series for junior dog show handlers called *Meet the Professionals*. She created this program as a means to help kids during COVID-19 feeling disconnected from their passion, dog shows. She also hosts handling workshops, offering herself as a holistic, nurturing guide for owner-handlers who share a passion for dogs, showmanship, and excellence.

In addition to writing and showing dogs, she is a certified life coach and operates Winall Coaching, coaching goal-oriental individuals and helping them reach their desired potential. She and her daughter, Gabrielle, reside in Fremont, New Hampshire, with their Doberman, Goose, and their Mini Wirehaired Dachshund, Dove. Kelly enjoys nature, reading, writing, exercising, and spending time with family and friends.

www.ingramcontent.com/pod-product-compliance
Lightning Source LLC
LaVergne TN
LVHW091718070526
838199LV00050B/2447